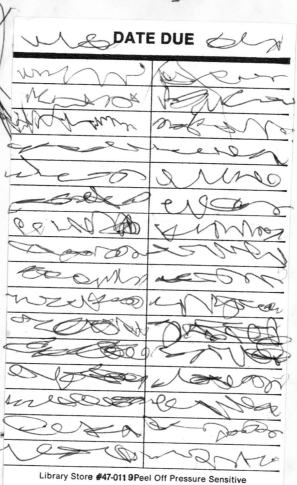

DATE DUE

A New True Book

VOLCANOES

By Helen J. Challand

*This "true book" was prepared
under the direction of
Illa Podendorf,
formerly with the Laboratory School,
University of Chicago*

CHILDRENS PRESS, CHICAGO

Trees covered with volcanic ash

PHOTO CREDITS

Joseph Antos—2

United States Department of Interior, National
Park Service—36

United States Geological Survey: J. Vallance—
4; K. Segerstrom—45; J.C. Ratté—6;
J. Rosenbaum—22; R.L. Schuster—25 (left);
D. McKnight—25

Office of Earthquake Studies, USGS—39
(2 photos)

Japan National Tourist Organization—11

Louise Lunak—cover, 16, 31 (bottom)

James P. Rowan—7, 19, 41

Tom Winter—35 (top)

Len Meents—9, 13, 15

Wide World, Associated Press Wire Photo—32

Historical Pictures Service, Inc.—18, 21

Hawaii Visitors Bureau—31 (top)

Wyoming Travel Commission—26, 35 (bottom)

Hillstrom Stock Photos: ©Jack Lund—29

Root Resources: ©Mary Root—43

Cover—Parícutin Volcano, Mexico

Library of Congress Cataloging in Publication Data

Challand, Helen J.
  Volcanoes.

  (A New true book)
  Includes index.
  Summary: Discusses what causes volcanoes, where
they are likely to occur, and how scientists study them.
    1. Volcanoes—Juvenile literature. [1. Volcanoes]
I. Title.
QE521.3.C453   1983   551.2'1   82-17888
ISBN 0-516-01690-3   AACR2

TABLE OF CONTENTS

When Mount St. Helens erupted the explosion ripped away
1,300 feet from the top of the volcano.

WHAT IS A VOLCANO?

A volcano is the name for two things. It can be the opening in the ground that shoots out hot rocks, gases, steam, or ashes. A volcano is also the name given to the hill or mountain formed by these materials.

Inside the earth the melted rock is called magma. After the melted rock comes out, it is lava. Lava is a red or white mixture. It is very hot. It flows like thick syrup.

A lava "waterfall" caused by an eruption of Kilauea Volcano.

Sunset Crater, Sunset Crater National Monument

A volcano often has a
crater or depression in the
center of it or along the
sides. This crater may fill
up with water and become
a lake when the lava stops
flowing.

DIFFERENT KINDS
OF VOLCANOES

Cinder cone volcanoes
blow out burning cinders,
ash, and steam. This
material shoots out from a
single tube. A cinder cone
volcano is often violent
and explosive. Sunset
Crater in Arizona, Parícutin
in Mexico, and Krakatoa
are cinder cone volcanoes.

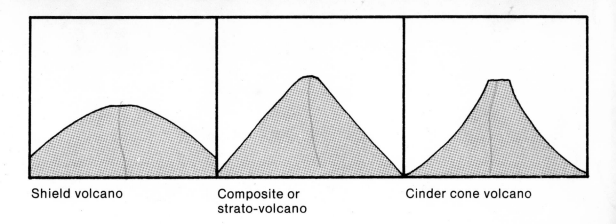

Shield volcano

Composite or
strato-volcano

Cinder cone volcano

Shield volcanoes form in
or along shores of oceans.
They spew out layer after
layer of lava from cracks
in the earth's surface.
Shield volcanoes are not
too explosive. The
Hawaiian Islands were
made by shield volcanoes.
They are also found in
Iceland.

Composite or strato-volcanoes are formed by hot broken rock, ash, and lava. These volcanoes are taller and more active than shield volcanoes. They are less explosive than cinder cone volcanoes. Mount Fuji in Japan, Mount Rainier in Washington, Mount Hood in Oregon, and Mount Shasta in California are composite volcanoes.

Mount Fuji is a composite volcano. These volcanoes often form along the areas where the oceans meet the continents.

WHAT CAUSES
A VOLCANO?

Scientists are not sure why magma blows up and out of the earth. They believe that it starts to form around sixty miles down in the ground. The temperature is so high here that rocks will melt. This forms magma.

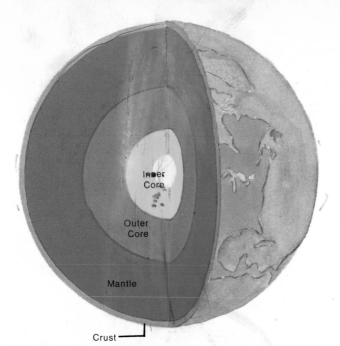

Inner Core

Outer Core

Mantle

Crust

Magma breaks through the earth's crust. When a volcano's magma is thick with lots of hot gases, its explosion will be great. Magma that is thin as water does not cause as much damage.

Solid rocks in the earth's crust hold magma down. Cracks form in the thin areas of the crust. As the pressure builds up the magma is forced through these cracks and a volcano is born.

WHERE ARE
THE VOLCANOES?

Most volcanoes are found along two major chains in the world. By the way, most earthquakes also happen in these same areas.

The Ring of Fire is a chain around the Pacific Ocean. There are over three hundred active volcanoes in this chain.

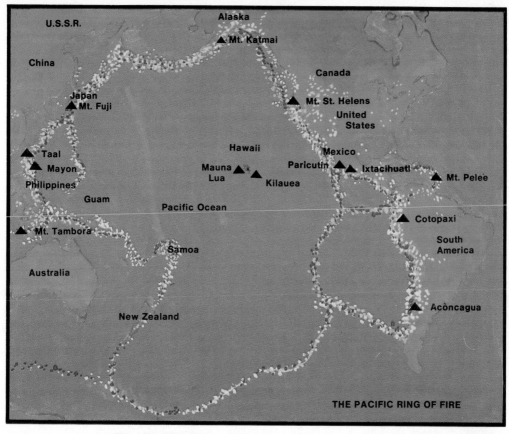

The Pacific Ring of Fire includes Japan; the Philippines; Papua New Guinea; New Zealand; the western coasts of South America, Central America, Mexico, and North America; Alaska and the Aleutian Islands.

The second chain of volcanoes forms a line along the Azores, Canary Islands, and then east

Parícutin Volcano in Mexico erupted in 1943.

through Europe and Asia.
There are a few volcanoes
in east-central Africa.

Volcanoes are found in
the sea. The earth is
indeed a restless place.

SOME REALLY BIG ONES

Mount Vesuvius was born maybe ten thousand years ago. It is found near the Bay of Naples in southern Italy. For hundreds, of years, people thought it was a dead volcano. They built towns nearby. Then in A.D. 79 Mount Vesuvius blew up.

The eruption from Mount Vesuvius buried Pompeii under one hundred feet of lava and ash.

The cities of Pompeii and Herculaneum were buried. The ruins of these towns can still be seen. Mount Vesuvius is still active. It has been resting now since 1944, but it will blow again.

Steam vents at Kilauea Volcano in the Hawaiian Islands.

The volcanoes that
formed the Hawaiian
Islands are the tallest in
the world. They start at the
bottom of the ocean, which
is around sixteen thousand
feet deep at that spot. The
islands are now almost

19

fourteen thousand feet above sea level. Add the two numbers together and you will know how tall they are today.

Another sleeping giant woke up in 1883 when Mount Krakatoa, a cinder cone volcano in Indonesia blew its top. The noise of the explosion was heard three thousand miles away. The ashes and dust blew so high the wind currents carried them around the

More than forty years after the island of Krakatoa was blown off the face of the earth by volcanic eruption, this volcanic island Anak Krakatoa, or Child of Krakatoa, raised its head above the sea.

whole earth. This blocked some of the sun's rays and the earth's temperature dropped more than ten degrees. The tidal waves caused by this volcano killed over thirty thousand people on Sumatra and Java.

21

Aerial view of the eruption of Mount St. Helens on May 18, 1980.

BLACK SUNDAY

On Sunday, May 18, 1980, Mount St. Helens let the world know it was still active. Its last big eruption was in 1831. But it was always restless.

During this last explosion the magma stayed inside the mountain. But ash and steam escaped. The ice on Mount St. Helens melted. Billions of gallons of water turned the ash into mud slides that flooded the valleys. Ash that stayed in the air from the blast was carried around the world in seventeen days. That morning it was as dark as night in the area.

Spirit Lake on the side of the volcano rose hundreds of feet. Temperatures in some rivers of mud heated up to over six hundred degrees. This killed all living things in the rivers. Thousands of acres of trees were knocked over like match sticks. Crops were smothered by ash. Over sixty people died. Thousands of deer, elk, mountain lions, black bears, and goats died, too.

It will take years for the trees (left) to grow back near Mount St. Helens, but within months millions of tree seedlings had taken root and plants, such as fireweed (right), were growing.

A few months after the eruption, life returned. Asters, ferns, and fireweed are growing in the barren ash. New ponds and lakes are forming. Wild animals are moving back in.

Old Faithful is in Yellowstone Park in Wyoming. This geyser shoots hot steam and water into the air every sixty-five minutes. Someday it will stop.

OLD FAITHFUL

Sometimes magma comes out of many cracks or holes in the ground. It does not form into a single hill or mountain. Instead it spreads out over large areas called lava fields.

In an active lava field the hot magma in the earth causes geysers and hot springs to form.

27

CRATER LAKE

Mount Mazama in
Oregon exploded about
seven thousand years ago.
It left a huge hole or basin
in the top of the mountain
six thousand feet above sea
level. It filled up with water
and is now two thousand
feet deep, the deepest
lake in the United States.

Wizard Island, Crater Lake

Then a thousand years ago
a small volcanic cone
formed in Crater Lake. It
was named Wizard Island.

HOUSE OF
EVERLASTING FIRE

Mauna Loa is a large
volcano in Hawaii. Kilauea
is a smaller one on the
side of Mauna Loa. Thin
lava boils and bubbles all
the time in its crater. It
erupted suddenly in 1982.

Above: Volcano
National Park,
Hawaii
Left: Haleakala
Crater,
Maui, Hawaii

Two smoking volcanoes in The Valley of Ten Thousand Smokes.

VALLEY OF TEN THOUSAND SMOKES

This scenic wonder is in Alaska. In 1912 two volcanoes blew out at the same time. Ash filled the sky. For three days, it was as dark as night. The acid rain from the ash burned people not only in Alaska but in western parts of Canada. The ground is still sending out hot gases and steam in thousands of places. That is how the area got its name.

DEAD VOLCANOES

A volcano grows old and dies when the hot magma inside it settles down. The cracks and openings seal over as the pressure inside the earth is reduced. Wind, rain, and other weather conditions wear down the hill or mountain.

The Cascade Range is part of the Rocky Mountains. This chain of old volcanoes was formed millions of years ago.

Ship Rock (above) in New Mexico and Devils Tower (left) in Wyoming are the only parts left of dead volcanoes.

Craters of the Moon National Monument in Idaho

The lava tubes in
Craters of the Moon
National Monument are
leftovers from ancient
volcanic activity, as are the
Palisades along the
Hudson River. Cones of

dead volcanoes are found in Sunset Crater in Arizona and in Lava Beds National Monument in California.

Some places in Arkansas might have been formed by volcanoes millions of years ago. We know that hot springs are the result of volcano activity. We also know that volcanoes leave huge deposits of mercury and diamonds. Hot springs, mercury, and diamonds are found in Arkansas.

STUDYING VOLCANOES

Scientists learn about
volcanoes by testing them.

A seismograph is a
device that records
earthquakes. As the hot
magma pushes rocks
around under the ground,
the earth begins to shake.
At first the shocks are little
ones. But when a volcano
is getting ready to break
through, the quakes get
stronger and are closer
together. This is a warning

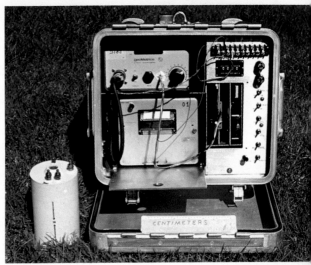

A strainmeter (left) is placed along cracks, or faults, in the earth's crust. It measures movement in the earth. The magnetometer (right) measures changes in the magnetic and electrical charges in the earth. The earth moves and changes before a volcano erupts.

that something will happen soon.

A tiltmeter measures the size of a volcano. A volcano will swell before it erupts. This swelling cannot be seen with the

naked eye. Tiltmeters are
placed around the sides
and near the top of a
volcano. They tilt, such as
a carpenter's level would,
as the shape of the slope
changes. This means that
magma is getting close to
breaking through the surface.

Scientists also use drills
to study the insides of a
volcano. They check the
change in temperature.
They study the makeup of

When lava cools, it turns back into solid rock or dust.
It can be brown, gray, or black.

the magma. They examine
the materials in the
trapped gases. All this
information tells scientists
if a volcano is dead, alive,
or just resting.

VOLCANOES
AREN'T ALL BAD

Millions of years ago volcanoes helped to form the surface of our earth. They blew carbon dioxide and water vapor into the air. This changed the atmosphere. Clouds formed. Rain fell. Oceans, seas, and lakes were formed. The first living things started in these ancient waters. Over time lava

Ferns grow in lichen-covered lava at Mauna Loa, Hawaii.

broke down into fertile soil
as minerals were added.
Higher plants, animals, and
humans followed.

Volcanoes send out tons
of minerals. Metals such
as tin, lead, zinc, and
mercury are removed from
volcanic rock. Diamonds

and a black glassy rock
called obsidian is formed.
Sulfur is brought out by
volcanoes and then mined
for use. Crushed lava
makes good bedrock for
highways and runways.

Ocean volcanoes make
new islands. This gives
plants, animals, and people
more space.

In Iceland the water
from hot springs is used to
heat buildings. Scientists

Glowing lava erupts from Parícutin Volcano.

know how to convert the heat from volcanoes into electricity. So you see good things can come from volcanoes.

WORDS YOU SHOULD KNOW

ancient(AIN • shent)—of times long ago

atmosphere(AT • muss • feer)—the air that surrounds the earth

barren(BAIR • en)—not being able to produce anything

basalt(beh • SALT)—a kind of rock formed after lava cools and hardens

basin(BAY • sin)—a large hole or depression in the ground

bedrock(BED • rock)—rock that is used as a support

composite(kom • POZ • it)—a kind of volcano that is formed by rocks, ashes, and lava

convert(kun • VERT)—to change something into something else

crater(KRAY • ter)—a low place in a volcano either at the top or along its side

crust(KRUSST)—the hard outer layer of the earth

depression(dih • PRESH • un)—an area in the volcano that is lower than the rest; crater

device(dih • VICE)—a machine or instrument

equator(ee • KWAY • ter)—the imaginary line that goes around the middle of the earth halfway between the North and South Poles

famine(FAM • in)—a great shortage of food

fertile(FER • till)—having raw materials necessary for plant growth

gorge(GORJ)—a deep, narrow valley with high sides

inactive(in • AK • tiv)—not in action, not working

lava(LAH • vah)—hot melted rock that flows from a volcano

level(LEV • ill)—a tool used to show whether or not a surface is flat

magma(MAG • mah)—hot melted rock found deep in the earth

molten(MOL • tin)—melted by heat

obsidian(ob • SID • ee • yan)—a rock that is glassy and formed from material from volcanoes

record(ree • KORD)—to register or indicate

reduce(ree • DOOCE)—to become less in amount or size

remnant(REM • nant)—remaining piece or part

reservoir(REZ • ih • vwahr)—an area in the ground where liquids are collected and stored

seismograph(SIZE • moh • graf)—an instrument that shows or records when and where an earthquake happens and how strong it is

smother(SMUH • ther)—to die from lack of air

spew(SPYOO)—to come forth, gush, or eject

tiltmeter(TILLT • me • tir)—an instrument used to measure the size of the swell of a volcano

INDEX

About the Author

Helen Challand earned her M.A. and Ph.D. from Northwestern University. She currently is Chair of the Science Department at National College of Education and Coordinator of Undergraduate Studies for the college's West Suburban Campus.

An experienced classroom teacher and science consultant, Dr. Challand has worked on science projects for Scott Foresman and Company, Rand McNally Publishers, Harper-Row Publishers, Encyclopedia Britannica Films, Coronet Films, and Journal Films. She is associate editor for the Young People's Science Encyclopedia *published by Childrens Press.*

Your All-in-One Resource

On the CD that accompanies this book, you'll find additional resources to extend your learning. The CD interface resembles the one shown here:

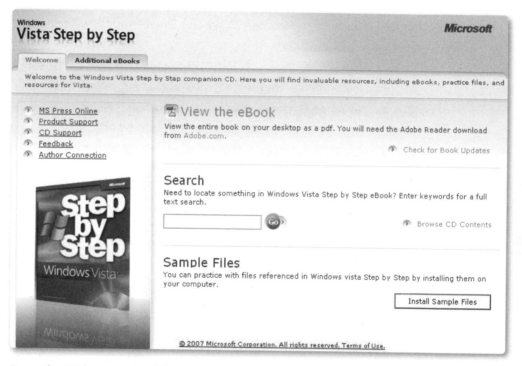

From the Welcome tab of the CD interface, you can access a variety of resources on the CD or online, including the following:

- Search or view the electronic version of this book.
- Install the book's practice files.
- Check for book updates.*
- Get product support or CD support.*
- Send us feedback.

* Requires Internet access

From the Additional eBooks tab of the CD interface, you can access electronic books and reference materials on the CD, including the following:

- *Microsoft Computer Dictionary, Fifth Edition*
- *Windows Vista Product Guide*
- Sample chapter from *Microsoft Office Live Small Business: Take your Business Online* (Katherine Murray, 2008)
- Sample chapter from *Beyond Bullet Points: Using Microsoft Office PowerPoint 2007 to Create Presentations That Inform, Motivate, and Inspire* (Cliff Atkinson, 2008)
- Sample chapter from *Microsoft Windows SharePoint Services 3.0 Step by Step* (Olga Londer, Penelope Coventry, Bill English, and Todd Bleeker, 2008)
- Sample chapter from *Working with Microsoft Dynamics 4.0, Second Edition* (Mike Snyder and Jim Stegar, 2008)

Microsoft

Microsoft Dynamics® CRM 4.0 Step by Step

Mike Snyder
Jim Steger
Kara O'Brien
Brendan Landers

PUBLISHED BY
Microsoft Press
A Division of Microsoft Corporation
One Microsoft Way
Redmond, Washington 98052-6399

Library of Congress Control Number: 2008929783

Printed and bound in the United States of America.

1 2 3 4 5 6 7 8 9 QWT 3 2 1 0 9 8

Distributed in Canada by H.B. Fenn and Company Ltd.

A CIP catalogue record for this book is available from the British Library.

Microsoft Press books are available through booksellers and distributors worldwide. For further information about international editions, contact your local Microsoft Corporation office or contact Microsoft Press International directly at fax (425) 936-7329. Visit our Web site at www.microsoft.com/mspress. Send comments to mspinput@microsoft.com.

Acquisitions Editor: Juliana Aldous Atkinson
Developmental Editor: Sandra Haynes
Project Editor: Rosemary Caperton
Editorial Production: Online Training Solutions, Inc.
Technical Reviewer: Sumit Virmani; Technical Review services provided by Content Master, a member of CM Group, Ltd.
Cover: Tom Draper Design

Body Part No. X14-95090

Contents

Part I Overview

1 Introduction to Microsoft Dynamics CRM 3

2 Getting Around in Microsoft Dynamics CRM 15

What do you think of this book? We want to hear from you!

Microsoft is interested in hearing your feedback so we can continually improve our books and learning resources for you. To participate in a brief online survey, please visit:

www.microsoft.com/learning/booksurvey/

Foreword

In these uncertain economic times, a company's ability to adequately manage its relationships with customers, partners, and vendors can determine whether it just survives or has the relationship capital to drive the business, and protect and grow revenue. No software application is better suited to helping companies address these challenges than Microsoft Dynamics CRM. In the 4.0 version, Microsoft Dynamics CRM delivers comprehensive Sales, Marketing, and Service functionality with its trademark user-friendly interface, powerful ability to meet the changing business processes and needs, as well as the ability to leverage all the other investments a company has already made in systems and infrastructure.

Companies large and small will find that Microsoft Dynamics CRM is a system that grows with them. The true measure of CRM success is the degree to which it is adopted by employees and how the system empowers users to drive business growth and success. Unlocking the power of CRM, however, is not always an easy task. With this book, Sonoma Partners delivers an extremely rich and easy-to-follow text for learning the Microsoft Dynamics CRM application.

For users of Microsoft Dynamics CRM, the well-organized content allows you to zero in on topics and learn quickly regardless of your level of experience with CRM. Whether you're a user, consultant, or implementer, this book equips you to extract the maximum value from your Microsoft Dynamics CRM system.

Sincerely,

Mark Corley

Senior Director

Microsoft Dynamics CRM

Introduction

Welcome to *Microsoft Dynamics 4.0 CRM Step by Step*! Chances are your organization has implemented—or is considering implementing—a Microsoft Dynamics CRM system, and you're ready to learn more about what the software can do.

Whether you're a sales associate following up with your top accounts, a marketing professional reaching out to prospects and customers, a customer service representative resolving customer requests and issues, or an executive manager seeking to analyze and understand all of your organization's customer interactions, Microsoft Dynamics CRM can help you do business better.

The intent of this book is to show you how to use key features in the software to understand your customers better, increase sales and productivity, and improve customer satisfaction. It's important to note that Microsoft Dynamics CRM allows administrators to easily customize the forms, fields, and other options in the software, so some of the names used in this book might not match your environment.

A Word About Sandbox Environments

If possible, ask your system administrator about setting up a second Microsoft Dynamics CRM environment—often referred to as a *sandbox environment*—that you can use to step through the exercises in this book. A sandbox environment allows you to modify records without affecting the data in your live system. Your organization might already have a staging or test environment that you can use.

About the Examples in This Book

The descriptions and procedures in this book are based on the default forms and views in Microsoft Dynamics CRM. As you'll learn in the chapters that follow, the software also offers several access options: CRM data can be accessed from a Windows Internet Explorer Web browser or from Microsoft Office Outlook by using the Microsoft Dynamics CRM Outlook feature. Most of the screenshots and examples in this book show the Web browser option.

Just like some of the forms, fields, and data described in this book, the security roles referenced throughout this book also might have been modified in or even removed from your system. If you do not have the access needed to view or assign security roles, talk to your system administrator about setting up a few roles for testing. For the purposes of this book, we assume the default roles included with Microsoft Dynamics CRM have not been modified.

Looking Forward

Microsoft Dynamics CRM is a fluid system that can adapt as your business grows and changes. By using the step-by-step processes laid out in these pages, you can explore whatever options you need to match the software with your requirements. We hope you find this book useful and informative as your organization moves into the future!

Acknowledgments

We want to thank all of the people that assisted us in writing this book. If we accidentally miss anyone, we apologize in advance. We want to thank these members of the Microsoft Dynamics CRM product team, Sonoma Partners colleagues, and friends who helped us at one point or another during the book project:

Andrew Bybee	Neil Erickson	Phillip Richardson
Andrew Becraft	Barry Givens	Ben Ryan
Kim Boeh	Kate Harper	Jim Schumacher
Mark Corley	Gretchen House	Derik Stenerson
Gerry Doyle	Ned Kandzor	Jay Michelle White
Rich Dickinson	Bill Patterson	Brad Wilson
Kate Egan	Manisha Powar	

Of course, we also want to thank the folks at Microsoft Press who helped champion and support us throughout the book-writing and publishing process, including Juliana Aldous, Sandra Haynes, and Rosemary Caperton.

And we want to thank Jean Trenary for managing the editing and production process and ensuring a successful delivery of the book. We extend our thanks to Joan Preppernau, Kathy Krause, and the rest of the OTSI team who contributed to our book.

Last but not least, we want to thank Sumit Virmani. As the technical editor for the book, Sumit worked around the clock to confirm the technical accuracy of the text. This included reviewing and testing all of our procedures and double-checking our facts.

Mike Snyder's Acknowledgments

I want to thank my wife, Gretchen, who supported me during this project. Writing this book required a significant time commitment above and beyond my normal work responsibilities, but Gretchen remained supportive from start to finish. I want also to thank my children for not deleting my completed work as they learned to play games on daddy's computer! I want to recognize my parents and my wife's parents who assisted my family with various babysitting stints. Lastly, thanks to all of my coworkers at Sonoma Partners who allowed me the time and understanding to work on this book.

Jim Steger's Acknowledgments

First and foremost, I wish to thank my beautiful wife, Heidi, for her patience and for continuing to support me during this arduous process again. I want to thank both of my children, who continue to grow, impress, and motivate me. I also received input from numerous members of the Microsoft Dynamics CRM product team, and I want to extend my thanks to them as well. Finally, I wish to express my gratitude to my associates at Sonoma Partners who really stepped up their effort and understanding while I was forced to prioritize my writing over some of my day-to-day duties.

Brendan Lander's Acknowledgments

I'd like to thank all the great people that made the writing process achievable, including my wife, Jennifer, my daughters, Caily, Shannon, and Cassidy, and my peers at Sonoma Partners.

Information for Readers Running Windows XP

The graphics and the operating system–related instructions in this book reflect the Windows Vista user interface. However, Windows Vista is not required; you can also use a computer running Windows XP.

Most of the differences you will encounter when working through the exercises in this book on a computer running Windows XP center around appearance rather than functionality. For example, the Windows Vista Start button is round rather than rectangular and is not labeled with the word *Start*; window frames and window-management buttons look different; and if your system supports Windows Aero, the window frames might be transparent.

In this section, we provide steps for navigating to or through menus and dialog boxes in Windows XP that differ from those provided in the exercises in this book. For the most part, these differences are small enough that you will have no difficulty in completing the exercises.

Managing the Practice Files

The instructions given in the "Using the Companion CD" section are specific to Windows Vista. The only differences when installing, using, uninstalling, and removing the practice files supplied on the companion CD are the default installation location and the uninstall process.

On a computer running Windows Vista, the default installation location of the practice files is *Documents\Microsoft Press\CRM4_SBS*. On a computer running Windows XP, the default installation location is *My Documents\Microsoft Press\CRM4_SBS*. If your computer is running Windows XP, whenever an exercise tells you to navigate to your *Documents* folder, you should instead go to your *My Documents* folder.

To uninstall the practice files from a computer running Windows XP:

1. On the Windows taskbar, click the **Start** button, and then click **Control Panel**.

2. In **Control Panel**, click (or in Classic view, double-click) **Add or Remove Programs**.

3. In the **Add or Remove Programs** window, click **Microsoft Dynamics CRM Step by Step**, and then click **Remove**.

4. In the **Add or Remove Programs** message box asking you to confirm the deletion, click **Yes**.

Important If you need help installing or uninstalling the practice files, please see the "Getting Help" section later in this book. Microsoft Product Support Services does not provide support for this book or its companion CD.

Navigating Dialog Boxes

On a computer running Windows XP, some of the dialog boxes you will work with in the exercises not only look different from the graphics shown in this book but also work differently. These dialog boxes are primarily those that act as an interface between Microsoft Dynamics CRM and the operating system, including any dialog box in which you navigate to a specific location. For example, here are the Open dialog boxes from Microsoft Dynamics CRM running on Windows Vista and Windows XP and examples of ways to navigate in them.

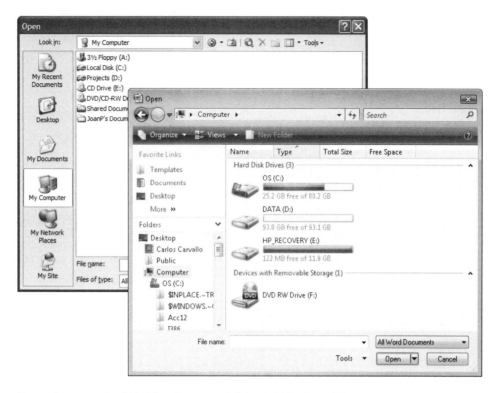

To navigate to the *WorkingAccounts* folder in Windows XP:

→ On the Places bar, click **My Documents**. Then in the folder content pane, double-click *Microsoft Press*, *CRM4_SBS*, and *WorkingAccounts*.

To move back to the *CRM4_SBS* folder in Windows XP:

→ On the toolbar, click the **Up One Level** button.

Features and Conventions of This Book

This book has been designed to lead you step by step through all the tasks you are most likely to want to perform in Microsoft Dynamics CRM 4.0. If you start at the beginning and work your way through all the exercises, you will gain enough proficiency to be able to create and work with all of the common modules and functionality of Microsoft Dynamics CRM 4.0. However, each topic is self contained. If you have worked with a previous version of Microsoft Dynamics CRM, or if you completed all the exercises and later need help remembering how to perform a procedure, the following features of this book will help you locate specific information:

- **Detailed table of contents.** Scan a listing of the book's topics and sidebars within each chapter.
- **Chapter thumb tabs.** Easily locate the beginning of the chapter you want.
- **Topic-specific running heads.** Within a chapter, quickly locate the topic you want by looking at the running head of odd-numbered pages.
- **Detailed index.** Look up specific tasks and features and general concepts in the index, which has been carefully crafted with the reader in mind.
- **Companion CD.** Install the practice files you use while working through the step-by-step exercises, and browse a fully searchable electronic version of this book and other useful resources.

In addition, we provide a glossary of terms for those times when you need to look up the meaning of a word or the definition of a concept.

You can save time when you use this book by understanding how the Step by Step series shows special instructions, keys to press, buttons to click, and other functionality.

Convention	Meaning
	This icon at the beginning of a chapter introduction indicates information about the practice files provided on the companion CD for use in the chapter.
USE	This paragraph preceding a step-by-step exercise indicates the practice files that you will use when working through the exercise.

(continued)

Convention	Meaning
BE SURE TO	This paragraph preceding or following an exercise indicates any require- ments you should attend to before beginning the exercise or actions you should take to restore your system after completing the exercise.
OPEN	This paragraph preceding a step-by-step exercise indicates files that you should open before beginning the exercise.
CLOSE	This paragraph following a step-by-step exercise provides instructions for closing open files or programs before moving on to another topic.
1 **2**	Large numbered steps guide you through hands-on exercises.
1 2	Small numbered steps guide you through procedures in sidebars and expository text.
→	An arrow indicates a procedure that has only one step.
See Also	These paragraphs direct you to more information about a given topic in this book or elsewhere.
Troubleshooting	These paragraphs explain how to fix a common problem that might prevent you from continuing with an exercise.
Tip	These paragraphs provide a helpful hint or shortcut that makes working through a task easier, or information about other available options.
Important	These paragraphs point out information that you need to know to complete a procedure.
Save	The first time you are told to click a button in a chapter, a picture of the button appears in the left margin. If the name of the button does not appear on the button itself, the name appears under the picture.
Enter	In step-by-step exercises, keys you must press appear as they would on a keyboard.
Ctrl + Tab	A plus sign (+) between two key names means that you must hold down the first key while you press the second key. For example, "Press Ctrl + Tab" means "hold down the Ctrl key while you press the Tab key."
Program interface elements and user input	In steps, the names of program elements, such as buttons, commands, and dialog boxes, and anything you are asked to type are shown in bold characters.
Glossary terms	Terms that are explained in the glossary at the end of the book are shown in bold italic characters.
Paths, URLS, and emphasized words	Folder paths, URLs, and emphasized words are shown in italic characters.

Using the Companion CD

The companion CD included with this book contains the practice files you'll use as you work through the book's exercises, as well as other electronic resources that will help you learn how to use Microsoft Dynamics CRM.

> Digital Content for Digital Book Readers: If you bought a digital-only edition of this book, you can enjoy select content from the print edition's companion CD.
>
> Visit *go.microsoft.com/fwlink/?LinkID=124659* to get your downloadable content. This content is always up-to-date and available to all readers.

CD Contents

The companion CD contains practice files necessary to complete the step-by-step exercises. The following table lists the practice files supplied on the companion CD.

Chapter	Folders\Files
Chapter 3: Working with Accounts and Contacts	*WorkingAccounts\Orders1.xls*
Chapter 18: Importing Data	*ImportingData\ContactImport1.csv*

In addition to the practice files, the CD contains the following resources in electronic format:

- *Microsoft Dynamics CRM 4.0 Step by Step* in eBook format
- *Microsoft Computer Dictionary, Fifth Edition*
- *Windows Vista Product Guide*
- Sample chapter from *Microsoft Office Live Small Business: Take Your Business Online* (Katherine Murray, 2008)

- Sample chapter from *Beyond Bullet Points: Using Microsoft Office PowerPoint 2007 to Create Presentations That Inform, Motivate, and Inspire* (Cliff Atkinson, 2008)

- Sample chapter from *Microsoft Windows SharePoint Services 3.0 Step by Step* (Olga Londer, Penelope Coventry, Bill English, and Todd Bleeker, 2008)

- Sample chapter from *Working with Microsoft Dynamics CRM 4.0, Second Edition* (Mike Snyder and Jim Steger, 2008)

> **Important** The companion CD for this book does not contain the Microsoft Dynamics CRM software. You must have access to a working Microsoft Dynamics CRM application before using this book.

Minimum System Requirements

To perform the exercises in this book, your computer should meet the following requirements:

- 700 megahertz (MHz) processor; 2 gigahertz (GHz) recommended

- 512 megabytes (MB) RAM; 1 gigabyte (GB) or more recommended

- CD or DVD drive

- For the eBooks and downloads, we recommend 3 GB of available hard disk space with 2 GB on the hard disk where the operating system is installed

> **Tip** Hard disk requirements will vary depending on configuration; custom installation choices might require more or less hard disk space.

- Monitor with 800 × 600 screen resolution; 1024 × 768 or higher recommended

- Keyboard and mouse or compatible pointing device

- Internet connection, 128 kilobits per second (Kbps) or greater, for accessing online Help topics, and any other Internet-dependent processes

- Windows Vista with Service Pack 1 (SP1), Windows XP with Service Pack 2 (SP2), or Windows Server 2003 with Service Pack 1 (SP1) or later

- Windows Internet Explorer 7 or Microsoft Internet Explorer 6 with service packs

Step-by-Step Exercises

In addition to the hardware, software, and connections required to run the 2007 Microsoft Office system, you will need the following to successfully complete the exercises in this book:

- Microsoft Office Word 2003 or 2007, Microsoft Office Excel 2003 or 2007, and Microsoft Office Outlook 2003 or 2007

- Microsoft Dynamics CRM for Outlook client installed for use with exercises in Chapter 5 and Chapter 8

- Sample product configured within Microsoft Dynamics CRM for use with an exercise in Chapter 9

- Sample relationship roles configured within Microsoft Dynamics CRM for use with an exercise in Chapter 3

- 1 MB of available hard disk space for the practice files

Installing the Practice Files

You need to install the practice files in the correct location on your hard disk before you can use them in the exercises. Follow these steps:

1. Remove the companion CD from the envelope at the back of the book, and insert it into the CD drive of your computer. If the **AutoPlay** window opens, click **Run startcd.exe**.

The Microsoft Software License Terms appear. To use the practice files, you must accept the terms of the license agreement.

2. Click **I accept the agreement**, and then click **Next**.

After you accept the license agreement, the CD interface appears.

> **Important** If the menu screen does not appear, click the Start button and then click Computer. Display the Folders list in the Navigation pane, click the icon for your CD drive, and then in the right pane, double-click the StartCD executable file.

3. Click **Install Practice Files**. If the **File Download** and/or **Internet Explorer Security** dialog boxes open, click **Run**.

4. On the **Welcome** page of the **InstallShield Wizard**, click **Next**. On the **License Agreement** page, click **I accept the terms in the license agreement**, and then click **Next**.

5. If you want to install the practice files to a location other than the default folder (*Documents\Microsoft Press\CRM4_SBS*), click the **Change** button, select the new drive and path, and then click **OK**.

> **Important** If you install the practice files to a location other than the default, you will need to substitute that path within the exercises.

6. On the **Custom Setup** page, click **Next**, and then on the **Ready to Install the Program** screen, click **Install**.

7. After the practice files have been installed, click **Finish**.

8. Close the **Step by Step Companion CD** window.

9. Remove the companion CD from the CD drive, and return it to the envelope at the back of the book.

Using the Practice Files

When you install the practice files from the companion CD that accompanies this book, the files are stored on your hard disk in chapter-specific subfolders under *Documents\Microsoft Press\CRM4_SBS*. Each exercise is preceded by a paragraph that lists the files needed for that exercise and explains any preparations needed before you start working through the exercise. Here is an example:

USE the Sonoma Partners account record you created earlier in this chapter, and the *Orders1.xls* practice file. This practice file is located in the *Documents\Microsoft Press\CRM4_SBS\WorkingAccounts* folder.

BE SURE TO use the Windows Internet Explorer Web browser to navigate to your Microsoft Dynamics CRM Web site, if necessary, before beginning this exercise.

You can browse to the practice files in Windows Explorer by following these steps:

1. On the Windows taskbar, click the **Start** button, and then click **Documents**.

2. In your *Documents* folder, double-click *Microsoft Press*, double-click *CRM4_SBS*, and then double-click a specific chapter folder.

Removing and Uninstalling the Practice Files

You can free up hard disk space by uninstalling the practice files that were installed from the companion CD. The uninstall process deletes any files that you created in the *Documents\Microsoft Press\CRM4_SBS* chapter-specific folders while working through the exercises. Follow these steps:

1. On the Windows taskbar, click the **Start** button, and then click **Control Panel**.

2. In **Control Panel**, under **Programs**, click the **Uninstall a program** task.

3. In the **Programs and Features** window, click **Microsoft Dynamics CRM Step by Step**, and then on the toolbar at the top of the window, click the **Uninstall** button.

4. If the **Programs and Features** message box asking you to confirm the deletion appears, click **Yes**.

See Also If you need additional help installing or uninstalling the practice files, see the "Getting Help" section later in this book.

> **Important** Microsoft Product Support Services does not provide support for this book or its companion CD.

Getting Help

Every effort has been made to ensure the accuracy of this book and the contents of its companion CD. If you do run into problems, please contact the sources listed in the following sections for assistance.

Getting Help with This Book and Its Companion CD

If your question or issue concerns the content of this book or its companion CD, please first search the online Microsoft Press Knowledge Base, which provides support information for known errors in or corrections to this book, at the following Web site:

www.microsoft.com/mspress/support/search.asp

Locate information specific to this book by searching for the book's ISBN, which is printed above the UPC code in the white box in the lower-left corner of the back cover of the book.

If you do not find your answer at the online Knowledge Base, send your comments or questions to Microsoft Press Technical Support at:

mspinput@microsoft.com

Getting Help with Microsoft Dynamics CRM 4.0

If your question is about Microsoft Dynamics CRM 4.0, and not about the content of this Microsoft Press book, your first recourse is the Microsoft Dynamics CRM Help system. You can find general or specific Help information in a couple of ways:

- In the Microsoft Dynamics CRM program window, you can click the Help button (labeled with a question mark) at the right end of the application toolbar to display the Microsoft Dynamics CRM Help window.

- In a dialog box, you can click the Help button at the right end of the dialog box title bar to display the Help window with topics related to the functions of that dialog box already identified.

Microsoft Dynamics CRM Help is context-sensitive; from the Microsoft Dynamics CRM Help menu, you can click Help On This Page to access the portion of the Help contents most relevant to the page you're currently viewing. For example, if you're viewing a lead record and you click Help On This Page, Microsoft Dynamics CRM automatically directs you to the Help topic titled "Work with Leads."

If you want to practice getting help, you can work through the following exercise, which demonstrates two ways of locating information.

BE SURE TO use the Windows Internet Explorer Web browser to navigate to your Microsoft Dynamics CRM Web site before beginning this exercise.

1. At the right end of the Microsoft Dynamics CRM application toolbar, click the **Help** button.

The Microsoft Dynamics CRM Help menu opens.

2. In the list of topics in the **Microsoft Dynamics CRM Help** menu, click **Help on this Page**.

Microsoft Dynamics CRM Help displays a list of topics related to the page from which you started the Help process.

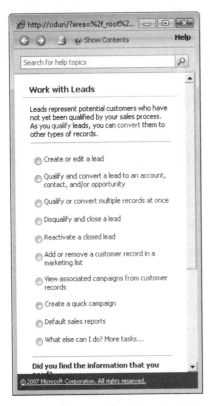

You can click any topic to display the corresponding information.

3. On the toolbar, click the **Show Contents** button.

The Contents appears in the left pane, organized by category, like the table of contents in a book.

Clicking any category (represented by a book icon) displays that category's topics (represented by help icons) as well as any available online training (represented by training icons).

Back   Forward

4. In the **Contents** area, click a few categories and topics. Then click the **Back** and **Forward** buttons to move among the topics you have already viewed.

Close

5. At the upper-right of the Internet Explorer window, click the **Close** button to close Help.

6. At the top of the **Microsoft Dynamics CRM Help** window, click the **Search for help topics** box, type **leads**, and then press the [Enter] key.

The Microsoft Dynamics CRM Help window displays topics related to the words you typed.

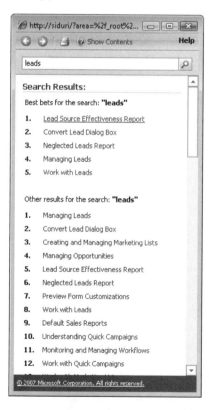

CLOSE the Microsoft Dynamics CRM Help window.

More Information

If your question is about Microsoft Dynamics CRM or another Microsoft software product and you cannot find the answer in the product's Help system, please search the appropriate product solution center or the Microsoft Knowledge Base at:

support.microsoft.com

In the United States, Microsoft software product support issues not covered by the Microsoft Knowledge Base are addressed by Microsoft Product Support Services. Location-specific software support options are available from:

support.microsoft.com/gp/selfoverview/

You can also click the Resource Center link, typically found at the bottom left of the Microsoft Dynamics CRM application. Or, you can access the same information via the Internet at the following locations:

Microsoft Dynamics CRM on-premise and service provider editions:

rc.crm.dynamics.com/rc/regcont/en_us/opdefault.aspx

Microsoft Dynamics CRM Online:

rc.crm.dynamics.com/rc/regcont/en_us/onlinedefault.aspx

Part I
Overview

Chapter at a Glance

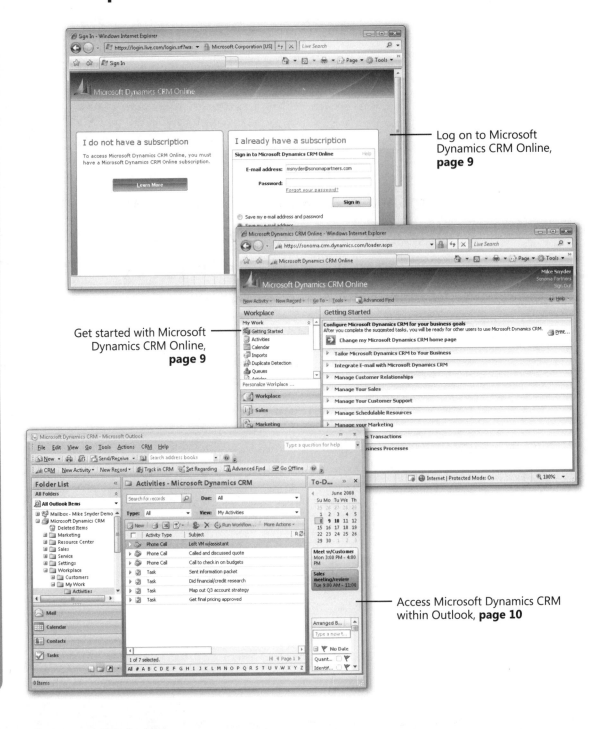

Log on to Microsoft Dynamics CRM Online, **page 9**

Get started with Microsoft Dynamics CRM Online, **page 9**

Access Microsoft Dynamics CRM within Outlook, **page 10**

1 Introduction to Microsoft Dynamics CRM

In this chapter, you will learn to:

✔ Understand key concepts in Microsoft Dynamics CRM.

✔ Understand the three deployment models for Microsoft Dynamics CRM.

✔ Understand how other Microsoft software products integrate with Microsoft Dynamics CRM.

✔ Log on to Microsoft Dynamics CRM.

✔ Log on to Microsoft Dynamics CRM Online.

✔ Access Microsoft Dynamics CRM by using Microsoft Dynamics CRM for Outlook.

Every successful organization relies on its customer base to sell products or services. Businesses that want to track and manage all of the various interactions with their customers frequently deploy a Customer Relationship Management (CRM) software system. With a CRM system, organizations can:

- Achieve a 360-degree view of the customer relationship.
- Automate common business processes to reduce manual tasks and common workflows.
- Deliver a more consistent customer experience by streamlining customer interactions.
- Enable executives to measure and report on key metrics related to their business so they can make better business and strategy decisions.

CRM software systems have been in existence for many years, but most of them earned a reputation for being difficult to use. Microsoft Dynamics CRM addresses the problems of previous CRM systems by providing an easy-to-use software application while still providing the flexibility and technical platform most businesses require. Microsoft Dynamics CRM works with most of the software products that organizations use today, such as Microsoft Office Outlook, Microsoft Office Word, and Microsoft Office Excel. Users do not need to learn a new software application to capture and work with Microsoft Dynamics CRM data; they can continue using the productivity tools they are comfortable using for other day-to-day business functions.

In this chapter, you will learn the core concepts of Microsoft Dynamics CRM. You'll also learn the different ways you can access Microsoft Dynamics CRM and other Microsoft products that integrate with Microsoft Dynamics CRM.

> **Important** Many of the examples in this book use a fictitious company named Adventure Works Cycle. This company manufactures and produces bicycle parts.

> **Important** There are no practice files for this chapter.

> **Troubleshooting** Graphics and operating system–related instructions in this book reflect the Windows Vista user interface. If your computer is running Windows XP and you experience trouble following the instructions as written, refer to the "Information for Readers Running Windows XP" section at the beginning of this book.

> **Important** The images used in this book reflect the default form and field names in Microsoft Dynamics CRM. Because the software offers extensive customization capabilities, it's possible that some of the record types or fields have been relabeled in your Microsoft Dynamics CRM environment. If you cannot find the forms, fields, or security roles referenced in this book, contact your system administrator for assistance.

> **Important** You must know the location of your Microsoft Dynamics CRM Web site to work the exercises in this book. Check with your system administrator to verify the Web address if you don't know it.

What Is Microsoft Dynamics CRM?

Microsoft Dynamics CRM is a business software solution that allows organizations of all sizes to track, manage, and report on customer or client interactions. Microsoft Dynamics CRM is part of the Microsoft Dynamics brand, which offers multiple software products to help businesses automate and streamline various operations, such as financial analysis, customer relationships, supply chain management, manufacturing, inventory, and human resources.

Microsoft Dynamics CRM includes the following three main modules:

- Sales
- Marketing
- Service

Within each module, Microsoft Dynamics CRM lets you track various customer information, as outlined in the following table.

Sales	Marketing	Service
Accounts	Accounts	Accounts
Contacts	Contacts	Contacts
Leads	Leads	Service Calendar
Opportunities	Marketing Lists	Cases
Marketing Lists	Campaigns	Knowledge Base
Competitors	Products	Contracts
Products	Sales Literature	Products
Sales Literature	Quick Campaigns	Services
Quotes		
Orders		
Invoices		
Quick Campaigns		

Your company might want to track only some of this data about your customers, and some of these might not apply to your business. Even though Microsoft Dynamics CRM includes only these three modules, many companies extend the system to track other types of related data such as projects, status reports, events, and facilities. The flexibility of the Microsoft Dynamics CRM platform allows businesses to capture almost any type of data related to their customers. In addition to customer data, you can utilize Microsoft Dynamics CRM to capture information about your prospects, partners, vendors, suppliers, and other related parties.

Microsoft Dynamics CRM is a Web-based application built on the Microsoft .NET Framework technology platform. Because of its native Web architecture, Microsoft Dynamics CRM can be accessed through the Windows Internet Explorer Web browser. In addition to the Web user experience (also known as the *Web client*), another possible access point for Microsoft Dynamics CRM is through Outlook, if your administrator installed the Microsoft Dynamics CRM for Outlook software on your computer.

> **Tip** Because Microsoft Dynamics CRM for Outlook is optional software, you might not be able to access Microsoft Dynamics CRM through Outlook. If you are not able to use Microsoft Dynamics CRM for Outlook, please contact your system administrator about getting it installed on your computer.

The Microsoft Dynamics CRM for Outlook software comes in two different versions:

- **Microsoft Dynamics CRM for Outlook.** This version is designed for use with desktop or notebook computers that will remain connected to the Microsoft Dynamics CRM server at all times.

- **Microsoft Dynamics CRM for Outlook with Offline Access.** This version is designed for users of laptop computers who must disconnect from the Microsoft Dynamics CRM server but who still need to work with CRM data when they are offline, just as they use Outlook for e-mail management, contact management, tasks and appointment management while working with no access to the Internet. The terms used by Microsoft Dynamics CRM to refer to the processes of connecting and disconnecting from the server are *going online* and *going offline*. The offline-enabled version of Microsoft Dynamics CRM for Outlook lets you work with Microsoft Dynamics CRM data offline; the software will synchronize your changes with the main database when you connect to the server again.

> **Tip** When we refer to Microsoft Dynamics CRM for Outlook in this book, we are referring to *both* the standard and offline versions. The two clients offer nearly identical functionality except that the version with offline access allows users to work while disconnected from the Microsoft Dynamics CRM server.

You can access almost all of the Microsoft Dynamics CRM system functionality from either the Web client or from Microsoft Dynamics CRM for Outlook. Therefore, you can decide which user interface method you prefer to use to access Microsoft Dynamics CRM. Microsoft Dynamics CRM for Outlook also allows you to synchronize your e-mail, tasks, contacts, and appointments from Outlook into your Microsoft Dynamics CRM system.

Microsoft Dynamics CRM Deployment Options

Microsoft Dynamics CRM is unique in the world of customer relationship management because it is one of the only applications that offers businesses multiple choices on how they can install and deploy the software. The three deployment options for Microsoft Dynamics CRM are:

- **On-premise.** A business purchases the Microsoft Dynamics CRM software and installs it on its local network. Depending on the configuration, employees can also access the Microsoft Dynamics CRM system over the Internet.

- **Microsoft Dynamics CRM Online.** A business uses the Microsoft Dynamics CRM software over the Internet on servers hosted by Microsoft.

- **Partner-hosted.** A business deploys the software at a third-party hosting environment.

The current release of Microsoft Dynamics CRM is the 4.0 version. The system functionality across all three deployment options is nearly identical, but differences do exist. The examples in this book apply to all three deployment options. If necessary, we will highlight any areas of the software in which the book examples vary by deployment type.

Integrating with Other Microsoft Products

In addition to the integration with Outlook discussed in the previous section, Microsoft Dynamics CRM integrates with several other Microsoft software applications:

- **Microsoft Office Excel.** You can export your CRM data into Excel with the click of one button and create Excel files that dynamically update when data in the CRM system changes.

- **Microsoft Office Word.** You can use Word to create mailings (such as letters and envelopes) to your customers by performing a mail merge in Microsoft Dynamics CRM. This integration also allows you to save copies of the mail merge documents.

- **Microsoft Office Communications Server.** You can access features of Microsoft Office Communications Server (such as instant messaging and presence information) directly within Microsoft Dynamics CRM to improve team collaboration.

Logging On to Microsoft Dynamics CRM

Before you can start using Microsoft Dynamics CRM, you will need to log on to the software. How you access Microsoft Dynamics CRM will depend on how your company chose to deploy the software. Prior to Microsoft Dynamics CRM 4.0, most companies deployed the software with an on-premise installation, but with the newest release of the software, many customers are choosing to deploy the software through Microsoft Dynamics CRM Online. If you are unsure how to access your Microsoft Dynamics CRM 4.0 system, contact your system administrator.

In this exercise, you will log on to the on-premise deployment of Microsoft Dynamics CRM through the Web client. In the next section, you will practice logging onto Microsoft Dynamics CRM Online. Select the exercise that matches your deployment model.

> **Troubleshooting** If your organization deploys the partner-hosted model, contact the hosting organization for specific instructions on how to log on to Microsoft Dynamics CRM.

OPEN the Windows Internet Explorer Web browser.

1. In the Internet Explorer address bar, type the Web address (also known as the URL) of your Microsoft Dynamics CRM site: **http://<*yourcrmserver/organization*>**.

   The <*yourcrmserver/organization*> portion of the URL is the name and organization name of the Microsoft Dynamics CRM site you will be using for the exercises in this book. Depending on how your Microsoft Dynamics CRM server is configured, you might need to include the organization portion in the address bar.

2. If Microsoft Dynamics CRM does not automatically log you on, enter your user name and password when prompted.

3. Click **OK**.

The start page of your Microsoft Dynamics CRM system appears. By default, the Activities page is the start page.

Logging On to Microsoft Dynamics CRM Online

If your company uses the Microsoft-hosted version of the software through Microsoft Dynamics CRM Online, you will need to use your Windows Live ID to log on to the system. Many users find that Windows Live ID is a convenient authentication method because they can use a single login and password through a wide variety of Web sites on the Internet. In this exercise, you'll log on to Microsoft Dynamics CRM Online.

OPEN the Internet Explorer Web browser.

1. In the address bar, type the following Web address (also known as the URL): **http://crm.dynamics.com**.

2. Click **Log In Here**.

3. Enter the e-mail address and password of your Windows Live ID.

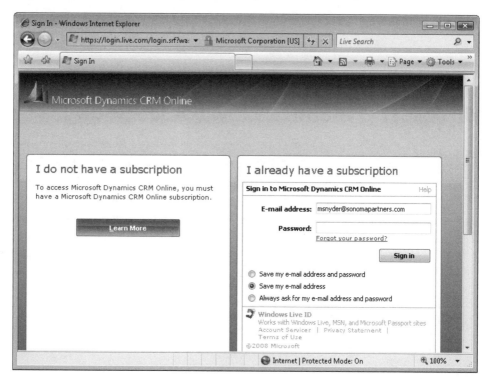

4. Click **Sign in**.

The Getting Started page of Microsoft Dynamics CRM Online appears.

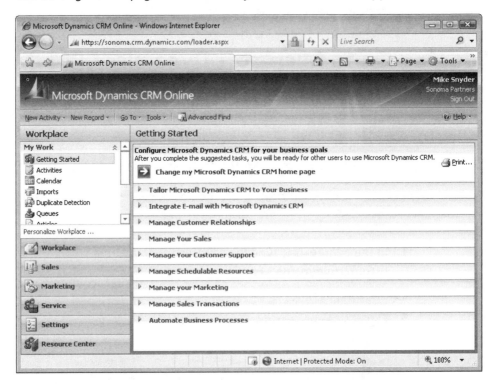

Accessing Microsoft Dynamics CRM by Using Microsoft Dynamics CRM for Outlook

In addition to the Web client, Outlook can be used to access Microsoft Dynamics CRM. Many users find accessing Microsoft Dynamics CRM within Outlook particularly convenient because they already spend a lot of time working within Outlook. The Microsoft Dynamics CRM integration with Outlook provides a single application to manage all of your customer sales, marketing, and service information. Many competing CRM software applications require users to open a second application to access their customer data. The Outlook integration of Microsoft Dynamics CRM is a unique benefit of the software that enables users to work more efficiently in a familiar software application.

See Also For more information on the integration between Microsoft Dynamics CRM and Outlook, refer to Chapter 5, "Microsoft Dynamics CRM for Outlook."

In this exercise, you will access Microsoft Dynamics CRM within Outlook.

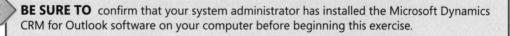

BE SURE TO confirm that your system administrator has installed the Microsoft Dynamics CRM for Outlook software on your computer before beginning this exercise.

1. Launch Outlook.

The CRM toolbar appears under the Outlook menu.

2. On the Outlook menu bar, click **Go**, and then click **Folder List**.

Microsoft Dynamics CRM for Outlook has added a set of Microsoft Dynamics CRM folders to your folder list.

3. In the **Microsoft Dynamics CRM** folder list, expand the **Workplace** folder.

4. Expand the **My Work** folder, and then click the **Activities** folder.

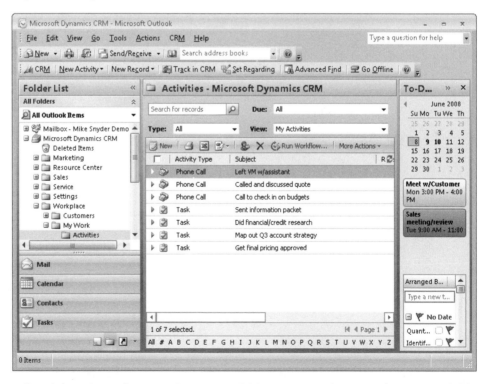

A list of the Microsoft Dynamics CRM activities appears. These are the same activities that you see when you log on to Microsoft Dynamics CRM through the Web client.

Key Points

- Microsoft Dynamics CRM is a Web-based application that lets businesses easily track and manage their customer data.

- The three modules of Microsoft Dynamics CRM are Sales, Marketing, and Service.

- You can access Microsoft Dynamics CRM data through Internet Explorer or Microsoft Dynamics CRM for Outlook.

- Microsoft Dynamics CRM integrates with other Microsoft products such as Microsoft Office Word, Microsoft Office Excel, and Microsoft Office Communications Server.

Chapter at a Glance

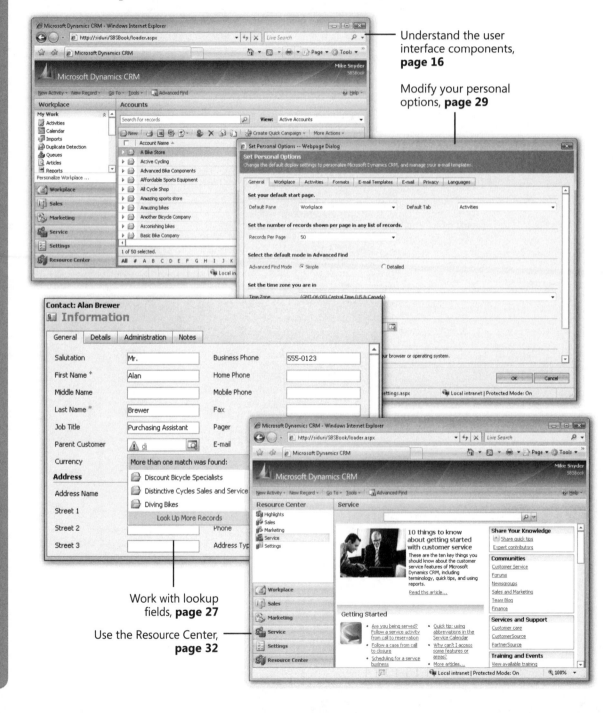

Understand the user interface components, **page 16**

Modify your personal options, **page 29**

Work with lookup fields, **page 27**

Use the Resource Center, **page 32**

2 Getting Around in Microsoft Dynamics CRM

In this chapter, you will learn to:

✔ Understand and work with the components of the user interface.

✔ Use Microsoft Dynamics CRM views to work with records.

✔ Use Quick Find to search for records in a view.

✔ Modify your personal options to suit your individual preferences.

✔ Work with lookup fields and use the automatic resolution feature.

✔ Use the Resource Center to learn more about Microsoft Dynamics CRM.

✔ Access software help within the system.

Before you can track and manage customer data in Microsoft Dynamics CRM, you need to know how to work in the user interface.

In this chapter, you will learn where to find the areas referenced in this book and how to navigate through the software. You'll also learn about the resources that can give you more information on how to work with the software.

> **Important** There are no practice files for this chapter.

> **Troubleshooting** Graphics and operating system–related instructions in this book reflect the Windows Vista user interface. If your computer is running Windows XP and you experience trouble following the instructions as written, refer to the "Information for Readers Running Windows XP" section at the beginning of this book.

> **Important** You must know the location of your Microsoft Dynamics CRM Web site to work the exercises in this book. Check with your system administrator to verify the Web address if you don't know it.

> **Important** The images used in this book reflect the default form and field names in Microsoft Dynamics CRM. Because the software offers extensive customization capabilities, it's possible that some of the record types or fields have been relabeled in your Microsoft Dynamics CRM environment. If you cannot find the forms, fields, or security roles referenced in this book, contact your system administrator for assistance.

Understanding the Microsoft Dynamics CRM User Interface

As you learned in Chapter 1, "Introduction to Microsoft Dynamics CRM," Microsoft Dynamics CRM offers two primary user interfaces: the Web client and Microsoft Dynamics CRM for Outlook. The exercises and examples in this book use the Web client unless otherwise specified. To help you better understand how to navigate the software, we will explain the various components of the user interface.

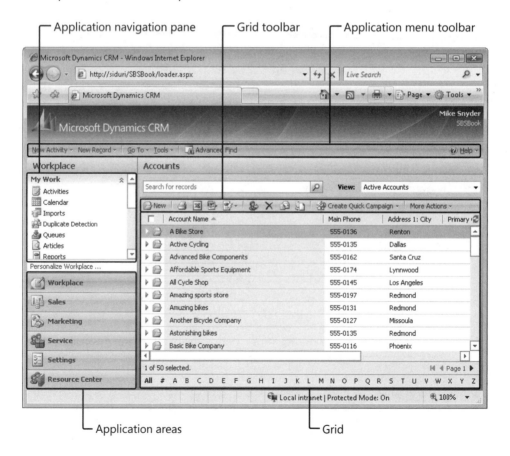

The following list describes the major components of the user interface:

- **Application menu toolbar.** This toolbar provides buttons that let you quickly create new activities or records. The Go To menu lets you navigate directly to other parts of the user interface. The Tools menu provides access to useful features such as importing data or setting your personal options. The Advanced Find button launches the Advanced Find interface, which you can use to perform ad-hoc data queries. You can also access the system help via a button on the application menu toolbar.

- **Grid.** The grid displays a list of records. Each record set is known as a data *view* in Microsoft Dynamics CRM. The grid consists of rows and columns of data. The bottom row of the grid provides information about the number of records in the view. The grid also includes an *index bar* that allows you to quickly filter records in the grid, based on the starting letter you select.

- **Grid toolbar.** The buttons in this toolbar allow you to take action on selected records in the grid. For example, if you select three records in a grid and click a button in the grid toolbar, Microsoft Dynamics CRM will apply that button's action to the three records you selected. You can also create new records by clicking the New button in the grid toolbar. The actions available in the toolbar vary depending on the type of records displayed.

- **Application navigation pane.** This portion of the user interface provides access to the various types of Microsoft Dynamics CRM data. Simply click a hyperlink in the application navigation pane to view that set of records.

- **Application areas.** Each application area provides a logical grouping of Microsoft Dynamics CRM records. The default application areas are Workplace, Sales, Marketing, Service, Settings, and Resource Center. If you click one of these buttons, Microsoft Dynamics CRM will update the application navigation pane to display the records grouped within that section.

Troubleshooting Your system administrator has the ability to add, delete, or rename buttons, so your system might look different than the one shown on the previous page.

When you open a record in Microsoft Dynamics CRM, you'll see additional parts of the user interface.

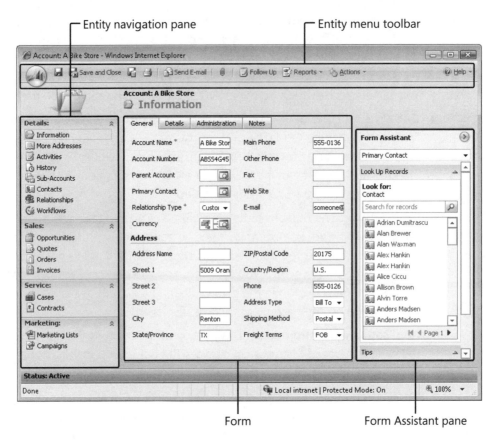

Entity navigation pane

Entity menu toolbar

Form

Form Assistant pane

Microsoft
Dynamics

- **Entity menu toolbar.** The buttons in this toolbar let you take action on the open record, such as saving or uploading an attachment. Click the Microsoft Dynamics button located in the upper-left corner of the record to access additional menu items related to the record.

- **Entity navigation pane.** Similar to the application navigation pane, the entity navigation pane displays different types of Microsoft Dynamics CRM records. However, the entity navigation pane displays only those records that are linked to the open record. For example, clicking the Contacts link in the entity navigation pane of an account record will display only those contacts that have the open account record listed as their parent customer.

- **Form.** The Microsoft Dynamics CRM form displays the data related to the open record. The fields on the entity form are often referred to as *attributes*.

- **Form Assistant pane.** This tool provides a quick way of locating related records for lookup fields and also allows you to create follow-up activities for the open record.

Using Views to Filter Data Records

Now that you understand the main components of the Microsoft Dynamics CRM user interface, you're ready to start working with data records. Microsoft Dynamics CRM uses a view to display a list of data records in a grid. You will spend a lot of time working with views, so it's important that you understand the utilities Microsoft Dynamics CRM offers to work with views of data.

Each view can contain an unlimited number of data records. Microsoft Dynamics CRM splits the view data into multiple pages of records, so you might need to click the page arrows located in the lower-right corner of the view to access the additional records contained in your view. If the page arrows are disabled, your view does not contain multiple pages of records.

> **Tip** Many users want to know how many total records or pages each view contains. Unfortunately, Microsoft Dynamics CRM does not provide this information within the user interface. To get a count of the total number of records in a view, export the data into Microsoft Office Excel and count the number of records in the data set.

In this exercise, you will change the data records that appear in the grid by selecting a different view of the data. You might want to change a view for many reasons. For example, you might want to change views to export the records from the view into Excel for a report, or you might want to perform a bulk edit of the records.

> **Tip** You can change the width of a view column by clicking the column divider and dragging it to the left or right. Resizing the column allows you to see more or less of the record's data.

 BE SURE TO use the Windows Internet Explorer Web browser to navigate to your Microsoft Dynamics CRM Web site before beginning this exercise.

1. In the application areas, click the **Sales** button.

2. In the application navigation pane, click the **Accounts** link.

   By default, Microsoft Dynamics CRM displays a view of all of the active account records in your system.

3. Click the arrow in the **View** list box.

   Microsoft Dynamics CRM displays a list of the views available for the account entity.

4. Click **My Active Accounts**.

Microsoft Dynamics CRM changes the records displayed in the grid to show only active accounts that list you as the owner of the record.

Sorting Records in a View

Within each view, you can sort the records to see them in a particular order. Each view contains a default sort order, but you can change the record order in any grid. When you're looking at a view, Microsoft Dynamics CRM includes visual indicators to show how it is sorting the records. In the column header, next to the column name, is a small triangle pointing up or down. This triangle indicates that the view records are sorted with this column's data. An upward-pointing triangle means that the records are displayed in ascending order (low to high or A to Z); a downward-pointing triangle means that the records are displayed in descending order (high to low or Z to A). In addition to the triangle in the column heading, Microsoft Dynamics CRM shades the column a light blue color in the background to visually indicate that the view is sorting on this column.

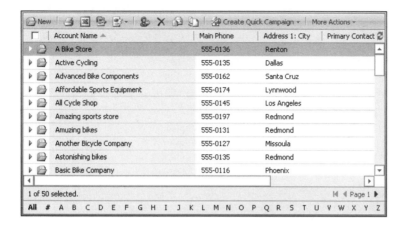

Changing the sort order of a column is very straightforward; all you need to do is click the column heading. Clicking the column heading toggles the sort order between ascending and descending.

You can also sort records by more than one column at a time. In this exercise, you will sort a view by using multiple columns.

> **Important** Even though you can display columns from related records in a view, you can sort only on columns that are attributes of the primary entity in the view. For example, if you have a Contact view that contains columns from the related account records, you can sort the Contact view only by clicking the columns that contain contact data; clicking the related account columns will not sort the records. You will not receive an error message when you click on the related columns; instead, Microsoft Dynamics CRM will not react at all.

BE SURE TO use the Internet Explorer Web browser to navigate to your Microsoft Dynamics CRM Web site, if necessary, before beginning this exercise.

OPEN a Web page that contains multiple records in a view.

1. Click the heading of the column by which you want to sort the records.

Microsoft Dynamics CRM adds the sort arrow with an ascending order and sorts the records in the view.

2. Hold down the ⎡Shift⎤ key and click the second column heading by which you want to sort the records.

Microsoft Dynamics CRM adds the sort arrow to this column with an ascending sort order, while preserving the first sort column.

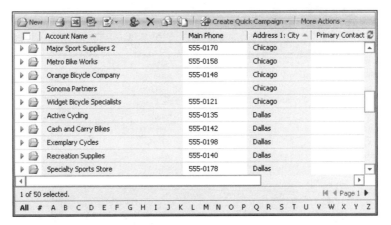

3. While keeping the ⬚Shift⬚ key down, click the second column heading again.

Microsoft Dynamics CRM switches the sort order to display the records in descending order.

Selecting and Refreshing Records in a View

As you learned earlier in this chapter, you can use the tools in the grid toolbar to perform actions on selected records in a view. Microsoft Dynamics CRM offers a few different ways to select records within a view. If you want to select one record, simply click the record row. Microsoft Dynamics CRM highlights the record with a blue background to indicate which record you selected. If you want to select all of the records, select the check box that appears in the upper-left corner of the view. Microsoft Dynamics CRM highlights all of the records that appear on the page. Selecting the check box again deselects all of the records.

> **Important** When you select the check box to select all of the records, you are only selecting the records on the page. You are not selecting all of the records in the view. For example, if your view contains 500 records and your page contains 25 records, selecting the check box selects only the 25 records displayed on the page. Some of the features in the entity toolbar, such as Export To Excel and Send Direct E-Mail, allow you to select all of the records from the view, but many of the features in the entity toolbar (such as assigning records and editing records in bulk) apply only to a single page of records. Unfortunately, in these scenarios, you will need to repeat the action on each page of records if your view contains multiple pages of records. Later in this chapter, we will explain how to display up to 250 records per page in a view (instead of the default value of 25 records per page). Displaying more records per page decreases the number of times you need to repeat an action on a set of records.

If you want to select more than one record in a view (but not all of them), you can do so by pressing the Ctrl and Shift keys. This technique should be familiar to users of Microsoft Office, because other applications such as Excel and Microsoft Office Outlook also allow users to select multiple records by holding down the Ctrl or Shift key while clicking the desired records.

As you work with the records in a view, you might find that the view does not refresh the data set as you expect. This might happen when you're working with different sets of records in multiple Internet Explorer windows or if a different user is editing the records in your view.

> **Tip** As a best practice, refresh the data in a view before performing any actions on the data set.

In this exercise, you will manually refresh the data that appears in a view, and then select multiple records in the view.

>
> **BE SURE TO** use the Internet Explorer Web browser to navigate to your Microsoft Dynamics CRM Web site, if necessary, before beginning this exercise.
> **OPEN** a Web page that contains multiple records in a view.

Refresh

1. In the upper-right corner of the view, click the **Refresh** button.

Microsoft Dynamics CRM refreshes the data in the view.

2. Click a record in the view.

Microsoft Dynamics CRM highlights the row, indicating that the record is selected.

3. To add one record to your selection, hold down the `Ctrl` key and click another record.

Microsoft Dynamics CRM highlights this new record as well, indicating that you've selected it.

4. To include multiple records in a selection, click one record, and then hold down the `Shift` key and select another record.

Microsoft Dynamics CRM selects and highlights all of the records listed between the original selection and the new selection. With the appropriate records selected, you can apply the desired action to the records.

Bulk Editing Records in a View

As you work with various records in a view, you might want to update the data in multiple records at one time. Microsoft Dynamics CRM includes a bulk edit feature that allows you to select multiple records in a view and edit them with one form instead of having to modify each record individually. This tool can provide a significant time savings if you need to modify a large number of records. Although this bulk edit feature is very convenient, it does contain a few notable restrictions:

- If a particular field contains programming script behind the scenes (as configured by your system administrator), you cannot edit the data in that field with the bulk edit tool.

- You cannot use the bulk edit tool to remove values from a field. You can only modify or add data to a field.

- You cannot use the bulk edit tool to edit certain fields in Microsoft Dynamics CRM, such as the Parent Customer field of an account or contact record.

- The bulk edit tool updates only the selected records on the page; you cannot use it to update all of the records in the view if the records span multiple pages.

- If a data field is read-only on the form, you cannot edit it with the bulk edit tool.

> **Tip** Even though you cannot edit the owner of a record by using the bulk edit tool, you can easily change the owner of multiple records at one time by using the Assign feature located in the entity menu toolbar.

In this exercise, you will use the bulk edit tool to update the State/Province field for multiple contacts.

 BE SURE TO use the Internet Explorer Web browser to navigate to your Microsoft Dynamics CRM Web site, if necessary, before beginning this exercise.
OPEN a view of Contacts that contains more than one record.

1. While holding down the Ctrl key, click two or more of the contact records.

   Microsoft Dynamics CRM highlights the records you click to indicate that they are selected.

2. In the entity menu toolbar, click **More Actions**, and then click **Edit**.

   The Edit Multiple Records dialog box opens. This dialog box is very similar to the contact form, with the same layout and fields.

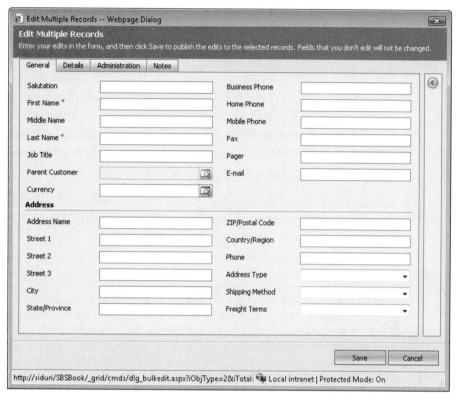

3. In the **State/Province** field, type **Illinois**.

4. Click the **Save** button.

Microsoft Dynamics CRM updates the State/Province field of the selected records and closes the Edit Multiple Records dialog box.

Using Quick Find to Search for Records in a View

Even with the sorting features in views, sometimes it can be time consuming to manually look for a particular record if the view contains a large number of records. To help address this concern, Microsoft Dynamics CRM includes a *Quick Find* feature that allows you to search for records by using keywords or wildcard characters. You can find the Quick Find search box above the grid and to the left of the View selector. To use it, enter a search phrase and press Enter on the keyboard or click the button with the magnifying glass to start the search. Even though Quick Find is simple to use, there are a few tips and tricks that will help you find records more efficiently.

Your system administrator can configure Microsoft Dynamics CRM to search for matching records across multiple columns. For example, you can search for particular contacts by name, phone number, or e-mail address. You can even include custom data fields as part of the search criteria.

When you enter search text, Microsoft Dynamics CRM searches for the value as it is entered. By default, it does not search for partial records. For example, if you search for a phone number by entering 555-1212 and the contact's phone number is (312) 555-1212, Microsoft Dynamics CRM does not consider that a match. It returns only those records that have 555-1212 as the start of their phone number.

Of course, there will be times when you don't know the exact value you're searching for. In these cases, you can enter an asterisk (*) as a wildcard character in your Quick Find search. In the previous example, if you did not know the exact phone number, you could search for *555-1212 and Microsoft Dynamics CRM would find the matching record.

> **Tip** You can enter the wildcard character anywhere in your search criteria: at the beginning, the middle, or the end. If you can't find the record you're looking for, be sure to try different combinations with the wildcard asterisk. Note that the Quick Find feature is not case-sensitive in its searches.

If you start a Quick Find search when you're working with a specific view, such as My Active Contacts, you might expect that Microsoft Dynamics CRM would search for matching records only within the My Active Contacts view. However, Quick Find always searches for matching records across all active records for that entity. Quick Find ignores inactive records.

> **Tip** To filter records within a specific view, you can click the letters in the index bar. Clicking a letter will update the view to show only those records whose entry in the current sort column starts with the selected letter. For example, if you're looking at the My Active Contacts view with the records sorted by City and you click B in the index bar, Microsoft Dynamics CRM shows you only those records in which the city starts with the letter B. If you then click the Full Name column to sort by that field and click the letter C in the index bar, Microsoft Dynamics CRM updates the My Active Contacts view to show only those records in which the Full Name entry starts with the letter C.

In this exercise, you will use the Quick Find feature to search for records in Microsoft Dynamics CRM.

BE SURE TO use the Internet Explorer Web browser to navigate to your Microsoft Dynamics CRM Web site, if necessary, before beginning this exercise.

OPEN a view of Contacts that contains more than one record.

1. In the **Quick Find** box, type ***bi**, and then press Enter .

Microsoft Dynamics CRM searches and returns all active contacts for matching records.

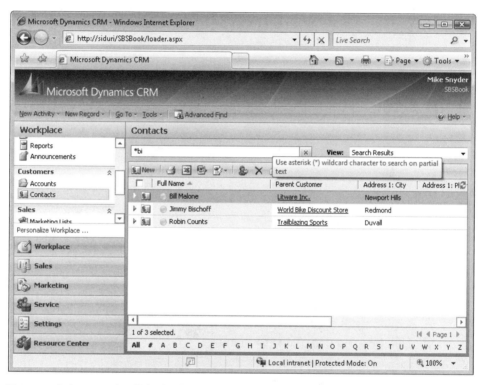

Cancel Search

2. To cancel the search, click the **Cancel Search** button to the right of the **Quick Find** box, or simply select a new view in the view selector.

Using Lookups and Automatic Resolution

One of the main benefits of any customer relationship management system is that you can use the software to create relationships between records in your database. These relationships allow you to understand the different types of data about your customers, vendors, and partners, and how they interact with one another. The Microsoft Dynamics CRM user interface displays the link between two records by using a *lookup*. The default contact form includes two lookups: one for the Parent Customer and one for the default Currency.

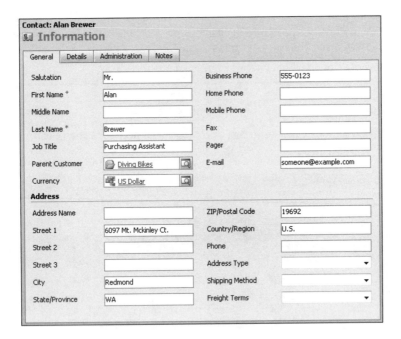

You can visually determine that a field is a lookup because:

- The text in the field is hyperlinked (blue and underlined).
- There is an icon to the left of the text that indicates the entity of the linked record.
- The field includes an icon with a window and a magnifying glass.

Look Up

Clicking the hyperlinked text in the field launches a new window displaying the linked record. Unlike the other fields on the form, in which you simply enter data into the field, lookup fields require you to select a record to link. You can link records in the lookup field by using one of two techniques:

- **Use the Look Up Records dialog box.** To use this technique, click the lookup icon. Microsoft Dynamics CRM then launches the Look Up Records dialog box that you can use to search for and select a specific record.
- **Use automatic resolution.** To use this technique, simply start typing the name of the linked record in the lookup field. After you enter all (or a portion) of the linked record's name, click a different form field or press the Tab key. Microsoft Dynamics CRM then tries to automatically resolve your entry to an existing record.

> **Tip** The automatic resolution feature in lookups can provide a significant time savings when you work with many different records.

Microsoft Dynamics CRM tries to match records in the lookup by using the find fields of the entity. The record name is usually included as a find field, but your administrator might configure additional find fields that you can use with automatic resolution. If Microsoft Dynamics CRM finds just one matching record during the automatic resolution, it populates a link to that record in the lookup field. If more than one match is found, the lookup field displays a yellow warning icon and colors the text you entered red. Click the warning icon to view the potential matches, and then select the record you want. Microsoft Dynamics CRM then uses that value for the lookup field.

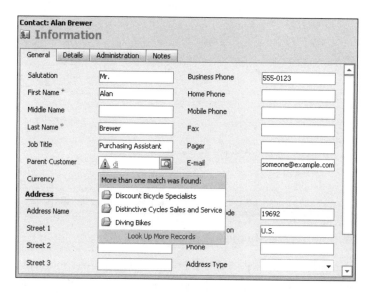

 If Microsoft Dynamics CRM does not find any potential matches, it colors the text red and displays a red circle with a white X.

If you want to remove a value from a lookup field, you can select the white portion of the field (without clicking the hyperlinked text) and then press the Backspace key or Delete key.

Setting Personal Options

Microsoft Dynamics CRM allows you to set personal options to modify the user interface. You can access your personal options by clicking the Tools button in the application menu toolbar and then clicking Personal Options. Although we won't review all of the personal options available, we do want to review a few common configuration options.

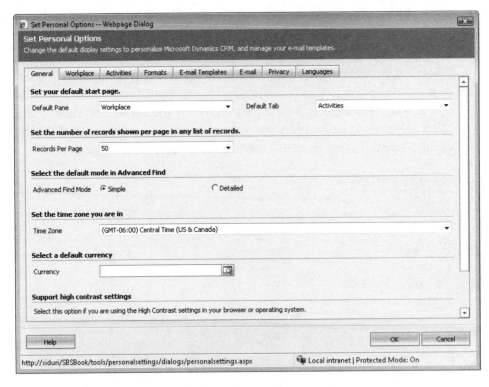

On the General tab, you can specify the following:

- **Default start page.** By changing this section, you can determine which page Microsoft Dynamics CRM starts on after you log on with the Web client. Select the pane and tab you use most frequently.

- **Records per page.** As we mentioned earlier, you might want to change the number of records that appear on a page. By displaying more records on a page, you can apply actions to a larger data set. However, you should be aware that users with a large number of records per page might experience slower performance as the page loads, so use caution with this setting.

- **Time zone.** Be sure to select the correct time zone to match the time zone of your computer. If this time zone setting does not match the time zone on your computer, you might find that appointments synchronized to Outlook are shifted by a few hours.

On the Workplace tab, you can select which application areas to display in the navigation pane. This setting appears only to you as an individual user; it does not apply to all users in the system. Therefore, feel free to set up the Workplace area in whatever manner is most comfortable for you.

In this exercise, you will modify your Workplace pane to include new areas of the user interface.

> **Tip** The Set Personal Options dialog box in Microsoft Dynamics CRM for Outlook provides additional configuration options when compared with the dialog box in the Web client. For more information about the personal options in Outlook, see Chapter 5, "Microsoft Dynamics CRM for Outlook."

 BE SURE TO log on to the Microsoft Dynamics CRM Web site through the Web client before beginning this exercise.

1. In the application menu toolbar, click **Tools**, and then click **Options**.

The Set Personal Options dialog box opens.

2. On the **Workplace** tab, select the **Sales** check box.

Microsoft Dynamics CRM updates the preview on the left side of the dialog box to include the Sales area.

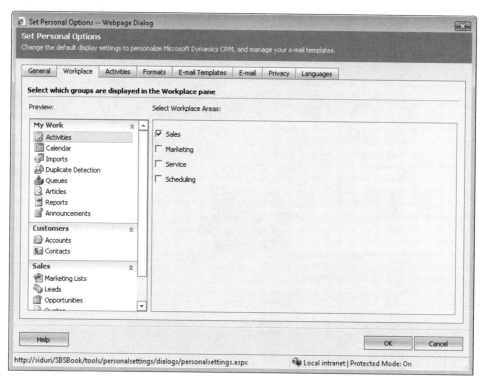

3. Click **OK**.

4. Click **Workplace** in the application areas.

Microsoft Dynamics CRM now includes the sales area that you just added in the application navigation pane.

Using the Resource Center

Microsoft Dynamics CRM includes a Resource Center that provides additional information about the software. The Resource Center contains dynamic content hosted on the Microsoft servers, and Microsoft provides continual updates to this content. You need an Internet connection to access content from the Resource Center. The Resource Center organizes information into five different sections:

- Highlights
- Sales
- Marketing
- Service
- Settings

Each section includes articles about working with Microsoft Dynamics CRM. Check the Resource Center periodically to see if there is any content that applies to you.

In addition to articles about using the software, the Resource Center contains links to other Microsoft Dynamics CRM resources such as newsgroups, blogs, and customer support.

Accessing Help in Microsoft Dynamics CRM

Even though most users indicate that Microsoft Dynamics CRM is intuitive and easy to learn, you might have questions about the software. Fortunately, Microsoft Dynamics CRM includes help guides for end users as well as administrators. To access Help, click the Help button on the application menu toolbar or the entity menu toolbar.

Microsoft Dynamics CRM Help is context-sensitive; you can click Help On This Page to access the portion of the Help contents most relevant to the page you're currently viewing. For example, if you're viewing a lead record and you click Help On This Page, Microsoft Dynamics CRM automatically directs you to the Help topic titled "Work with Leads."

> **Tip** Your system administrator can customize the Help content that appears in Microsoft Dynamics CRM to include specific instructions about your unique Microsoft Dynamics CRM deployment.

Key Points

- To sort records in a view, click the column heading to toggle the records in ascending or descending order. To sort by more than one column, hold down the Ctrl key and click a second column header.

- To select records in a view, use the Ctrl or Shift key to select multiple records. Selecting the check box selects all of the records on the page, but not all of the records in the view.

- Bulk editing allows you to modify multiple records at once, but you can only bulk edit records one page at a time.

- The Quick Find feature allows you to search for records in a view. You can use the asterisk (*) as a wildcard character in your searches.

- Lookups link records in the user interface. You can use the automatic resolution feature by typing text directly into the lookup field.

- You can modify your personal options to specify your preferences, including the start page when Microsoft Dynamics CRM first loads or the number of records displayed on each page.

- Microsoft Dynamics CRM includes additional information about using the software in the Resource Center and in the Help section.

Chapter at a Glance

Link contacts to an account, **page 41**

Attach files to an account, **page 47**

Track additional customer relationships, **page 45**

Share a contact with other users, **page 51**

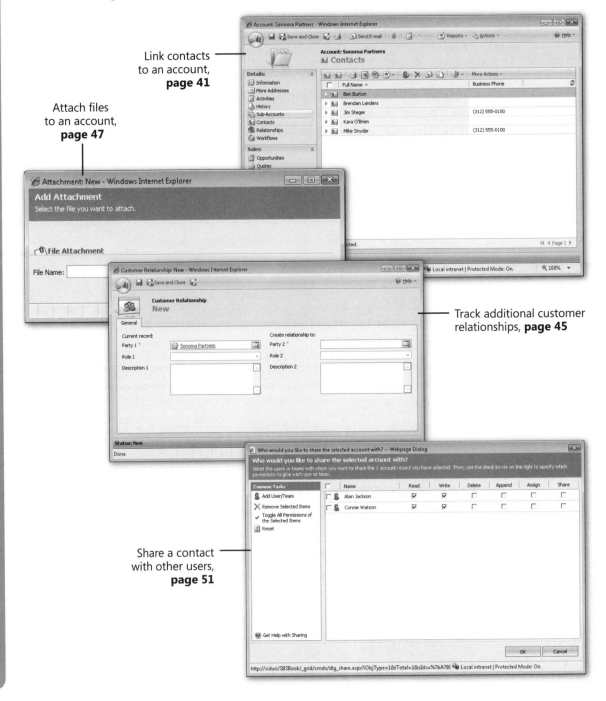

3 Working with Accounts and Contacts

In this chapter, you will learn to:

✔ Create an account.

✔ Link accounts to sub-accounts.

✔ Create a contact.

✔ Create links between accounts and contacts.

✔ Create additional relationships between accounts and contacts.

✔ Attach files to accounts and contacts.

✔ Share accounts and contacts with other users.

✔ Assign accounts and contacts to other users.

✔ Merge account or contact records.

The previous chapters covered a lot of the background information about Microsoft Dynamics CRM. In this chapter, you'll start working with customer records. *Accounts* and *contacts* are two of the most important and frequently used types of records in the system. As you learned in Chapter 1,"Introduction to Microsoft Dynamics CRM," CRM stands for *Customer Relationship Management*, and capturing the relationships between the accounts and contacts that work with your organization is one of the most valuable benefits of the Microsoft Dynamics CRM system.

In Microsoft Dynamics CRM, an account is a company or other business entity that interacts with your organization. If your business sells products and services to other businesses, accounts might represent your customers. Contacts in Microsoft Dynamics CRM represent specific individuals, who might or might not have a relationship with an account record. If your organization's target customers include consumers, you'll appreciate the fact that Microsoft Dynamics CRM lets you manage contact records without any association to specific account records. In addition to tracking customers, you might also want to track the other organizations and people that interact with your company, such as competitors, consultants, partners, suppliers, and vendors. This chapter will teach you how to distinguish between these different types of records.

You'll also learn how to link contacts to accounts so that you can track how each person relates to different businesses. By capturing as much data as possible about accounts and contacts, you can begin to develop a 360-degree view of each person and business related to your organization. When you understand all of the interactions with each account and contact, you will be able to work more efficiently, make better decisions, and provide improved customer service.

For example, assume you're a sales representative using Microsoft Dynamics CRM, and you want to approach an existing customer about purchasing an additional product from your company. Before you pick up the phone to call the customer, it would be ideal for you to know whether the customer is experiencing any problems or issues with the product she purchased from you last year. A happy customer without any service issues will be more likely to purchase from you than a customer who is experiencing a lot of problems. Now let's assume that your customer service department is also using Microsoft Dynamics CRM and tracking all of the service requests in the same system you're using to track sales and marketing activities. When you view the customer record in Microsoft Dynamics CRM, you will be able to easily view all of your sales information *and* all of the customer service requests. If sales and service were using two different systems, you might have to make multiple phone calls or check in two different places to get the full picture of a customer's dealings with your organization. Microsoft Dynamics CRM allows you to quickly review a customer record to understand the whole picture before you approach the customer about purchasing additional products or services.

In this chapter, you will create accounts and contacts within Microsoft Dynamics CRM and then work with them to track business relationships, attach related files, and share permissions for the customer data with another member of your sales team.

Important In this chapter, you will work with accounts and contacts by using the Web client, not the Microsoft Dynamics CRM for Outlook client. Both clients share almost all of the concepts and steps for working with accounts and contacts. However, Microsoft Dynamics CRM for Outlook includes some additional account and contact functionality that you will learn about in Chapter 5, "Microsoft Dynamics CRM for Outlook."

See Also One of the most important benefits of Microsoft Dynamics CRM for Outlook is the ability to synchronize contacts from Microsoft Dynamics CRM with your Microsoft Office Outlook contact list. This lets you synchronize your Microsoft Dynamics CRM contacts in Outlook to a mobile or handheld device. Chapter 5 discusses the Outlook synchronization process in detail.

> **Important** Before you can use the practice files in this chapter, you need to install them from the book's companion CD to their default location. See "Using the Companion CD" at the beginning of this book for more information.

> **Troubleshooting** Graphics and operating system–related instructions in this book reflect the Windows Vista user interface. If your computer is running Windows XP and you experience trouble following the instructions as written, refer to the "Information for Readers Running Windows XP" section at the beginning of this book.

> **Important** The images used in this book reflect the default form and field names in Microsoft Dynamics CRM. Because the software offers extensive customization capabilities, it's possible that some of the record types or fields have been relabeled in your Microsoft Dynamics CRM environment. If you cannot find the forms, fields, or security roles referenced in this book, contact your system administrator for assistance.

> **Important** You must know the location of your Microsoft Dynamics CRM Web site to work the exercises in this book. Check with your system administrator to verify the Web address if you don't know it.

Creating an Account

Accounts represent businesses or organizations in Microsoft Dynamics CRM. You can access account information from the Sales, Marketing, and Service areas. The Account form consists of multiple tabs, each of which contains data fields known as *attributes*.

In all of the types of records in Microsoft Dynamics CRM, required attributes are marked with a red asterisk (*) to the right of the field name. The red asterisk indicates that you must enter a value in that field before you can create or save the record. If you try to create or save a record in which a required field does not contain data, Microsoft Dynamics CRM will prompt you to enter data in the field, and it will not save your changes.

A blue plus (+) symbol to the right of a field's name indicates that the field is recommended. You can still create or edit records without entering data in a recommended field.

In this exercise, you will create a new account record.

BE SURE TO use the Windows Internet Explorer Web browser to navigate to your Microsoft Dynamics CRM Web site before beginning this exercise.

New Account

1. In the **Sales** area, click **Accounts**.

2. In the grid toolbar, click the **New Account** button to launch the **New Account** form.

3. In the **Account Name** field, enter **Sonoma Partners**. If your system includes additional required fields (as indicated by the red asterisk), enter values into those fields as well.

4. In the **Relationship Type** list, select **Supplier**.

5. In the **Street 1** field, enter **525 W. Monroe St**.

6. In the **City** field, enter **Chicago**.

7. In the **State/Province** field, enter **IL**.

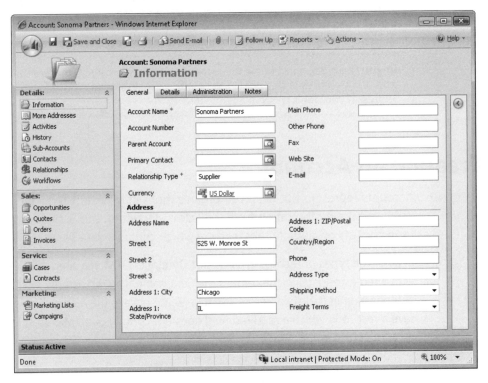

Save

8. Click the **Save** button to create the account.

> **Tip** You can also create an account by clicking the New Record menu item in the application menu toolbar and selecting Account.

Using Parent Accounts and Sub-Accounts

In the previous example, you created a new account named Sonoma Partners. Now let's assume that Sonoma Partners is a division of a much larger organization named Contoso. Knowing a relationship exists between Sonoma Partners and Contoso might be beneficial when you're working with either company. Microsoft Dynamics CRM allows you to capture and record this type of relationship by using *parent accounts* and *sub-accounts*. In this example, you would specify Contoso as the parent account of Sonoma Partners. When you do so, Microsoft Dynamics CRM automatically denotes that Sonoma Partners is a sub-account of Contoso.

> **Important** You can use parent accounts and sub-accounts to record a link between two organizations. Specifying one account as the parent account automatically makes the other a sub-account. Each account can have only one parent account, but you can specify as many sub-accounts as necessary.

Most companies that use Microsoft Dynamics CRM use parent accounts and sub-accounts to denote a legal or ownership relationship between two accounts. When one or more sub-accounts are related to a parent account, all of the activities and history for the sub-accounts are rolled up to the parent account. Therefore, when you look at the history of the Contoso account, Microsoft Dynamics CRM also displays the history of records attached to the Sonoma Partners account. This provides a complete picture of the interactions between the various records in your system, allowing your organization to understand your customers and tailor your sales, marketing, and customer service efforts accordingly.

See Also For more information on how to track activities, see Chapter 4, "Working with Activities and Notes."

In this exercise, you will create a new Contoso account and link it to the Sonoma Partners account created in the previous example.

USE the Sonoma Partners account record you created in the previous exercise.

BE SURE TO use the Internet Explorer Web browser to navigate to your Microsoft Dynamics CRM Web site, if necessary, before beginning this exercise.

1. In the application menu toolbar, click **New Record**, and select **Account** to launch the **New Account** form.

2. In the **Account Name** field, enter **Contoso**.

Save and Close

3. Enter values in any other required fields marked by a red asterisk, and then click the **Save and Close** button.

4. In the application navigation pane, click **Accounts**, and double-click the **Sonoma Partners** record.

5. In the box next to **Parent Account**, enter **Contoso**, and then press the Tab key.

   Microsoft Dynamics CRM automatically resolves the text you entered to the Contoso record. The association is indicated by the underline and blue text color of the parent account name.

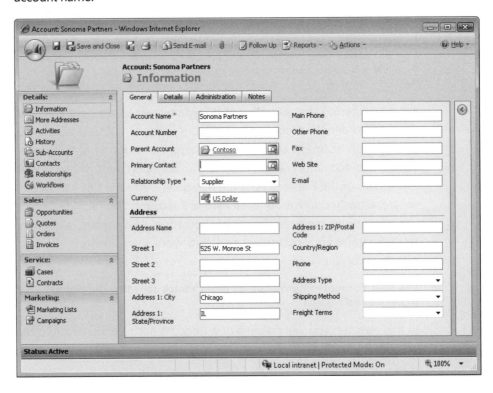

6. Click **Save**.

> **Tip** You also could have used the lookup window to select the Contoso record as the parent account.

Creating a Contact

Contacts represent the various people with whom you do business. For each contact record, you can specify one (and only one) account as its parent customer. Most companies use the Parent Customer field to record the contact's employer, but you are not obligated to do so.

By specifying a parent customer for a contact, you create a relationship between those two records. When you create relationships between accounts and contacts, you can view all of an account's contacts by clicking the Contacts link in the account's left navigation pane. This list of contacts related to the account is known as the contact associated view.

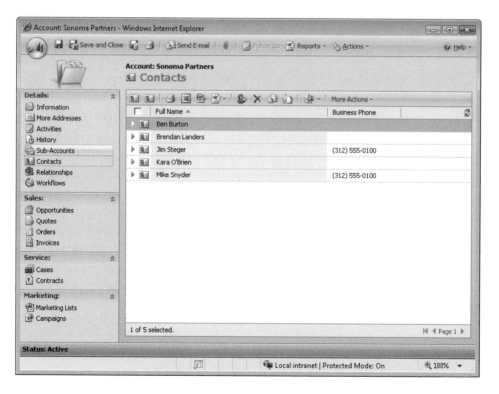

Similar to linking sub-accounts and parent accounts, linking contacts to an account allows you to view the contacts related to an account, including a roll-up of the activities from the related contacts to the parent account. Therefore, if you log a phone call activity with the Mike Snyder contact record, whose parent account is Sonoma Partners, you will be able to view that phone call record when you're looking at the Sonoma Partners record.

> **Tip** By default, Microsoft Dynamics CRM lists the contact's full name and business phone number when you're looking at the contacts related to an account. Your system administrator can customize this contact associated view to include additional columns, such as title, city, or e-mail address.

As with accounts, you can use several methods of creating a contact, such as the following:

- Create a contact from the application menu toolbar by clicking New Record and selecting Contact.
- Create a contact by navigating to a contact view and clicking the New Contact button in the grid toolbar.
- Create a contact by clicking the New Contact button in the grid toolbar of the contact associated view of an account.
- Create a contact by clicking the New button in the contact's Look Up Records dialog box.

One benefit of creating a contact from the contact associated view is that Microsoft Dynamics CRM automatically populates several fields on the contact record, based on the account record you're currently viewing. For example, if you have the Sonoma Partners account record open and you then click the New Contact button in the contact associated view, Microsoft Dynamics CRM fills out many of the fields on the new contact record—Street 1, Street 2, City, Business Phone, and others—with data from the Sonoma Partners account record. Microsoft Dynamics CRM also automatically fills out the Parent Customer field of the new contact as Sonoma Partners. This concept of populating data fields is known as field mapping. Your system administrator can determine how fields are mapped between two types of records.

> **Tip** Creating a new contact from the contact associated view automatically fills out the mapped fields, such as the Parent Customer field and the address fields. Using this technique saves you time if the contact shares the same address information with the account.
>
> If you create a new contact record by using one of the first two methods described previously, Microsoft Dynamics CRM will not automatically fill out the mapped fields for you. This can be useful when the contact has different address information than the account (as could be the case when an employee works from home).

Although field mapping populates the contact record with data from the parent account, it will not maintain an ongoing link between the two records. If the account address changes because the business moves to a new office, you will need to explicitly update the address of the contacts related to that account. The bulk edit feature located on the More Actions menu on the grid toolbar of the contact associated view allows you to update the address of multiple contacts at the same time.

For each account record, you can specify a primary contact. As you would expect, the primary contact denotes the individual that your organization should initiate interactions with. Although most of the time the primary contact works for the account as an employee, this is not a requirement. You can select any contact in the system as the primary contact for an account. Consequently, assigning a primary contact to an account does not automatically map the data fields and populate the mapped values.

> ## Why Is It Called Parent Customer?
>
> In the examples in this chapter, you set an account as the *parent customer* of the contact. However, most companies that use Microsoft Dynamics CRM use this field to track the *employer* of the contact. Why does Microsoft Dynamics CRM call this field the parent customer? The **customer** field is special in Microsoft Dynamics CRM, because you can use it to select either an account or a contact record. The customer field appears in multiple places throughout the system (in cases and opportunities, for instance) in which you might want to select an account *or* a contact, depending on how your organization tracks customers in Microsoft Dynamics CRM. Your system administrator can rename this field to Parent Account if necessary.

In this exercise, you will create two new contacts for the Sonoma Partners account. First, you will create a contact from the contact associated view, which will populate certain values in the contact. Then you will use a different method, in which Microsoft Dynamics CRM does not populate the mapped fields.

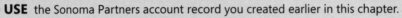

USE the Sonoma Partners account record you created earlier in this chapter.

BE SURE TO use the Internet Explorer Web browser to navigate to your Microsoft Dynamics CRM Web site, if necessary, before beginning this exercise.

1. Navigate to **Accounts** and open the **Sonoma Partners** record.

2. In the left navigation pane, click the **Contacts** link.

New Contact

3. In the grid toolbar, click the **New Contact** button.

   Microsoft Dynamics CRM opens a new window. Note that the following fields already contain data: Parent Customer, Street 1, City, and State/Province.

4. In the **First Name** field, enter **Ben**, and in the **Last Name** field, enter **Burton**.

5. Click **Save and Close**.

   The Ben Burton contact now appears in the contact associated view of the Sonoma Partners account record.

6. Click the **New Records** menu item in the application menu bar, and select **Contact** to launch the **New Contact** form.

7. In the **First Name** field, enter **Alan**, and in the **Last Name** field, enter **Jackson**.

8. In the **Parent Customer** field, enter **Sonoma Partners**, and then press ⌨Tab.

9. Click **Save and Close**.

   Now both Ben Burton and Alan Jackson are linked to the Sonoma Partners account record, but Microsoft Dynamics CRM populated the mapped fields only in the Ben Burton record because you created it from the contact associated view.

Creating Additional Relationships Between Accounts and Contacts

As you just learned, you can link multiple contacts to a single account by using the Parent Customer field. This relationship typically indicates an employer-employee relationship between the records. In addition, you can link two accounts by using the parent account and sub-account functionality. These relationships typically indicate some sort of legal ownership between the accounts. But what if you want to capture additional types of relationships between accounts and contacts outside of the ones we just described? For example, what if you wanted to record that Company A is the networking consultant for Company B? Clearly, that relationship wouldn't fit into the parent account/ sub-account structure, but it is still valuable information.

Fortunately, Microsoft Dynamics CRM allows you to link accounts and contacts by using *customer relationships*. Because each type of business will want to track different types of relationships, Microsoft Dynamics CRM allows your administrator to configure the types of account and contact relationships that your business will track.

In this example, you will create a customer relationship between two accounts to indicate that one account is the customer and the other is the networking consultant.

> **USE** the Sonoma Partners account record you created earlier in this chapter.
>
> **BE SURE TO** have your system administrator import the sample relationship roles included in the practice files, or create your own relationship roles in your Microsoft Dynamics CRM environment. Use the Internet Explorer Web browser to navigate to your Microsoft Dynamics CRM Web site, if necessary, before beginning this exercise.

1. Open the **Sonoma Partners** account record.

2. In the left navigation pane, click **Relationships**.

New Customer
Relationship

3. In the grid toolbar, click the **New Customer Relationship** button to launch the **New Customer Relationship** dialog box.

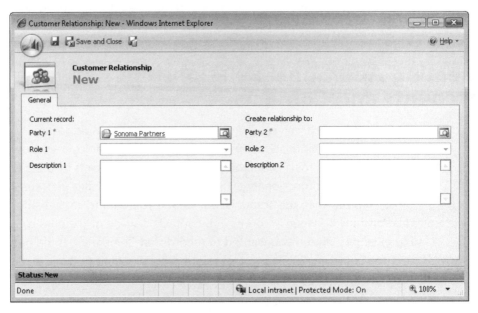

Look Up

4. In the **Party 2** field, click the **Look Up** button, and select any account record.

5. After you select a value for **Party 2**, notice that Microsoft Dynamics CRM enables the **Role 1** and **Role 2** lists. In the **Role 1** list, select **Customer**.

6. In the **Role 2** list, select **Networking Consultant**. If you want, you can add more information about the relationship in the **Description 1** and **Description 2** boxes.

7. Click **Save and Close** to create the relationship.

   Microsoft Dynamics CRM now displays the relationship that you created between the Sonoma Partners account and the account you selected in step 4.

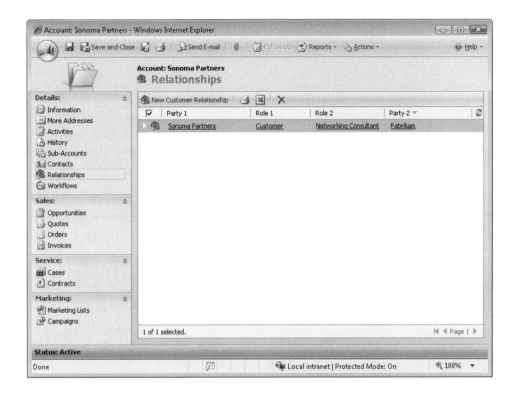

Important The values that appear in the Role 1 and Role 2 lists depend on the values configured by your system administrator. He or she can also set up certain types of relationships that apply only to account-to-account, account-to-contact, or contact-to-contact relationships. For example, you might want to track a family relationship between two contacts, but this type of relationship would never apply to an account-to-account or an account-to-contact relationship.

Attaching Files to Accounts and Contacts

In addition to entering information about accounts and contacts in the forms, you can attach files (such as a Microsoft Office Excel spreadsheet or an Adobe Acrobat PDF file) to the record. Microsoft Dynamics CRM allows you to easily upload and save files about accounts and contacts so that you can refer to them later.

In this exercise, you will save a file as an attachment to an account and download it for viewing. You can follow a similar sequence of steps to attach a file to a contact record.

> **USE** the Sonoma Partners account record you created earlier in this chapter, and the *Orders1.xls* practice file. This practice file is located in the *Documents\Microsoft Press\ CRM4_SBS\WorkingAccounts* folder.
>
> **BE SURE TO** use the Internet Explorer Web browser to navigate to your Microsoft Dynamics CRM Web site, if necessary, before beginning this exercise.

1. Navigate to the **Accounts** view, and open the **Sonoma Partners** record.

Attach a File

2. In the toolbar, click the **Attach a File** button to launch the **Add Attachment** window.

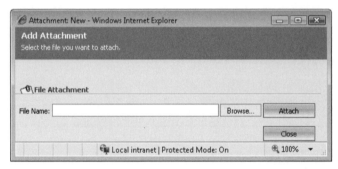

3. Click **Browse**, and navigate to the *Documents\Microsoft Press\CRM4_ SBS\ WorkingAccounts* folder.

4. Select *Orders1.xls*, and click **Open**.

   The navigation window closes.

5. Click **Attach** to upload the file to the account.

6. Click **Close**.

7. In the **Sonoma Partners** record, click the **Notes** tab.

   Microsoft Dynamics CRM has now attached the *Orders1.xls* file to the account record and has automatically recorded the name of the user who uploaded the attached file, in addition to the date and time.

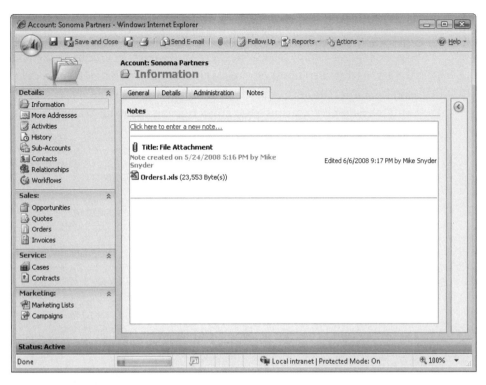

8. To open the attachment, click the file name, and select either **Open** or **Save**.

Deactivating and Activating Records

Most of the records in Microsoft Dynamics CRM include values for status and status reason. A record's status defines the state of the record. The most common status values are *Active* and *Inactive*. However, some types of records include additional status values. For example, case records can have a status value of *Active, Resolved,* or *Canceled*. Records that do not have a status value of *Open* or *Active* are considered to be deactivated (also referred to as "inactive"). Microsoft Dynamics CRM retains deactivated records in the system; it does not delete them. However, inactive records will not appear in several areas throughout the user interface, such as in Quick Find searches or lookup windows.

> **Important** Microsoft Dynamics CRM removes inactive records from parts of the user interface. Also, you cannot use an inactive record's form to edit the record.

A record's status reason provides a description of the record's status. Status reasons vary by type of record and status value. In the case example, a record with an Active status value can have one of several status reason values: In Progress, On Hold, Waiting For Details, or Researching. Trying to understand the difference between a record's status and its status reason can cause confusion, but you should make sure you get familiar with these important concepts. The following table illustrates how status and status reason values can vary by record type.

Record type	Status value	Status reason value
Account	*Active*	*Active*
	Inactive	*Inactive*
Contact	*Active*	*Active*
	Inactive	*Inactive*
Case	*Active*	*In Progress* *On Hold* *Waiting For Details* *Researching*
	Resolved	*Problem Solved*
	Canceled	*Canceled*
Phone Call	*Open*	*Open*
	Completed	*Made* *Received*
	Canceled	*Canceled*

By default, all new records that you create have an active status, but there are many reasons you might deactivate a record. For example, you might want to deactivate a record if:

- A contact has changed companies or does not work for the account anymore.
- An account has gone out of business.
- A duplicate of the account or contact record already exists in the system.
- You do not want to continue tracking interactions with the account or contact.

In this exercise, you will deactivate a contact record and then reactivate it.

> **USE** the Ben Burton contact record you created earlier in this chapter.
>
> **BE SURE TO** use the Internet Explorer Web browser to navigate to your Microsoft Dynamics CRM Web site, if necessary, before beginning this exercise.

1. Click the **Sales** application area. In the navigation pane, click **Contacts**.

2. In the **Quick Find** box, type **Burton**, and then press ⌈Enter⌋.

The Ben Burton record appears in your results.

3. Click the record to select it. On the grid toolbar, click the **More Actions** button and select **Deactivate**. In the dialog box that opens asking you to confirm, click **OK**.

Microsoft Dynamics CRM deactivates the record.

4. In the **Quick Find** box, type **Burton**, and then press ⌈Enter⌋.

The Ben Burton record does not appear in your results because you deactivated the record. Microsoft Dynamics CRM does not include inactive records in the Quick Find results. Now you will reactivate the contact record.

5. In the view selector, select **Inactive Contacts**.

The list of deactivated contacts that appears includes the Ben Burton record.

6. Double-click the **Ben Burton** record to open the contact record.

Note that Microsoft Dynamics CRM disables the fields on the form so that you cannot edit the inactive record.

Actions

7. In the toolbar, click the **Actions** button, and then click **Activate Contact**. In the dialog box that opens asking you to confirm, click **OK**.

Microsoft Dynamics CRM activates the contact and enables the form fields so that you can edit it.

Sharing Accounts and Contacts with Other Users

Microsoft Dynamics CRM includes a robust security model that allows an administrator to set up and configure which users can view or perform actions on the different types of records in a system. If you want to share a particular account or contact record with a different user because he or she cannot access it, Microsoft Dynamics CRM allows you to easily share records, assuming that your system administrator has given you permission to do so. Microsoft Dynamics CRM allows your organization to create *teams* of users, which can be beneficial when your organization wants to share records, because team members can belong to any business unit within your organization.

> **Important** Microsoft Dynamics CRM allows you to share records on an ad-hoc basis with a specific user or a team of users. When you share records, you can also determine which types of security privileges you want to grant with the shared record(s). You can grant privileges to other users only if you already have those permissions on the shared record.

In this example, you will share a contact record with two different users so that they can view and edit the record. You can follow a similar process to share account records.

> **USE** the Ben Burton contact record you created earlier in this chapter.
>
> **BE SURE TO** use the Internet Explorer Web browser to navigate to your Microsoft Dynamics CRM Web site, if necessary, before beginning this exercise.

1. Navigate to a contact view, and open the **Ben Burton** contact.

2. In the toolbar, click **Actions**, and then click **Sharing**.

   A new window opens.

3. In the **Common Tasks** pane, click **Add User/Team**.

   A new window opens.

4. Because you are sharing this contact record with a user, leave the **Look for** list value set to **User**. Select any two active users in your system, and then click the >> button.

5. Click **OK**.

   Microsoft Dynamics CRM lists the selected users. Within this window, you can decide what types of privileges you want to grant each user for the Ben Burton contact record.

6. Because you want these users to have permission to edit the contact record, select the **Write** check boxes for both of the users you selected.

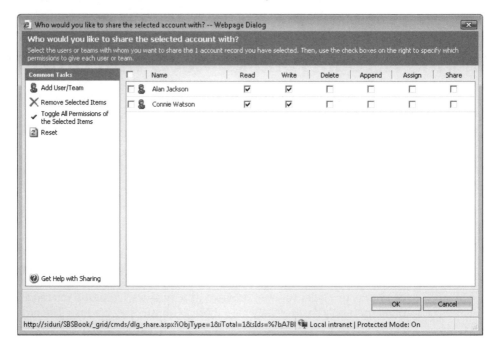

7. Click **OK**.

Microsoft Dynamics CRM updates the security permissions and closes the sharing window.

8. To view the current share permissions on a record, click **Actions**, and then click **Sharing**.

A new window opens that displays the sharing information that you just configured.

> **Tip** When you are working collaboratively with other users on a record, you might want to send someone a specific record to review. To simplify the process of referencing a specific record, Microsoft Dynamics CRM offers a Web address shortcut (URL) for each record. Users can click the record shortcut to automatically open that record in the system without having to look for it in the user interface.
>
> To copy the shortcut address to your Clipboard, click Actions on the toolbar, and select Copy Shortcut. Now you can paste the record's address into another application, such as an e-mail message or a document, by using Ctrl+V. Microsoft Dynamics CRM includes shortcuts for almost every type of record in the system, including accounts, contacts, cases, and activities.

Assigning Accounts and Contacts to Other Users

In addition to sharing records with other users, you can change the ownership of a record. Most of the records in Microsoft Dynamics CRM (such as accounts, contacts, leads, cases, and opportunities) are "owned" by a user, and the record owner is a key component of the security model within the system. Microsoft Dynamics CRM allows you to change the record owner (or *assign the record*) by using multiple techniques in the user interface:

- Open the record and change the value in the **Owner** field.
- Open the record, click **Actions** in the toolbar, and then click **Assign**.
- In the grid toolbar, select one or more records, and then click **Assign**.

Regardless of the technique you use, you will follow the same steps to assign account, contact, and most other records in Microsoft Dynamics CRM.

> **Tip** Only users in Microsoft Dynamics CRM can own records; a team or group of users cannot own a record. However, you can assign some types of records, such as cases and activities, to a *queue*, which represents a group of users. See Chapter 13, "Working with Contracts and Queues," for more information on using queues. You can usually find the name of the owner of a particular record on the Administration tab. You cannot change the owner of a record with the bulk edit tool.

In this exercise, you will change the ownership of a contact record by assigning it to a different user by using the second technique mentioned on the previous page.

USE the Ben Burton contact record you created earlier in this chapter.

BE SURE TO use the Internet Explorer Web browser to navigate to your Microsoft Dynamics CRM Web site, if necessary, before beginning this exercise.

1. Open the **Ben Burton** contact record.

2. In the toolbar, click **Actions**, and then click **Assign**.

The Assign Account dialog box opens.

3. Click **Assign to another user**.

4. Select a different user by typing the user's name directly in the box or by clicking the Look Up button.

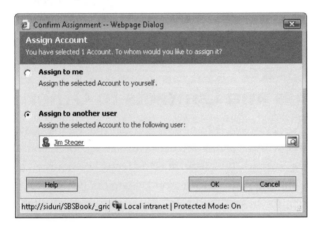

5. Click **OK**.

The dialog box closes, and Microsoft Dynamics CRM updates the record owner to the value you selected.

Tip Inactive users can own records, but you can assign records only to active users. If a user record is deactivated, records will remain assigned to the inactive user, but no other records can be assigned to the user as long as it is inactive in Microsoft Dynamics CRM.

Merging Account or Contact Records

When you are working with account and contact records in Microsoft Dynamics CRM, you might notice that two or more records appear very similar. For example, your system might contain more than one contact record for the same person in your system. Although you wouldn't knowingly enter two records for the same person, it is possible that your system might contain duplicate records.

See Also Microsoft Dynamics CRM includes many tools to help you avoid creating duplicate records in your system. For more information on configuring the duplicate check features, see Chapter 14, "Detecting Duplicate Records."

Even though Microsoft Dynamics CRM includes powerful tools that help you to avoid duplicates, you will undoubtedly find a few duplicate records within your system. Fortunately, Microsoft Dynamics CRM includes a Merge tool that allows you to consolidate two different records into a single merged record. When merging two records, you specify one record as the master record, and Microsoft Dynamics CRM treats the other record as the child record. Microsoft Dynamics CRM deactivates the child record and copies all of the related records (such as activities, notes, and opportunities) to the master record. During the merge process, Microsoft Dynamics CRM presents you with a dialog box that allows you to populate data from individual fields in the child record so that you can preserve the data in the surviving master record. By merging duplicate records, you can maintain a clean customer database that will help with sales, marketing, and service productivity.

> **Tip** You can merge lead records as well as accounts and contacts.

In this exercise, you will create a new contact record and merge it with an existing contact record. The same process is used to merge account and lead records.

> **USE** the Ben Burton contact record you created earlier in this chapter.
> **BE SURE TO** use the Internet Explorer Web browser to navigate to your Microsoft Dynamics CRM Web site, if necessary, before beginning this exercise.

1. In the application menu tool bar, on the **New Record** menu, click **Contact**.

2. In the **First Name** field, enter **Ben**, and in the **Last Name** field, enter **Burton**. In the **Fax** field, enter **(312) 555-0100**. In the **Parent Customer** field, type **Sonoma Partners**.

The Parent Customer field should automatically resolve to the Sonoma Partners account record, as indicated by the underline and blue text color that the account name appears in.

3. In the contact toolbar, click **Save and Close**.

4. Click the **Sales** application area. In the navigation pane, click **Contacts**.

5. In the **Quick Find** text box, enter **Burton**, and then press ⎙Enter⎙.

Microsoft Dynamics CRM lists the contact you just created and the Ben Burton contact record you created previously.

Merge

6. Holding the ⎙Shift⎙ key down, click both **Ben Burton** records in the grid so that they are highlighted. In the grid toolbar, click the **Merge** button.

The Merge Records dialog box opens. In this dialog box, you choose the master record by clicking the contact record you want to use. You can also select the data fields you want to keep from the child record in the surviving master record.

7. In the **Fax** field, click **(312) 555-0100**. When you do this, Microsoft Dynamics CRM keeps this fax data on the final record.

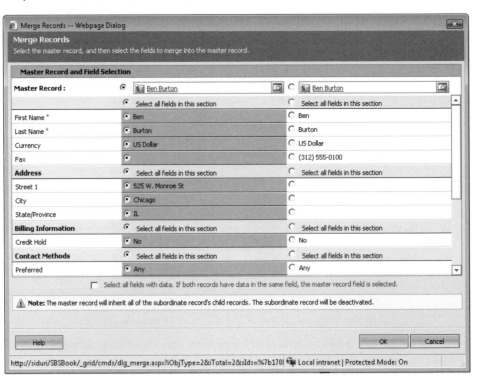

8. Click **OK**.

Microsoft Dynamics CRM merges the two records by updating the master record and deactivating the child record. When the process is complete, Microsoft Dynamics CRM displays an alert window telling you that the selected records have been merged and the subordinate record has been deactivated.

9. Click **OK**.

Microsoft Dynamics CRM closes the Merge Records dialog box.

Key Points

- You can create accounts and contacts by clicking the New button in the grid toolbar or by using the New Record option in the application menu bar.

- You can link multiple accounts by specifying one account as the parent account, which automatically makes the other a sub-account.

- Each account can have only one parent account, but accounts can have as many sub-accounts as you need.

- You can use customer relationships to create additional links between accounts and contacts.

- Microsoft Dynamics CRM allows you to upload file attachments to many records, such as accounts and contacts.

- Sharing accounts with other users or teams allows you to grant security privileges to groups that might not otherwise have access.

- Most records in Microsoft Dynamics CRM, such as accounts and contacts, have a single user as the record owner. Record ownership helps determine security settings. You can change record owners by assigning the record to a different user.

- You can use the Merge tool to consolidate duplicate records into a single record while preserving the history of both records.

Chapter at a Glance

Create a follow-up activity,
page 67

View open and completed
activities for a record,
page 70

Create a note,
page 77

Send direct e-mail messages,
page 83

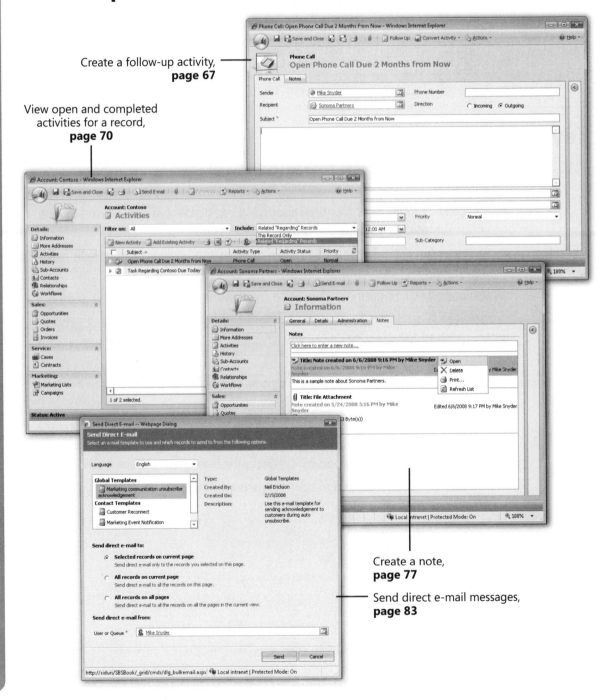

4 Working with Activities and Notes

In this chapter, you will learn to:

✔ Understand different activity types.

✔ Understand the Regarding field.

✔ Create follow-up activities.

✔ View open and completed activities.

✔ Create a note.

✔ Manage your activities.

✔ Send direct e-mail messages.

In the previous chapters, you learned how to create and manage accounts and contacts in Microsoft Dynamics CRM. In this chapter, you will learn how to record, manage, and report on the *activities* and *notes* related to those records. The word *activity* is a generic term that Microsoft Dynamics CRM uses to describe business interactions, such as phone calls, tasks, and e-mail messages. Notes are comments or other descriptive text related to a record.

Tracking activities and notes allows you and your company to:

● Record the phone calls to and from a particular person or account.

● Track customer service calls regarding a product or service.

● Assign tasks to ensure a sales representative follows up with new leads in a timely fashion.

● Save copies of the e-mail correspondence on a particular topic.

● Understand the marketing activities a prospect or customer participated in during his or her history with your firm.

Think back to a time when you called a company with a question, and each time you called about the same topic the representative acted as though you had never spoken with the company before. This type of situation causes frustration for the customer and for the company. If that company had recorded calls and notes related to your request in a customer relationship management system, the representatives could resolve your subsequent calls more quickly because they could access the history of your interaction with the company.

Capturing all of the interactions with your customers and prospects as activities allows you to provide a higher level of customer service, improve sales efficiency, make better business decisions, and market more effectively.

Creating Activities by Using Microsoft Dynamics CRM Workflow

Although you can create activities one at a time, Microsoft Dynamics CRM also allows you to create and assign activity records automatically using workflow rules. You can think of Microsoft Dynamics CRM workflow as an application or service that runs in the background, 24 hours a day, 7 days a week, constantly evaluating your Microsoft Dynamics CRM data and the multiple workflow rules in your deployment. When the workflow service encounters a trigger event, it fires the appropriate workflow rules to run the workflow actions. Typical workflow actions include sending an e-mail message, creating a task, and updating a data field in a record. Workflow rules are usually set up by system administrators to automate follow-up tasks or other actions in Microsoft Dynamics CRM at key milestones during sales or other business processes.

Creating activities with workflow helps your business ensure that everyone follows a consistent process when dealing with customers. Contact your system administrator about creating workflow rules to ensure that important follow-up activities are created when key events occur in Microsoft Dynamics CRM, such as assigning a follow-up task when a new lead is created or sending a birthday e-mail to a preferred customer.

See Also Creating and designing workflow rules is beyond the scope of this book, but you can learn more about workflow rules in *Working with Microsoft Dynamics CRM 4.0*, by Mike Snyder and Jim Steger (Microsoft Press, 2008).

In this chapter, you will learn how to capture tasks, e-mail messages, faxes, appointments, and other customer interactions in Microsoft Dynamics CRM, and then relate them to customer and other records to gain a full picture of how your organization communicates with its customers.

Important The exercises in this chapter require only records created in earlier chapters; none are supplied on the companion CD. For more information about practice files, see "Using the Companion CD" at the beginning of this book.

Troubleshooting Graphics and operating system–related instructions in this book reflect the Windows Vista user interface. If your computer is running Windows XP and you experience trouble following the instructions as written, refer to the "Information for Readers Running Windows XP" section at the beginning of this book.

Important The images used in this book reflect the default form and field names in Microsoft Dynamics CRM. Because the software offers extensive customization capabilities, it's possible that some of the record types or fields have been relabeled in your Microsoft Dynamics CRM environment. If you cannot find the forms, fields, or security roles referenced in this book, contact your system administrator for assistance.

Important You must know the location of your Microsoft Dynamics CRM Web site to work the exercises in this book. Check with your system administrator to verify the Web address if you don't know it.

Understanding Activity Types

Microsoft Dynamics CRM uses the term *activity* to describe several types of interactions. The types of activities are:

- **Phone Call.** Use this to record a received or initiated telephone call.
- **Task.** Use this to record a to-do or follow-up item.
- **E-Mail.** Use this to record a received or sent e-mail message.
- **Letter.** Use this to record the mailing of a physical letter or document.
- **Fax.** Use this to record a received or sent facsimile.
- **Appointment.** Use this to record a meeting or appointment. Many companies use appointments to track conference calls or online meetings, in addition to face-to-face meetings.
- **Service Activity.** Use this to record a service that you performed for a customer.

> **Tip** To create and use service activities, you must first ensure that your administrator has set up and configured the services, sites, and resources that your company offers. Service activities do not apply to every type of business; they are best suited to businesses that need to schedule customer services in specific time slots. Your business might not use service activities at all.

- **Campaign Response.** Use this to record a customer or prospect response to a marketing campaign. For example, you might create a campaign response to record that a customer registered for a seminar.

    See Also Campaign responses offer unique marketing functionality that differs from that of the other activities. See Chapter 10, "Working with Campaign Activities and Responses," to learn more about this activity type.

Tracking activities and notes on customer records helps you and others in your organization understand all of the communication your organization has had with each customer. You can also create search queries, views, and reports to track activities by customer or activity type. For example, a sales manager can view information about her team's phone calls for review during a weekly sales meeting, or a customer service manager can view the open service activities scheduled for an upcoming week to ensure that his team is available.

See Also For more information about analyzing data and creating reports in Microsoft Dynamics CRM, see Chapter 16, "Using the Report Wizard."

The most commonly used data fields in activity records include those listed in the following table.

Data field	Description
Subject	A brief description of the activity
Regarding	The customer or other record to which the activity is related
Description	Additional notes or information about the activity
Status	The status of the activity, such as Active, Completed, or Canceled
Duration	The estimated time it will take for the activity to be completed
Actual Duration	The actual time it takes for the activity to be completed
Scheduled Start	The estimated start date of the activity
Due Date	The estimated completion date of the activity
Actual Start	The date the activity was started
Actual End	The date the activity was completed

Each activity record also includes data fields specific to the activity type. For example, only phone call activities contain information about the phone number or the call direction.

> **Tip** Even though the activity forms include category and sub-category fields, Microsoft Dynamics CRM categories are not related to the categories configured in Microsoft Office Outlook. Consequently, updating an activity's category in Microsoft Dynamics CRM will *not* update the activity's Outlook category. Even though they share the same name, Microsoft Dynamics CRM categories are unrelated to Outlook categories.

Understanding the Regarding Field

You can track to-dos and other follow-up activities as tasks in Microsoft Dynamics CRM, much as you can in Outlook. When you create an activity in Microsoft Dynamics CRM, you can use the ***Regarding field*** to specify a customer or other record to which the activity is associated. When you enter a value in the Regarding field, you create a link between the activity and the selected record so that the activity is displayed from the specified record. Using the Regarding field provides additional data about your activities, and this data might help your organization better understand how employees spend their time in addition to categorizing the various customer interactions.

By default, you can set an activity to be regarding any of the following records:

- Account
- Campaign Activity
- Case
- Contact
- Contract
- Invoice
- Lead
- Opportunity
- Order
- Quick Campaign
- Quote

> **Tip** You might be able to track activities and notes to other record types if your system administrator has configured custom entities in your Microsoft Dynamics CRM environment.

By properly setting the Regarding field for activity records, you can more easily look up and reference customer information. For example, if you set all of your tasks so they are regarding an account record, it would be cumbersome to find a particular task if you have several hundred activities for that account record. However, if you set activities so they are regarding certain records related to the account (such as quotes or cases), you can find all of the activities related to those other entities without having to sort through hundreds of activities.

> **Tip** It is a best practice to use the Regarding field to link activities to records in Microsoft Dynamics CRM.

In this exercise, you will create a task regarding the Sonoma Partners account created in the previous chapter and then mark it as Completed.

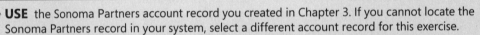 **USE** the Sonoma Partners account record you created in Chapter 3. If you cannot locate the Sonoma Partners record in your system, select a different account record for this exercise.

BE SURE TO use the Windows Internet Explorer Web browser to navigate to your Microsoft Dynamics CRM Web site before beginning this exercise.

1. In the application menu toolbar, click the **New Activity** button, and then select **Task** to launch the **New Task** form.

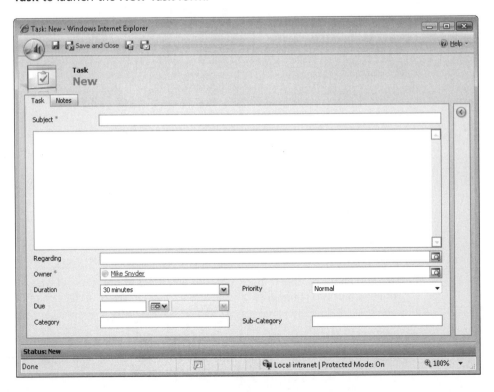

2. In the **Subject** field, enter **Send information to the customer**.

By default, the Subject and Owner fields are the only data fields in which you must enter values before you can create a task.

3. In the **Description** field, enter **Sample description of the task**.

Look Up

4. In the **Regarding** field, click the **Look Up** button. In the **Look Up** dialog box that opens, leave **Account** selected in the **Look for** field and enter **Sonoma Partners** in the box. Press the ⎡Enter⎤ key to submit your search.

> **Tip** Although only one record can be entered in the Regarding field for each activity, the selected record can be one of many different types—a lead, an account, an opportunity, or a case, for example. Because the Regarding field links to several types of records, you must click the Look Up button to select the Regarding record; you cannot type in the Regarding field as you can with some of the other lookup fields in Microsoft Dynamics CRM.

The Look Up dialog box filters the records to show the accounts that match your search phrase.

5. Click the **Sonoma Partners** record, and then click **OK**.

Calendar

6. In the **Due** field, click the **Calendar** button, and select the date by which you want this task completed.

After you have selected a date, a drop-down list of times is activated on the form so you can select the specific time of day by which you want the task completed.

7. Select **1:00 PM**.

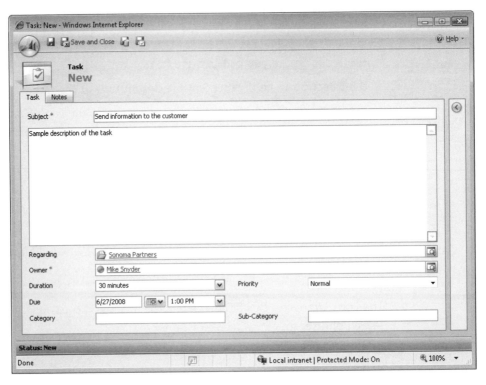

Save

8. Click the **Save** button to create the task.

9. You can mark the task as completed in two ways. First, in the form toolbar, on the **Actions** menu, click **Close Task**.

10. In the **Close Task** dialog box, click the **Status** list arrow to show the possible values.

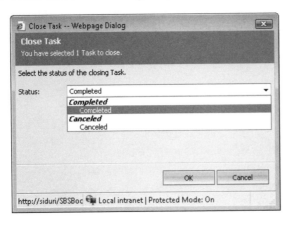

With this technique, you can mark the task as Completed or Canceled. You would cancel the task if you did not complete the task but want to remove it from your list of open tasks. After you select the value you want, you would click the **OK** button to close the task.

11. For this exercise, click **Cancel** to keep the task active.

You will use an alternative method to close the task.

Save as
Completed

12. In the toolbar, click the **Save as Completed** button.

Microsoft Dynamics CRM marks the task as Completed and closes the task window. Using this technique will save you a few clicks, but you can't use it to mark a task as Canceled.

> **Tip** You can also upload attachments to an activity record, which can be useful if you need to reference a specific file. Uploading a file to an activity follows the same process as uploading an attachment to an account, as explained in Chapter 3, "Working with Accounts and Contacts."

Creating Follow-Up Activities

Activities can be created from customer or other records as well as from the application menu toolbar in Microsoft Dynamics CRM. Because activities are critical to developing a complete view of each customer's interaction with your company, you'll find several locations from which you can quickly create new activities. You can even schedule follow-up activities from an existing activity! For instance, you can enter notes from a phone call with a client contact, and then schedule a follow-up appointment activity based on a time and date discussed with the customer during your call. By doing so, you can save the phone call activity as Completed while also ensuring that the dialog with your customer continues by scheduling the future appointment.

In all record types for which you can create activities, Microsoft Dynamics CRM provides the following ways to create a new activity:

- You can click the Follow Up button in the entity menu toolbar to open the Form Assistant pane, which displays the necessary fields to quickly create an activity.

- You can use the Actions menu in the entity menu toolbar to open an Add Activity submenu that allows you to quickly select the activity type you want to create.

- You can use the Activities option in the left navigation area of the form. From this view, you can click the New Activity button in the grid toolbar to create an activity.

Any time an activity is created from a specific record, that record is automatically populated in the new activity's Regarding field. When you create a new activity from an existing lead, account, or contact, Microsoft Dynamics CRM can also populate other activity fields in a record, such as the phone number in a phone call or the recipient in an e-mail message.

In this exercise, you will create a phone call activity from a contact record. When you create a phone call record by using this technique, Microsoft Dynamics CRM automatically populates the mapped fields, such as the call recipient, the phone number, and the phone call's Regarding value.

USE the Mike Snyder contact record you created in Chapter 3. If you cannot locate the Mike Snyder record in your system, select a different contact record for this exercise.

BE SURE TO use the Internet Explorer Web browser to navigate to your Microsoft Dynamics CRM Web site before beginning this exercise.

1. Navigate to the **Contacts** view and open the **Mike Snyder** contact record or any contact record in your system. Ensure that the contact record includes a phone number in the **Business Phone** field.

Actions

2. In the toolbar, click the **Actions** button, and then click the **Add Activity** submenu. On the submenu, click **Phone Call**.

A phone call record opens and is populated with data from the contact record.

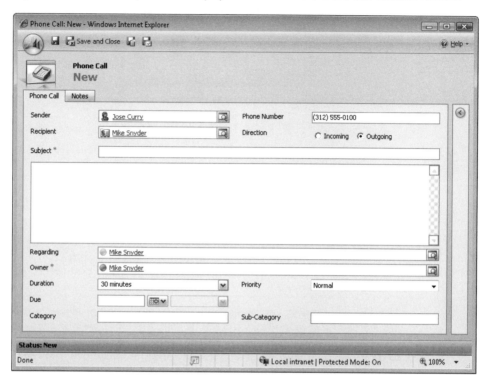

3. Click **Incoming** near the upper right of the form.

   Microsoft Dynamics CRM automatically switches the values in the Sender and Recipient fields. This direction field indicates whether you placed the call or the contact called you.

4. In the **Subject** field, type **Spoke with customer**.

5. In the form toolbar, click **Save**.

6. Click **Actions** in the toolbar, and then click **Close Phone Call**.

   The Close Phone Call dialog box opens.

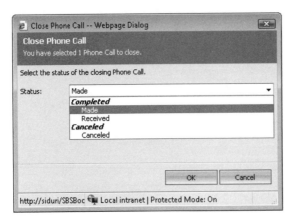

In this dialog box, you can select a value to record how you closed out the phone call.

7. Select **Made**, and then click **OK**.

Microsoft Dynamics CRM closes the phone call as a completed activity.

> **Tip** The other types of activities can be created by using processes similar to those you just learned for creating tasks and phone calls; therefore, we won't repeat the exercises for each activity type. Chapter 5, "Microsoft Dynamics CRM for Outlook," shows how to create appointments, tasks, and e-mail messages in Outlook that can be saved into Microsoft Dynamics CRM.

> **Tip** Certain activity types can be converted to opportunities and cases. You can convert phone calls, faxes, e-mail messages, appointments, and letters to sales opportunities or service requests by clicking the Convert Activity button on the form toolbar. Opportunities are detailed in Chapter 6, "Working with Leads and Opportunities," and cases are covered in Chapter 11, "Tracking Service Requests."

Viewing Open and Completed Activities for a Record

When you track activities related to your customers, you and other employees can reference that information to understand the complete history of interactions with those customers. Imagine a scenario in which a customer has been working with one person from your office, but that employee leaves for a week's vacation. If the customer calls your office when that person is out, you could look up the customer's record in Microsoft Dynamics CRM and read the activity history to get up to speed on the customer.

As you learned earlier in this chapter, all of the activity types share some common data fields. One of the shared data fields across all activity types is the Status field. The default status values for activity records are:

- *Open*
- *Scheduled*
- *Completed*
- *Canceled*
- *Closed*

When you look up activities related to a customer, you will notice that Microsoft Dynamics CRM splits the activities into two categories: Activities and History. The *Activities* section displays all of the activities related to the record that need to be completed. Only activities with a status of Open or Scheduled appear in the Activities display. The *History* section lists all of the completed, closed, or canceled activities related to the record.

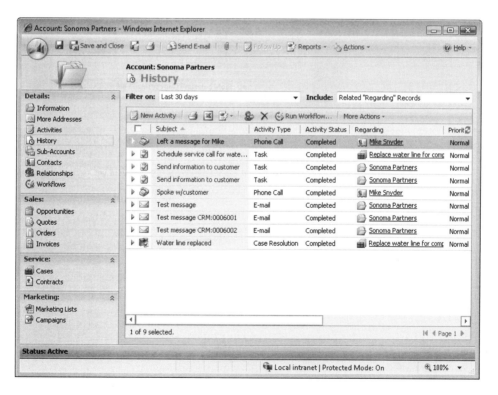

> **Tip** If your view contains a large number of records, you can use the Filter On list to show only those activities within a specific date range. You can also sort the columns in the record list just like you can sort the other grids.

In addition to displaying a view of all activities related to the record, Microsoft Dynamics CRM performs an activity rollup so that you can see the activities of records related to the record you're viewing. For example, the Sonoma Partners account lists nine different closed activities, but only five of those activities are regarding the Sonoma Partners account. The other completed activities are regarding records that are related to the Sonoma Partners account. For example, two phone calls are regarding the Mike Snyder contact. They appear in this view because Mike Snyder's parent account is Sonoma Partners. In addition, this view lists two completed activities regarding a case opened by Sonoma Partners. If you want to see only the activities regarding the Sonoma Partners account, you can use the Include list to select the *This Record Only* value. The Microsoft Dynamics CRM activity rollup works on both open and closed activities.

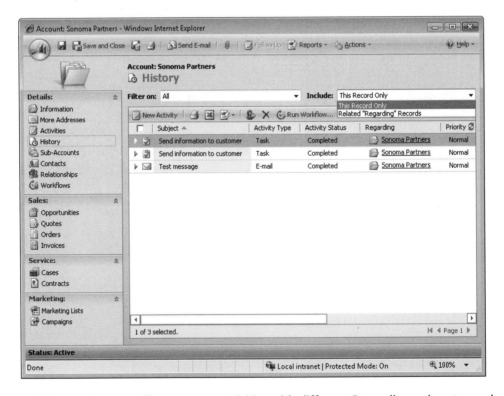

In this exercise, you will create two activities with different Regarding values to see how Microsoft Dynamics CRM displays those records in the Activities and History sections.

USE the Sonoma Partners and Contoso account records you created in Chapter 3. If you cannot locate these records in your system, select two different account records for this exercise.

BE SURE TO use the Internet Explorer Web browser to navigate to your Microsoft Dynamics CRM Web site before beginning this exercise.

1. Navigate to the **Accounts** view and open the **Sonoma Partners** account record.

2. In the menu toolbar, click **Actions**, select **Add Activity**, and then click **Phone Call**.

A new window opens.

3. In the **Subject** field, enter **Open Phone Call Due 2 Months from Now**.

Note that because you created this phone call from the Sonoma Partners record, Microsoft Dynamics CRM automatically populates the Regarding field with the Sonoma Partners account.

4. In the **Due** field, select a date two months from today.

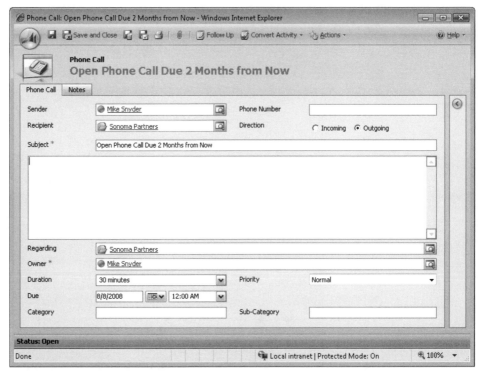

Save and Close

5. Click the **Save and Close** button.

The window closes and you are returned to the Sonoma Partners account record.

6. In the **Parent Account** field, select the Contoso account record that you created in Chapter 3, and then save the **Sonoma Partners** account. (Remember, if you cannot locate the Contoso record in your system, select a different account record.)

7. Click the account you selected in the **Parent Account** field to view the details of the parent account record.

8. In the menu toolbar, click **Actions**, select **Add Activity**, and then click **Task** to launch the **New Task** form.

Note that, because you created this task from the parent account record, Microsoft Dynamics CRM automatically populates the Regarding field with the parent account.

9. In the **Subject** field, enter **Task Regarding Contoso Due Today**.

10. In the **Due** field, select today's date.

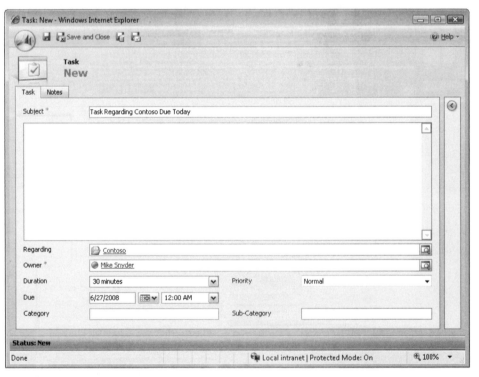

11. Click **Save and Close**.

The window closes, and you are returned to the parent account record.

12. In the left navigation pane, click **Activities**.

The activity list displays the task that you just created, but the phone call record does not appear. By default, Microsoft Dynamics CRM shows activities within the next 30 days for open activities, or the previous 30 days for closed activities. Because you entered a due date two months from today for the phone call, that record doesn't fit the filter criteria.

13. To view the phone call, click the **Filter On** list arrow, and select **All**.

The view updates to show the phone call.

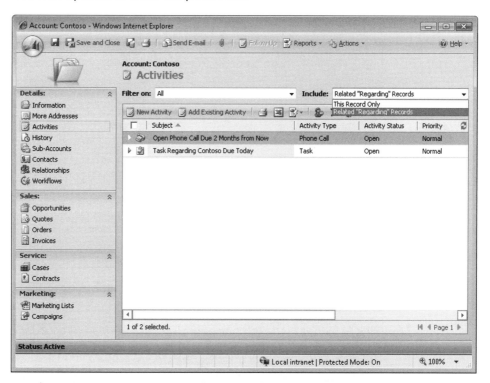

This example shows the activity rollup in action. You created two activities regarding two different records, but you can see them in a single view because the Sonoma Partners record lists Contoso as its parent.

14. To view only those activities regarding the parent account, click the **Include** list arrow, and select **This Record Only**.

The view updates again to display only the task regarding Contoso.

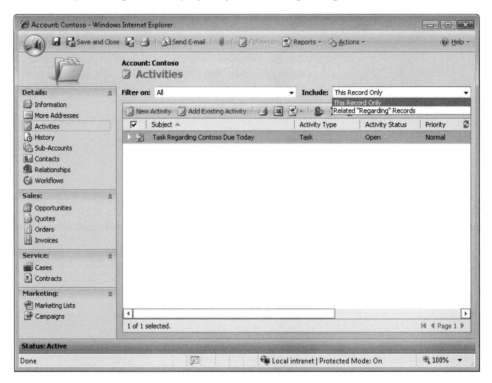

15. Double-click the task regarding the parent account to open that record. Click **Save as Completed** to mark the task as completed.

16. Click **Activities** in the left navigation pane of the parent account record.

The task record does not appear anymore because you just closed it.

17. To view the closed task, click **History** in the left navigation pane.

The view shows the task you just completed.

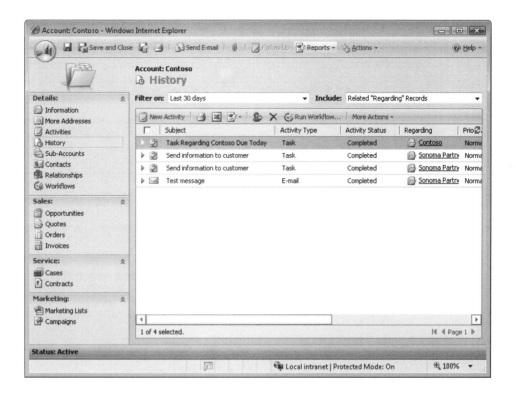

Creating a Note

In addition to using activities to capture the interactions with your customers and prospects, you might find that you want to jot down some notes about a record. For example, imagine that you read an article in the newspaper about one of your accounts, and the article includes some important information about the account's growth plans. You'd like to capture that information in Microsoft Dynamics CRM. Because you didn't interact with the customer or anyone else, the action of recording this data doesn't fit the "activity" concept. Fortunately, Microsoft Dynamics CRM allows you to create *notes* and link those notes to the various records in your system.

As you learned in Chapter 3, you can upload file attachments to a record. Microsoft Dynamics CRM displays the notes you enter about a record in the same area of the user interface.

In this exercise, you will create a note about an account.

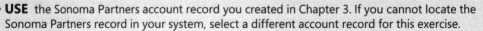

USE the Sonoma Partners account record you created in Chapter 3. If you cannot locate the Sonoma Partners record in your system, select a different account record for this exercise.

BE SURE TO use the Internet Explorer Web browser to navigate to your Microsoft Dynamics CRM Web site before beginning this exercise.

1. Navigate to the **Accounts** view and open the **Sonoma Partners** record.

2. Click the **Notes** tab.

3. Click in the box that displays **Click here to enter a new note**.

Microsoft Dynamics CRM inserts a new row and positions the cursor in it so you can begin typing.

4. Enter **This is a sample note about Sonoma Partners**.

5. Press ⌷Enter⌷. Notice that Microsoft Dynamics CRM moves the cursor to a new row. To complete your note, press the ⌷Tab⌷ key or click anywhere on the screen outside the current note.

6. To delete the note, right-click the **Note** title.

> **Important** To delete a note, you must have a security role that has delete privileges. If you are unable to perform this step, contact your system administrator about deleting the note.

A new menu appears.

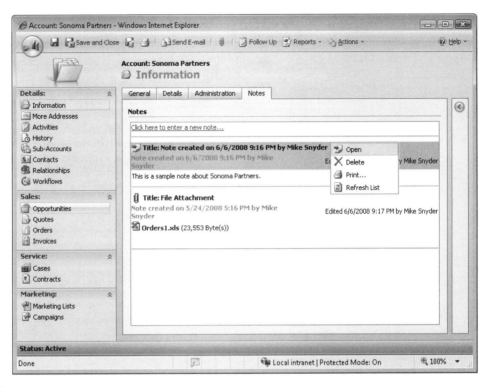

7. Click **Delete** to delete the note.

> **Tip** Unlike activities, notes do not roll up from related records. You will see only those notes regarding the record you're viewing.

Managing Your Activities

Now that you understand how to create and work with activities for a particular record, we'll review how you can manage your activities on a daily basis. For example, after you arrive at the office and log on to Microsoft Dynamics CRM, where should you start your day? What calls do you need to make? Which tasks do you need to complete? What does your schedule look like? Microsoft Dynamics CRM includes a *Workplace* that you can use to manage all of your activities.

The Workplace contains many different sub-areas, but the two related to managing activities are the Calendar and Activities areas. The Calendar displays a list of appointments that you can view by day, week, or month.

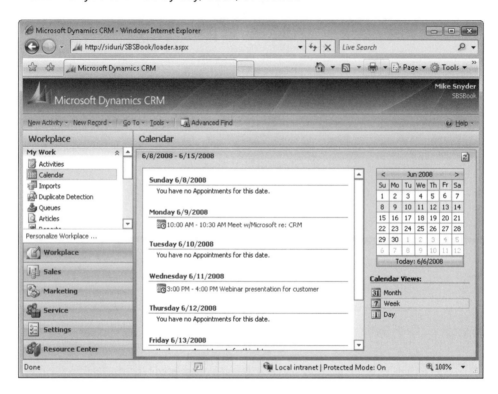

> **Important** The Calendar shows only those appointments from Microsoft Dynamics CRM; it does not show activities from your personal Outlook calendar. The Calendar also does not display other activity record types, such as tasks or phone calls.

The Activities area provides a list of all of the activity records you have privileges to view within Microsoft Dynamics CRM. You can access different views of the activity data in addition to filtering the records by activity type and due date. You can also use Quick Find to search for specific terms or keywords within the activities.

By using a combination of the Calendar and Activities views, you can quickly prioritize your open activities.

In this exercise, you will toggle the filters on the Activities view to see how they dynamically update.

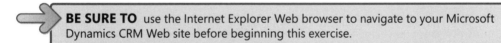

BE SURE TO use the Internet Explorer Web browser to navigate to your Microsoft Dynamics CRM Web site before beginning this exercise.

1. In the **Workplace** pane, click **Activities**.

2. Click the **View** field arrow to view the list of activity views that apply to all of the activity types that are displayed. Leave this option set to **My Activities**.

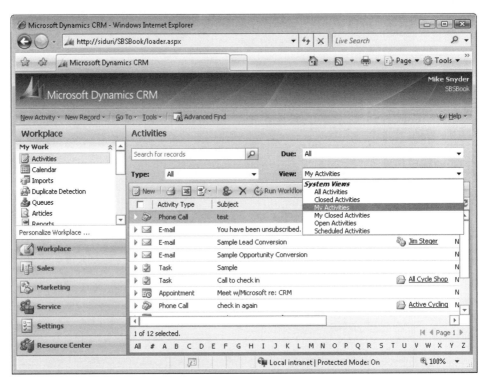

3. In the **Type** list, select **Phone Call**.

4. Click the **View** list arrow again.

Microsoft Dynamics CRM has updated the **View** list to show only those views specific to phone call records.

5. Now select **Task** in the **Type** list.

6. Click the **View** list arrow again.

Microsoft Dynamics CRM has updated the view list to show only those views specific to task records.

Sending Direct E-Mail Messages

Another very important activity type is e-mail. Because Microsoft Dynamics CRM integrates with Outlook, most users write and read e-mail messages within Outlook. However, one feature that many users want to take advantage of is the ability to send an e-mail message to a large list of recipients so that each message is individually addressed (in other words, sending an e-mail message to 500 people generates 500 different e-mail messages). Microsoft Dynamics CRM refers to this mass e-mailing as *direct e-mail*, and you can access this feature only within the Web client.

Sending a direct e-mail message requires you to select an *e-mail template*. Microsoft Dynamics CRM includes several e-mail templates by default, so you can use one of those for the exercise in this section. However, you will probably want to create new e-mail templates specific to your business and use those for your e-mail communications.

To send a direct e-mail message, select one or more records in a view and click the Send Direct E-Mail button in the grid toolbar. Microsoft Dynamics CRM will open a dialog box that allows you to select an e-mail template. If you selected a view with several pages of records, you can choose to send the direct e-mail message to just the selected records, all the records on the page, or all the records on all of the pages. Finally, you can send the e-mail message from someone other than yourself. You might want to do this if you want the e-mail to come from a generic address, such as *info@sonomapartners.com*, instead of a person.

> **Tip** The Direct E-Mail feature will not send messages to records if their Bulk E-Mail preference is set to Do Not Allow. Direct E-Mail will simply exclude those records from the mailing list.

In this exercise, you will send a direct e-mail message to contacts by using one of the out-of-the-box e-mail templates.

> **BE SURE TO** use the Internet Explorer Web browser to navigate to your Microsoft Dynamics CRM Web site before beginning this exercise.

1. Navigate to the **Contacts** view.

2. Select one or more records in the view, making sure to select records with sample or test e-mail addresses instead of real customers.

Send Direct
E-mail

3. In the grid toolbar, click the **Send Direct E-mail** button.

   The Send Direct E-Mail window opens.

4. Select the **Customer Reconnect** template. Leave the other default options.

5. Click **Send**.

   Microsoft Dynamics CRM submits the e-mail message for immediate delivery. If you view the history of the contact records you selected, you will see the e-mail message you just sent.

Key Points

- Activities are used to track interactions with customers, prospects, vendors, and other record types.

- Microsoft Dynamics CRM allows you to track many different kinds of activities, including tasks, phone calls, faxes, letters, e-mail messages, appointments, service activities, and campaign responses.

- You can create an activity from the application menu toolbar or from an individual record. Creating the activity from the individual record maps the Regarding field to the corresponding record.

- You can view the activities associated with a record by clicking Activities or History in the navigation pane. The Activities link displays open or scheduled activity records, and the History link shows completed or canceled records.

- Microsoft Dynamics CRM automatically rolls up activities between related records so that you can view related activities in a single view. You can toggle the activity rollup while you are working with an activity view.

- In addition to activities, you can view notes about the records in your system. Microsoft Dynamics CRM displays notes attached to a record in the same place that it displays files attached to that record.

- Microsoft Dynamics CRM includes a Calendar and an Activity view to allow you to manage a large list of activities.

- You can use the Web client and the Direct E-Mail feature to send mass e-mail messages to leads, contacts, and accounts in your system.

Chapter at a Glance

Access Microsoft Dynamics CRM data within Outlook, **page 89**

Track e-mail messages sent from Outlook in Microsoft Dynamics CRM, **page 97**

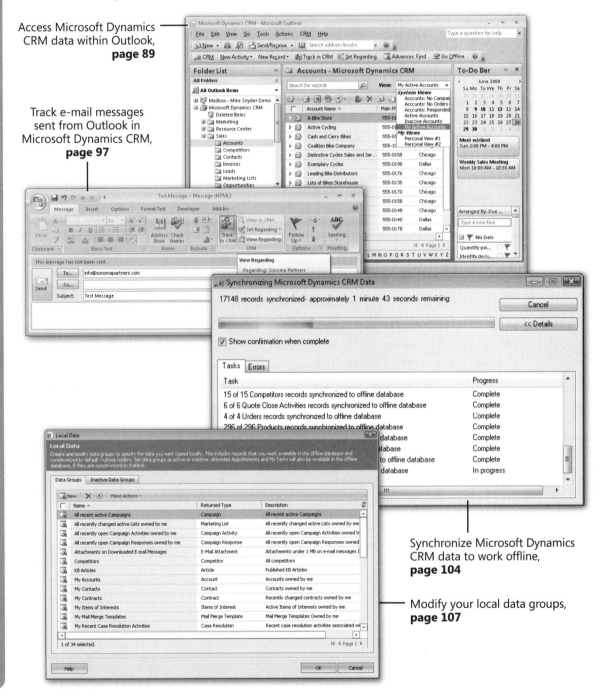

Synchronize Microsoft Dynamics CRM data to work offline, **page 104**

Modify your local data groups, **page 107**

5 Microsoft Dynamics CRM for Outlook

In this chapter, you will learn to:

✔ Access Microsoft Dynamics CRM records within Microsoft Dynamics CRM for Outlook.

✔ Synchronize contacts, tasks, and appointments between Microsoft Dynamics CRM and Outlook.

✔ Create and track Microsoft Dynamics CRM contacts, tasks, and appointments in Outlook.

✔ Send and track e-mail messages in Microsoft Dynamics CRM for Outlook.

✔ Delete records in Microsoft Dynamics CRM for Outlook.

✔ Go offline with Microsoft Dynamics CRM for Outlook.

✔ Configure a local data group.

Microsoft Dynamics CRM offers a Microsoft Dynamics CRM for Outlook interface in addition to the Web client interface. Without a doubt, the integration with Microsoft Office Outlook generates the most excitement and interest among Microsoft Dynamics CRM users. Information workers love being able to work directly with their Microsoft Dynamics CRM data in Outlook without needing to open a second software application. More importantly, users do not need to learn a new software application to perform their day-to-day functions. The Microsoft Dynamics CRM for Outlook user experience closely matches the rest of the functions that users already know how to perform in Outlook. This chapter will highlight many of the key steps and processes you'll use when working with Microsoft Dynamics CRM for Outlook.

> **Important** Before you can use Microsoft Dynamics CRM for Outlook, you or your system administrator must install the software on your computer. In this chapter, we assume that the Microsoft Dynamics CRM for Outlook software is already installed and connecting properly to your Microsoft Dynamics CRM server.

Your company can deploy one of two versions of the Microsoft Dynamics CRM for Outlook software:

● Microsoft Dynamics CRM for Outlook

● Microsoft Dynamics CRM for Outlook with Offline Access

Both versions offer almost identical functionality, but the Offline Access version allows you to work offline, disconnected from the Microsoft Dynamics CRM server. In this chapter, we will assume that you are using the Offline Access client.

> **Important** The exercises in this chapter require only records created in earlier chapters; none are supplied on the companion CD. For more information about practice files, see "Using the Companion CD" at the beginning of this book.

> **Troubleshooting** Graphics and operating system–related instructions in this book reflect the Windows Vista user interface. If your computer is running Windows XP and you experience trouble following the instructions as written, refer to the "Information for Readers Running Windows XP" section at the beginning of this book.

> **Important** The images in this chapter show Microsoft Dynamics CRM for Outlook with Outlook 2007, but Microsoft Dynamics CRM also supports Outlook 2003. If you are using Outlook 2003, the exercise steps will be the same, but the user interface will look a little different than the one shown in the images.

> **Important** The images used in this book reflect the default form and field names in Microsoft Dynamics CRM. Because the software offers extensive customization capabilities, it's possible that some of the record types or fields have been relabeled in your Microsoft Dynamics CRM environment. If you cannot find the forms, fields, or security roles referenced in this book, contact your system administrator for assistance.

> **Important** You must know the location of your Microsoft Dynamics CRM Web site to work the exercises in this book. Check with your system administrator to verify the Web address if you don't know it.

In this chapter, you will learn how to use the integration between Microsoft Dynamics CRM and Outlook to create contacts, tasks, appointments, and e-mail messages in Outlook and track them in Microsoft Dynamics CRM. You'll also learn how to work with Microsoft Dynamics CRM records while disconnected from the server and how to configure a local data group.

Using Microsoft Dynamics CRM for Outlook to Access Records

With Microsoft Dynamics CRM for Outlook, you can access Microsoft Dynamics CRM records directly within Outlook. Many users prefer to access their Microsoft Dynamics CRM data through Outlook instead of using the Web client because they are already working in Outlook to manage e-mail and other tasks. Microsoft Dynamics CRM for Outlook installs additional folders to your Outlook file, creating a folder for each area of the Microsoft Dynamics CRM user interface. Therefore, to access a list of accounts within Microsoft Dynamics CRM for Outlook, you would navigate the folder list to drill into the Sales folder and find the Account folder.

You will notice that Microsoft Dynamics CRM creates a folder for each of the application areas and then creates sub-folders for each entity contained within that application area. When you're viewing a list of records within Microsoft Dynamics CRM for Outlook, you can perform the same actions that you can in the Web client, such as searching for and opening records, exporting to Microsoft Office Excel, changing views, and running reports.

In this exercise, you will display a list of opportunities within Microsoft Dynamics CRM for Outlook.

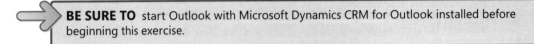

BE SURE TO start Outlook with Microsoft Dynamics CRM for Outlook installed before beginning this exercise.

1. On the Outlook menu bar, click **Go**, and then click **Folder List**. Scroll down past your mailbox to see the **Microsoft Dynamics CRM** folder. Click the + symbol to expand the folder.

2. Locate the **Sales** folder and click the + symbol next to it to expand the folder.

3. Click **Opportunities**.

   Microsoft Dynamics CRM for Outlook displays a list of opportunities within Outlook.

Synchronizing Contacts, Tasks, and Appointments

One of the main benefits of Microsoft Dynamics CRM for Outlook is that the system automatically synchronizes your contacts, tasks, and appointments between Outlook and Microsoft Dynamics CRM. If you create a new contact in the Microsoft Dynamics CRM Web client, the system can automatically download a copy of that contact into Outlook. Likewise, if you update a contact's information (with a new address or phone number, for example) in Outlook, the system updates the Microsoft Dynamics CRM database. If other users of your system synchronize the updated contact to their Outlook file, they receive your updates in the next sync process. This bi-directional update of contact information between Outlook and Microsoft Dynamics CRM means that you and other users can always access the latest information. In addition to synchronizing contacts, Microsoft Dynamics CRM for Outlook can perform a similar update for Outlook appointments and tasks. If you use a mobile device and synchronize it with Outlook, you can access Microsoft Dynamics CRM contacts, appointments, and tasks on your mobile device.

> **Important** Microsoft Dynamics CRM can also synchronize other activities, such as phone calls, letters, and faxes to Outlook. Because Outlook does not include phone calls, letters, or faxes, the synchronization software copies all of these activities into Outlook as tasks.

Microsoft Dynamics CRM for Outlook does not synchronize *all* of the contacts, appointments, and tasks from your Outlook file; rather, it synchronizes only the records that you track in Microsoft Dynamics CRM. If you have personal records in Outlook that you do not want to copy into the Microsoft Dynamics CRM database, you do not need to track those records in Microsoft Dynamics CRM. You can determine whether a particular record is tracked in Microsoft Dynamics CRM by opening the record and looking for the *Track In CRM* button in the CRM group of the record's menu bar. If the Track In CRM button is clicked, the record will be part of the Microsoft Dynamics CRM for Outlook synchronization process.

In addition, records tracked in Microsoft Dynamics CRM will display a different icon than the standard Outlook icon when you view a list of records in Outlook.

Default contact icons

Icons of contacts that are
tracked in Microsoft Dynamics CRM

When you first install Microsoft Dynamics CRM for Outlook, the software uses its default
settings for the synchronization process. One of these settings sets the system to perform
the synchronization process in the background every 15 minutes. This automatic background sync provides you with the convenience of not having to remember to explicitly
sync your records. If you want, you can change your options to increase the amount of
time between automatic synchronizations, but you cannot make it less than 15 minutes.

> **Tip** When you are connected to the server, changes made to contacts, tasks, and appoint-
> ments in Outlook synchronize to the Microsoft Dynamics CRM server when the record is saved.
> However, changes made to the Microsoft Dynamics CRM server in the Web client will not
> appear in Outlook until the completion of the next synchronization process.

If don't want to wait for the next scheduled synchronization interval, you can manually
kick off the synchronization process. In this exercise, you will manually synchronize
Outlook records with the Microsoft Dynamics CRM server.

BE SURE TO start Outlook with Microsoft Dynamics CRM for Outlook installed before beginning this exercise.

→ In the Outlook menu bar, click **CRM**, and then select **Synchronize with CRM**.

A progress indicator appears. When the software finishes the synchronization process, the window closes.

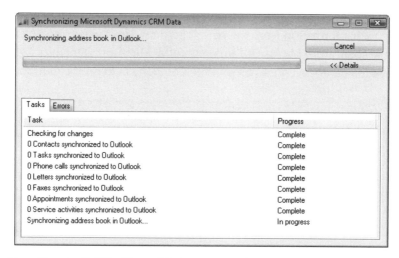

See Also Chapter 3, "Working with Accounts and Contacts," describes how to create contacts by using the Web client.

Creating and Tracking Contacts

Microsoft Dynamics CRM can synchronize your existing contacts from the Microsoft Dynamics CRM server so they appear in your Outlook contacts file. However, as you continue to work with the system, you will want to create and track new contact records. To create contacts in Outlook and track them in Microsoft Dynamics CRM, create the record in Outlook as you normally would, click the Track In CRM button, and then save the contact. Doing so creates the contact record in Microsoft Dynamics CRM and includes the record as part of future data synchronizations. When creating contacts in Outlook, you also can link the contact record to a parent account in Microsoft Dynamics CRM by clicking the Set Parent button in the Contact menu bar in Outlook.

> **Troubleshooting** Filling out the Company field in the Outlook contact record does not automatically link the contact to that company's account record in Microsoft Dynamics CRM. For new contacts that you create in Outlook and track in Microsoft Dynamics CRM, you must explicitly link the record to a parent account.

As is the case when you create a contact in the Web client, when you create a new contact in Outlook, track it in Microsoft Dynamics CRM, and link it to an existing parent account, the mapped fields (such as address and phone) in the contact record do *not* automatically update with information from the parent account. However, if you link a contact to a parent account from Microsoft Dynamics CRM, Microsoft Dynamics CRM for Outlook can save the parent account name in the Company field on the Outlook contact.

> **Tip** Microsoft Dynamics CRM for Outlook allows you to decide whether you want the Microsoft Dynamics CRM parent account to overwrite the Company field in Outlook. To update this preference, click the CRM menu in Outlook and select Options. On the Synchronization tab of the Options window, locate the Update The Company Field For Outlook Contacts section and select the check box if you want to automatically update the Company field with the parent account name.

When you track a contact in Microsoft Dynamics CRM, you can access additional information about the record from Outlook by clicking one of the following links in the contact record's menu bar:

- View In CRM opens the contact record in the Microsoft Dynamics CRM Web client. This allows you to view all of the details and related records that you're tracking in Microsoft Dynamics CRM.

- View Parent opens the account record of the parent record. Typically, the parent is the company for which the contact works.

In this exercise, you will create two new contacts (one from Outlook and one from the Web client) to see how the different options impact the contact data. You will also update the contact records and manually kick off the synchronization process.

USE the Sonoma Partners account record you created in Chapter 3. If you cannot locate the Sonoma Partners record in your system, select a different account record for this exercise.

BE SURE TO start Outlook with Microsoft Dynamics CRM for Outlook installed, if necessary, before beginning this exercise.

New

1. In the Outlook menu bar, click the **New** button, and select **Contact** to open the new contact form.

Track in CRM

Set Parent

2. Enter **Chris Perry** as the contact name.

3. Click the **Track in CRM** button.

4. Click the **Set Parent** button, and then select **Account**.

A Microsoft Dynamics CRM lookup window opens.

5. In the text field, enter **Sonoma Partners,** and then press the ⎡Enter⎤ key to search for the account in Microsoft Dynamics CRM. Select the appropriate account in the results, and then click **OK**.

The Sonoma Partners account name appears in the Company field of the Chris Perry Outlook contact.

> **Troubleshooting** If the parent account name does not appear in the Company field, check your preference setting in the Microsoft Dynamics CRM for Outlook options. For information about how to update this preference, see the Tip earlier in this section.

Save

6. Click the **Save** button.

This record is now tracked in Microsoft Dynamics CRM, as indicated by the selected Track In CRM button.

7. Close the contact.

8. Open Windows Internet Explorer and browse to the address of your Microsoft Dynamics CRM system.

9. Navigate to the account records and open the **Sonoma Partners** account or other parent account selected in step 5.

10. In the navigation pane, click **Contacts**.

The Chris Perry record appears linked to this account.

11. Double-click the **Chris Perry** record to open it. In the **Business Phone** field, enter **(312) 555-1212**.

Save and Close

12. Click the **Save and Close** button.

Microsoft Dynamics CRM closes the window and returns you to the list of contacts associated with the account.

New Contact

13. In the grid toolbar, click the **New Contact** button to launch the **New Contact** form.

14. In the **First Name** field, enter **Jose**. In the **Last Name** field, enter **Curry**.

Note that, because you created this contact from the account, the contact record includes the mapped address fields from the parent account record.

15. Click the **Save and Close** button.

16. Close Internet Explorer.

17. In Outlook, click **CRM** in the menu bar, and select **Synchronize in CRM**.

A window opens, indicating that Microsoft Dynamics CRM for Outlook is updating data.

18. In the Outlook menu, click **Go**, and select **Contacts**. In the search box, enter **Jose Curry**.

The contact you created in the Web client now appears in your Outlook file (with the mapped fields from the account).

19. In the search box, enter **Chris Perry**.

Outlook shows the Chris Perry record, which now includes the phone number that you entered in the Web client.

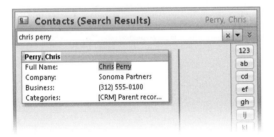

Creating and Tracking Tasks and Appointments

In addition to synchronizing contacts, Microsoft Dynamics CRM for Outlook can synchronize tasks and appointments between Microsoft Dynamics CRM and Outlook. The process of creating and tracking tasks and appointments follows the same rules as previously outlined for contacts. You can create the task and appointment records in Outlook by using the standard Outlook tools, and then click the Track In CRM button to save a copy to Microsoft Dynamics CRM. As you learned in previous chapters, you can also specify a Regarding value for activities such as tasks and appointments.

If you create tasks or appointments in the Web client, Microsoft Dynamics CRM for Outlook can also synchronize those records from the server into your Outlook file.

> **Tip** You can modify many of the Microsoft Dynamics CRM for Outlook synchronization settings. To access the personal settings page, click CRM in the Outlook menu bar, and then select Options. You can view the sync settings on the Synchronization tab.

Sending and Tracking E-Mail Messages in Microsoft Dynamics CRM for Outlook

Even though you can create and send Microsoft Dynamics CRM e-mail messages with the Web client, most users prefer to create and reply to their e-mail messages by using Outlook. Copies of your Outlook e-mail messages can be saved to Microsoft Dynamics CRM so that you can go back later and see a complete history of the communications. Much like creating contacts, tasks, and appointments in Outlook, you can create e-mail messages as you normally would in Outlook and save a copy of each message to Microsoft Dynamics CRM by clicking the Track In CRM button. When processing the e-mail message, Microsoft Dynamics CRM for Outlook reviews the list of message participants and automatically looks for matching e-mail records in the Microsoft Dynamics CRM database. If it finds matching e-mail addresses, the system appends the e-mail message to the matching records as a completed e-mail activity. This e-mail matching process searches for matching e-mail addresses across those record types that contain e-mail addresses in Microsoft Dynamics CRM, such as contacts, accounts, leads, queues, users, and facilities/equipment.

> **Troubleshooting** If Microsoft Dynamics CRM cannot find a matching e-mail address for your message participants, you will need to manually resolve the participant to an existing record to get the message to appear in the record's history.

In addition to linking the e-mail message to the participants, you can specify which Microsoft Dynamics CRM record the e-mail message is regarding. For example, you might send multiple e-mails to a single customer, but one e-mail might be about an existing order, whereas a different e-mail might be about a customer service issue. By specifying the Regarding field of each message (one is regarding an order, and one is regarding a service issue), you can split up the communication history to the appropriate records. This will save you time when viewing the activity history related to each record. Microsoft Dynamics CRM for Outlook saves a list of your recently used Regarding values so you can quickly track e-mail messages regarding recent topics.

See Also For more information about tracking e-mail messages and other activities in Microsoft Dynamics CRM, see Chapter 4, "Working with Activities and Notes."

When you create an e-mail message in Outlook, Microsoft Dynamics CRM for Outlook also allows you to access an Outlook address book that contains your Microsoft Dynamics CRM records. The Microsoft Dynamics CRM address book provides you quick access to the e-mail addresses of your Microsoft Dynamics CRM records directly in Outlook, without forcing you to look up their e-mail addresses from the Web client. In addition, the Microsoft Dynamics CRM address book can include e-mail information about non-contact records, which you cannot synchronize to Outlook.

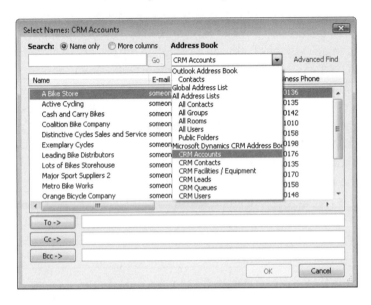

> **Tip** You can configure additional settings for the Microsoft Dynamics CRM address book in the Microsoft Dynamics CRM for Outlook options.

In addition to tracking e-mail messages sent from Outlook, Microsoft Dynamics CRM for Outlook allows you to track e-mail messages that you receive. To track these types of messages, you can open the message and click the Track In CRM button, or you can select the e-mail message in your Inbox and then click the Track In CRM button in the CRM group on the menu bar. You can set the Regarding value of the message by using the Set Regarding button in the CRM toolbar.

> **Important** You can select up to 20 e-mail messages at a time and click the Track In CRM button. Depending on your e-mail system and your Microsoft Dynamics CRM tracking con-figuration, Microsoft Dynamics CRM can automatically track all of the e-mail messages in a subject thread so that you don't have to manually track every message. Contact your system administrator to determine your exact system configuration.

In this exercise, you will create an e-mail message in Outlook and track it in Microsoft Dynamics CRM. You will also manually resolve an unmatched e-mail address to an existing record.

USE the Chris Perry contact record you created earlier in this chapter and the Sonoma Partners account record you created in Chapter 3. If you cannot locate the Sonoma Partners record in your system, select a different account record for this exercise.

BE SURE TO start Outlook with Microsoft Dynamics CRM for Outlook installed, if necessary, before beginning this exercise.

1. In the Outlook menu bar, click the **New** button, and select **Mail Message**.

A blank e-mail message opens.

2. In the **To** field, enter any e-mail address that does not already exist in your Microsoft Dynamics CRM database. You need to use a new e-mail address to complete steps 11 through 14 of this exercise.

3. In the **Subject** field, enter **Test Message**.

4. In the menu bar, click the **Track in CRM** button.

Set Regarding

5. Click the **Set Regarding** button, and then select **More**.

A Microsoft Dynamics CRM lookup window opens.

6. In the lookup window, click the list to see the possible entities you can link to the e-mail message. Select **Account**.

7. In the search box, enter **Sonoma Partners**, and press Enter to search for the account in Microsoft Dynamics CRM. Select the appropriate account in the results, and then click **OK**.

8. In the e-mail message, move your mouse over the **View Regarding** button to preview the **Regarding** value of the message. You can see that this message is regarding the Sonoma Partners account.

View Regarding

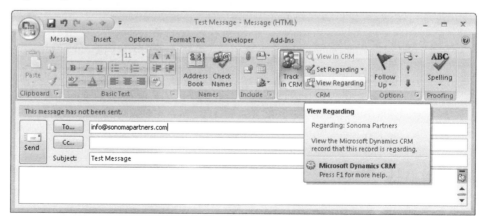

Send

9. Click the **Send** button.

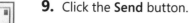

View in CRM

10. Click the **Sent Items** link in the folder list to display a list of your sent e-mail messages. Double-click the test e-mail message you just sent. When the message opens, click the **View in CRM** button.

The e-mail message now opens in the Web client. Assuming that you entered an e-mail address not already in your database, the sample e-mail address is colored red in the To field. This record color indicates that Microsoft Dynamics CRM could not find a matching e-mail address in your system.

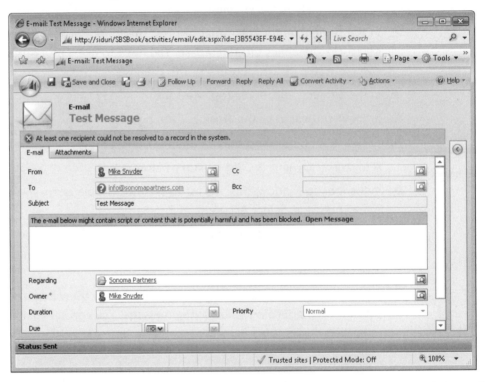

11. To manually resolve this e-mail message to a particular contact record, click the red e-mail address.

A Resolve Address dialog box opens. From this dialog box, you can resolve the e-mail participant to an existing record or create a new record. Let's assume that you want to resolve this message to the Chris Perry contact record you created earlier in this chapter.

12. In the text field under **Resolve to an existing record**, type **Chris Perry**, and then press the Tab key.

Microsoft Dynamics CRM formats the text you entered as blue and underlines it, indicating that it has successfully found the matching record.

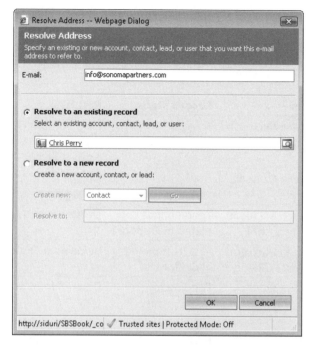

13. Click **OK**.

    In the e-mail message, Microsoft Dynamics CRM replaced the sample e-mail address with the Chris Perry contact.

14. In the menu bar, click the **Save** button.

    Now if you view the history of the Chris Perry contact or the Sonoma Partners account, you can view a copy of this e-mail message.

> **CLOSE** all open windows of Internet Explorer.

Deleting Records in Microsoft Dynamics CRM for Outlook

After Microsoft Dynamics CRM for Outlook completes its initial synchronization process with your Outlook file, special rules apply to how the synchronization process handles deleted records. For example, deleting a contact record in Outlook does *not* delete that contact record in Microsoft Dynamics CRM. Conversely, deleting a contact in Microsoft Dynamics CRM removes the synchronized contact from Outlook for all users except for the Outlook user who owns the record in Microsoft Dynamics CRM.

With respect to deleted records, Microsoft Dynamics CRM for Outlook follows rules and conditions to determine how the synchronization process should update Outlook and Microsoft Dynamics CRM. Microsoft Dynamics CRM for Outlook processes deleted records as outlined in the following table.

Record type	Action	Record state	Result
Contact	Delete in Microsoft Dynamics CRM	Any	Deleted from Outlook for all users except contact owner. Remains in contact owner's Outlook file.
Contact	Delete in Outlook	Any	No change in Microsoft Dynamics CRM.
Task	Delete in Microsoft Dynamics CRM	Pending (not completed in Outlook)	Deleted from Outlook.
Task	Delete in Microsoft Dynamics CRM	Past (completed in Outlook)	Remains in Outlook.
Task	Delete in Outlook	Pending (open in Microsoft Dynamics CRM)	Deleted from Microsoft Dynamics CRM.
Task	Delete in Outlook	Past (completed or canceled in Microsoft Dynamics CRM)	No change in Microsoft Dynamics CRM.
Appointment	Delete in Microsoft Dynamics CRM	Pending (open in Microsoft Dynamics CRM)	Deleted from Outlook if appointment start time is in the future.
Appointment	Delete in Microsoft Dynamics CRM	Past (completed or canceled in Microsoft Dynamics CRM)	Remains in Outlook.
Appointment	Delete in Outlook	Pending (open in Microsoft Dynamics CRM)	Deleted from Microsoft Dynamics CRM if deleted by appointment owner or organizer. Not deleted from Microsoft Dynamics CRM if deleted in Outlook by non-owners or non-organizers.
Appointment	Delete in Outlook	Past (completed or canceled in Microsoft Dynamics CRM)	No change in Microsoft Dynamics CRM.

If you delete a contact in Outlook (which does not delete the contact from Microsoft Dynamics CRM) and then someone subsequently modifies that contact record in Microsoft Dynamics CRM, Microsoft Dynamics CRM for Outlook recreates that contact in the Outlook file, even though you previously deleted it.

On a related note, deactivating contact records in Microsoft Dynamics CRM does not remove the contacts from Outlook. You must manually delete the deactivated contacts from Microsoft Dynamics CRM if you don't want them to appear in your Outlook file any longer.

In this exercise, you will delete several records to see how the synchronization process treats each scenario.

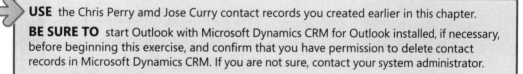

USE the Chris Perry amd Jose Curry contact records you created earlier in this chapter.
BE SURE TO start Outlook with Microsoft Dynamics CRM for Outlook installed, if necessary, before beginning this exercise, and confirm that you have permission to delete contact records in Microsoft Dynamics CRM. If you are not sure, contact your system administrator.

1. In the Outlook menu bar, click the **Go** menu, and then select **Contacts**.

2. In the search box, type **Chris Perry** to locate the contact record.

Delete

3. Select the **Chris Perry** record and, in the Outlook menu bar, click the **Delete** button.

4. Open Microsoft Dynamics CRM in Internet Explorer, and navigate to the account list. Locate the **Sonoma Partners** account (or the alternate parent account record, if you assigned a different parent account to the record earlier in this chapter) and double-click it to open it.

5. Click **Contacts** in the left navigation pane.

A list of contacts associated with the account appears. Note that even though you deleted the Chris Perry contact from Outlook, Microsoft Dynamics CRM for Outlook did not delete the record on the server.

6. Click the **Jose Curry** record, and click the **Delete** button in the grid toolbar. In the **Contact Delete Confirmation** dialog box, click the **Delete** button, and then click **OK** in the secondary confirmation dialog box.

7. Close Internet Explorer.

8. Open Outlook, click **CRM** in the menu bar, and then click **Synchronize with CRM**.

9. In the **Contact** search box, type **Jose Curry**. Outlook displays the matching contact record. Double-click the record to open the contact.

Note that Microsoft Dynamics CRM for Outlook did not delete the Jose Curry contact from your Outlook file, because you are listed as the owner of this record. However, this contact record is no longer tracked in Microsoft Dynamics CRM. If you delete a contact record owned by a different user, Microsoft Dynamics CRM for Outlook removes that record from your Outlook file.

Going Offline with Microsoft Dynamics CRM for Outlook

If you install Microsoft Dynamics CRM for Outlook with Offline Access, you have the option to work with your Microsoft Dynamics CRM data when you are disconnected from the server. This feature is useful if you need to travel for onsite customer meetings or other activities, because you can look up your existing notes, add new notes, run reports, and do much more without needing an Internet connection. The concept of disconnecting from the Microsoft Dynamics CRM server is known as *going offline*. When you go offline, Microsoft Dynamics CRM for Outlook copies a subset of the Microsoft Dynamics CRM database to your computer. While offline, you can perform almost all of the Microsoft Dynamics CRM functionality just the same as when you're online. When you are able to connect to the Microsoft Dynamics CRM server again, you *go online* to synchronize your offline database with the main Microsoft Dynamics CRM database. When you go online, Microsoft Dynamics CRM for Outlook automatically determines which records it should upload to the Microsoft Dynamics CRM database and which records it needs to synchronize with your local database.

Because some Microsoft Dynamics CRM databases can get quite large, going offline does not copy *all* of the data to your computer. Instead, Microsoft Dynamics CRM for Outlook uses *local data groups* to determine which subsets of the database it should copy to the offline database. The use of local data groups provides better performance and faster synchronization times than if you were using the entire Microsoft Dynamics CRM database.

> **Tip** You can configure Microsoft Dynamics CRM for Outlook with Offline Access to perform a background update of your local data as often as every 15 minutes. Setting up this option in the Microsoft Dynamics CRM for Outlook options allows you to go offline more quickly in the future, in addition to allowing you to access relatively updated offline data in case you forget to explicitly go offline.

In this exercise, you will go offline and confirm you are disconnected from the Microsoft Dynamics CRM server.

> **BE SURE TO** start Outlook with Microsoft Dynamics CRM for Outlook installed, if necessary, before beginning this exercise.

Go Offline

1. In the Outlook **CRM** toolbar, click the **Go Offline** button.

A progress window appears, showing you the status of the synchronization process.

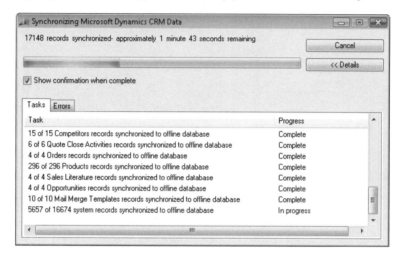

When the process is complete, the Go Offline button on the CRM toolbar is renamed Go Online. This indicates that you are now working with data from the local database instead of data from the Microsoft Dynamics CRM server.

2. In the Outlook menu bar, click the **Go** menu, and select **Folder List**. Scroll down past your mailbox to the **Microsoft Dynamics CRM** folder. Click the + symbol to expand the folder.

3. Click the + symbol to expand the **Sales** folder, and then click the **Accounts** folder.

You will see a list of accounts, just as if you were viewing them while connected to the Microsoft Dynamics CRM server. Depending on your local data groups, you might see only a subset of all of the Microsoft Dynamics CRM accounts.

4. To confirm that you are working offline, double-click an account record to open it. When the account record is open in Internet Explorer, press ⌗F11 on the keyboard.

The Internet Explorer address bar appears. If you examine the Web address of the account record, you will notice that it starts with *http://localhost:2525* instead of the typical Web address that you use to access Microsoft Dynamics CRM. This *localhost* address references the offline version of Microsoft Dynamics CRM, so you know that you're working offline.

Go Online

5. Click the **Go Online** button to reconnect to the Microsoft Dynamics CRM server.

Configuring a Local Data Group

As you learned in the previous section, local data groups define which data Microsoft Dynamics CRM for Outlook with Offline Access copies from the server to your offline database. During the installation process, Microsoft Dynamics CRM creates approximately 30 different local data groups for the records in your system. If you plan to work offline frequently, you should examine these default local data groups to make sure you'll have access to the information you need when offline.

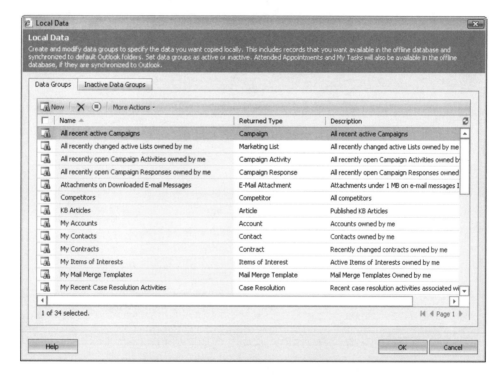

Two common modifications to the default local data groups are:

- Including all reports to run offline, because the default local data group downloads only the reports you own to the offline database.

- Including custom entities, because the default local data group does not include any custom entities.

> **Important** You can modify your local data group settings only when you are online.

If your computer uses the online-only version of Microsoft Dynamics CRM for Outlook, your system still contains local data groups, but the software uses them for a different purpose. If you are an online-only user of Microsoft Dynamics CRM for Outlook, you can configure your local data groups to specify which contacts the software should copy from the server to your Outlook file. By default, Microsoft Dynamics CRM for Outlook includes a data group that copies contacts that you own from the Microsoft Dynamics CRM server into your Outlook file.

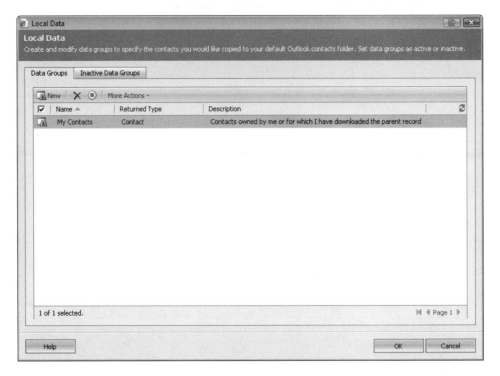

You can delete, deactivate, or modify this default local data group, or add entirely new data groups if you want. Some users like to create local data groups so that Microsoft Dynamics CRM copies all of the contacts for the accounts and opportunities that they own.

In this exercise, you will modify the local data group for Microsoft Dynamics CRM for Outlook with Offline Access to include all of the reports in your offline database.

> **Important** When you run reports offline, the reports will include only data from the offline database, which is typically a subset of the entire database. If you need to report on the entire database, make sure you go online first.

BE SURE TO start Outlook with Microsoft Dynamics CRM for Outlook installed, if necessary, before beginning this exercise.

1. In the Outlook menu bar, click **CRM**, and then click **Modify Local Data Groups**.

The **Local Data** dialog box opens.

2. Scroll down the list to locate the **My Reports** row. Double-click this record to open the **Data Group** dialog box.

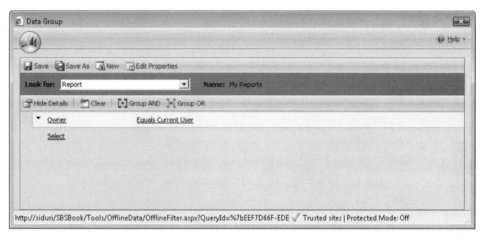

Clear

Save As

3. You can see that this data filter will download only the reports that list you as the owner. To change this setting, click the **Clear** button in the toolbar.

4. Now click the **Save As** button to save this local data group with a new name.

A new window opens.

5. In the **Name** field, remove the existing text and enter **All Reports**. In the **Description** field, remove the existing text and enter **All reports**. Click **OK** to close the window.

6. In the **Data Group** dialog box, click the **Save** button, and then close the window.

The new local data group you created appears in the data group list.

7. Click **OK** to close the window.

8. In the **CRM** toolbar, click the **Go Offline** button.

When the progress window appears, notice that Microsoft Dynamics CRM is downloading the reports to your offline database.

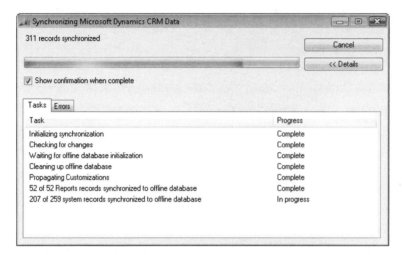

9. In the Outlook menu bar, on the **Go** menu, click **Folder List**. Scroll down past your mailbox to the **Microsoft Dynamics CRM** folder. Click the + symbol to expand the folder.

10. Click the + symbol to expand the **Workplace** folder, click the + symbol to expand the **My Work** folder, and then click the **Reports** folder.

   A list of the Microsoft Dynamics CRM reports that you can run while working offline appears.

 BE SURE TO go back online when you have finished this exercise.

Key Points

- Microsoft Dynamics CRM for Outlook provides integration between Outlook and Microsoft Dynamics CRM.

- Microsoft Dynamics CRM for Outlook is available in two versions: one for online use only, and one with offline access so that you can work while disconnected from the server.

- Microsoft Dynamics CRM for Outlook performs a bi-directional synchronization of tracked contacts, tasks, and appointments between Outlook and the Microsoft Dynamics CRM server.

- To create contacts, tasks, and appointments in Outlook that will appear in the Microsoft Dynamics CRM database, simply click the Track In CRM button in the Outlook menu bar.

- You can create and reply to e-mail messages in Outlook and track those communications to the appropriate Microsoft Dynamics CRM records by clicking the Track In CRM button.

- Synchronized records follow a unique set of processing rules regarding deletion, depending on their ownership, status, and other variables.

- Microsoft Dynamics CRM for Outlook with Offline Access allows users to copy data to a local database and work offline.

- Local data groups define which records are synchronized to your Outlook file. In offline mode, you can configure any record type that you want to access while offline. For online-only use, local data groups define the contacts that are synchronized to your Outlook file.

- You can create new local data groups or modify existing data groups according to your needs.

Part II
Sales

Chapter at a Glance

Qualify or disqualify a lead, **pages 120 and 121**

Create a lead, **page 118**

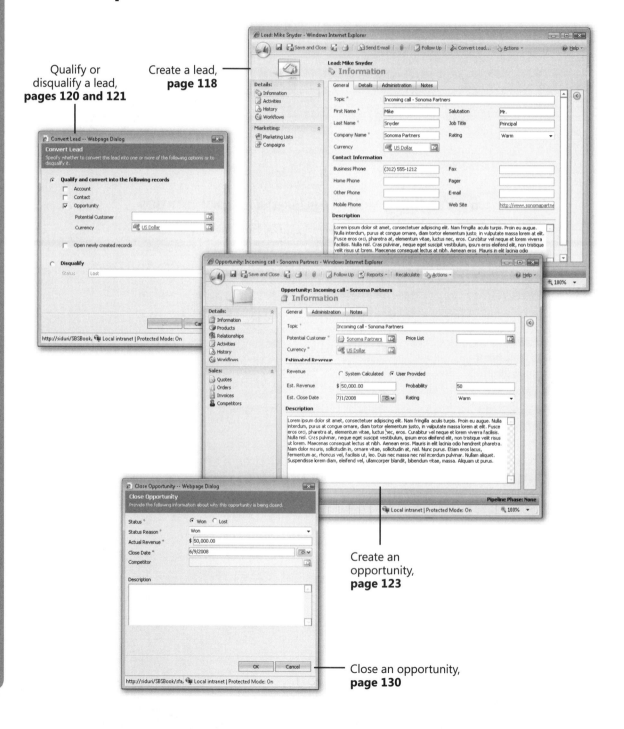

Create an opportunity, **page 123**

Close an opportunity, **page 130**

6 Working with Leads and Opportunities

In this chapter, you will learn to

✔ Understand the difference between leads and opportunities.

✔ Create a lead.

✔ Qualify a lead.

✔ Disqualify a lead.

✔ Create an opportunity.

✔ Use opportunities to forecast potential sales.

✔ Close an opportunity.

✔ Reopen an opportunity.

✔ Convert an e-mail message to a lead.

By now you should understand many of the basics of Microsoft Dynamics CRM and how to navigate within the software. Microsoft Dynamics CRM includes three main modules: Sales, Marketing, and Service. This chapter will take a deeper look at some of the sales management capabilities in the software. As you would expect, the sales portion of Microsoft Dynamics CRM helps organizations track and manage revenue-generating activities such as lead management, opportunity forecasting, and quotes.

In this chapter, you will learn how to work with leads and opportunities in Microsoft Dynamics CRM so that you can manage your organization's sales data more efficiently. You will learn how to create and convert leads, in addition to creating and closing opportunities. Quotes are detailed in Chapter 7, "Working with Quotes."

> **Important**   The exercises in this chapter require only records created in earlier chapters; none are supplied on the companion CD. For more information about practice files, see "Using the Companion CD" at the beginning of this book.

> **Troubleshooting**   Graphics and operating system–related instructions in this book reflect the Windows Vista user interface. If your computer is running Windows XP and you experience trouble following the instructions as written, refer to the "Information for Readers Running Windows XP" section at the beginning of this book.

> **Important**   The images used in this book reflect the default form and field names in Microsoft Dynamics CRM. Because the software offers extensive customization capabilities, it's possible that some of the record types or fields have been relabeled in your Microsoft Dynamics CRM environment. If you cannot find the forms, fields, or security roles referenced in this book, contact your system administrator for assistance.

> **Important**   You must know the location of your Microsoft Dynamics CRM Web site to work the exercises in this book. Check with your system administrator to verify the Web address if you don't know it.

Understanding Leads and Opportunities

Many CRM software systems use the terms lead and opportunity to describe different types of sales records, but sometimes these expressions can cause confusion for new users. *Leads* represent prospective customers that your sales representatives need to qualify or disqualify. Depending on your organization's sales and marketing processes, leads can come from many different sources—Web site requests, purchased lists, trade shows, or incoming phone calls. Many organizations try to qualify or disqualify lead records as quickly as possible to determine whether they represent potential customers. Because lead records are not intended to be used for the long term, they use a flat data structure in which the data about an individual and his or her company reside in a single record.

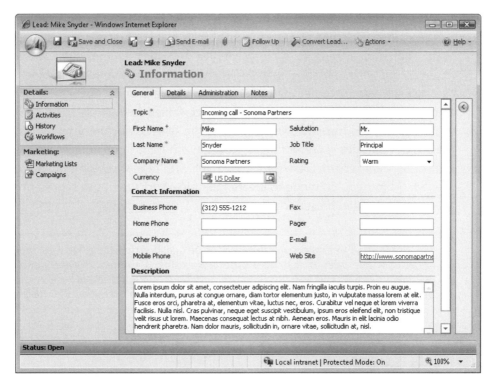

Each organization defines its own lead qualification criteria, but typical qualifying questions asked by businesses include:

- Is the lead located in a geographic region that we sell to?
- Does the lead fit the financial profile of customers that we sell to?
- Does the lead have a need or desire for our products or services?

If you determine that the lead meets your sales criteria, you convert the lead to one or more different types of records in Microsoft Dynamics CRM:

- Account
- Contact
- Opportunity

As you learned in Chapter 3, "Working with Accounts and Contacts," accounts represent businesses, and contacts represent people. By using accounts and contacts instead of leads to track prospects and customers, you can model additional relationships within Microsoft Dynamics CRM to capture the various people in each account.

Opportunities represent potential revenue-generating events for your organization. Most organizations track data about a potential sales opportunity, such as estimated close date, estimated revenue, sales representative, and sales stage. You link each opportunity to an account or a contact, depending on how you want to track the potential customer. Because a single customer might purchase multiple products or services from your organization, a single customer record can be linked to multiple opportunities. Each potential sale can have its own data about the sales opportunity, and you can even have different sales representatives pursuing different opportunities for the same contact or account record. Likewise, as you work with repeat customers over an extended period of time, you continue to create multiple opportunities to represent new sales opportunities while preserving the historical opportunity data.

> **Tip** Use leads to track prospects that need to be qualified or disqualified. Use opportunities to track potential sales to qualified prospects or existing customers. Not every organization uses leads. For example, businesses and organizations that sell their products and services to a small, defined customer base might not use lead records at all in Microsoft Dynamics CRM.

Creating a Lead

Leads come from many different sources, depending on your sales and marketing processes. Your corporate Web site might generate leads automatically, or marketing personnel might import leads into Microsoft Dynamics CRM with a batch process. However, you can also manually create lead records. When working with a lead, you can use Microsoft Dynamics CRM activities such as tasks, phone calls, and e-mail messages to track your interactions with the lead during the qualification process. The type of data that you capture about each lead depends on your business needs and any customizations your system includes, but most organizations track the person's name and address information.

See Also If you need to create many leads at the same time by importing a data file, refer to Chapter 18, "Importing Data," for more details on that process.

Many organizations also want to capture the marketing source from which the lead originated. If your organization captures the *lead source* for each record, sales and marketing managers can run reports to determine which lead-generation tactics are most effective. For example, you might find that a lead source such as the trade show circuit generates a large number of leads, but only a small percentage of them qualify as potential customers. Meanwhile, another marketing tactic such as a Web site might generate a smaller number of leads, but a high percentage of them qualify as potential customers. Understanding the source of your leads will help your company make better decisions on where to invest in future sales and marketing efforts.

In this exercise, you will create a lead to track a new prospect who found out about your organization from a Web site.

> **BE SURE TO** use the Windows Internet Explorer Web browser to navigate to your Microsoft Dynamics CRM Web site before beginning this exercise.

New Lead

1. In the **Sales** area, click **Leads**.

2. In the grid toolbar, click the **New Lead** button to launch the **New Lead** form.

3. In the **Topic** field, enter **New Lead – Mike Snyder**.

4. In the **First Name** field, enter **Mike**.

5. In the **Last Name** field, enter **Snyder**.

6. In the **Company Name** field, enter **Sonoma Partners**.

7. Click the **Details** tab. In the **Lead Information** section, click the **Lead Source** arrow, and then select **Web**.

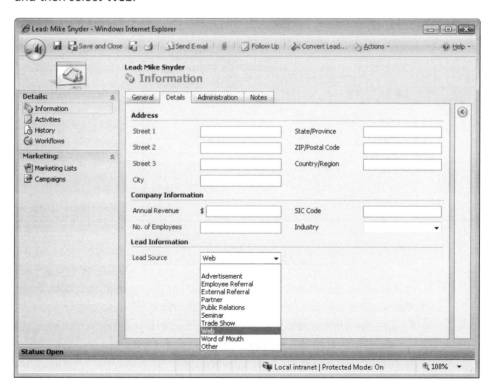

Save

8. In the form toolbar, click the **Save** button.

> **Tip** Your system administrator can customize the list values for the Lead Source field, in addition to all of the other lead fields.

Qualifying a Lead

Leads represent potential customers that can be qualified or disqualified based on criteria set by your organization. After you work with a lead record and determine whether or not the lead fits your lead qualification criteria, you *convert the lead*. When you convert the lead, you specify whether or not the lead is qualified or disqualified.

When you qualify the lead, you create one or more of the following record types: account, contact, or opportunity.

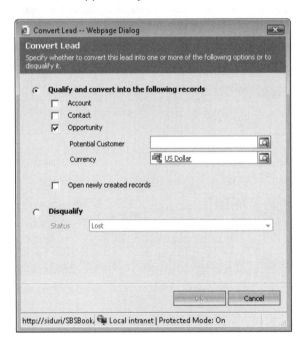

Your business process should dictate which of the records to create. For example, if your organization sells to businesses, you will probably want to create an account and a contact. If your organization sells to individual consumers, you might not want to create an account. Likewise, you might not always create an opportunity when you qualify a lead. You might determine that a lead fits your qualification criteria but that an immediate sales opportunity does not exist.

In addition to creating new accounts and contacts, you can convert a lead to a new opportunity that will be linked to an existing customer record in Microsoft Dynamics CRM. You might want to do this if a matching account or contact already exists in your Microsoft Dynamics CRM database.

When you qualify a lead, you can mark a check box to open the newly created records, which will open the new account, contact, or opportunity records created during the convert lead process so that you can work with them right away, saving you a few clicks.

> **Tip** Microsoft Dynamics CRM will populate data fields in the account, contact, and opportunity records you create from a qualified lead, based on the mapped data fields.

In this exercise, you will convert a lead as qualified and create a new account, contact, and opportunity.

> **USE** the Mike Snyder lead record you created in the previous exercise.
>
> **BE SURE TO** use the Internet Explorer Web browser to navigate to your Microsoft Dynamics CRM Web site, if necessary, before beginning this exercise.

Convert Lead

1. Open the **Mike Snyder** lead record.

2. On the form toolbar, click the **Convert Lead** button.

   A new dialog box opens.

3. Select the check boxes next to **Account**, **Contact**, and **Opportunity**.

4. Select the **Open newly created records** check box.

5. Click **OK**.

   Microsoft Dynamics CRM opens three new windows in addition to deactivating the lead record.

Disqualifying a Lead

Not every lead will meet your qualification criteria, so you will need to disqualify leads from time to time. Disqualifying a lead does not delete the record from your system. Instead, it deactivates the lead to indicate that no one needs to follow up with it. Likewise, converting a lead as qualified does not delete the record; it deactivates the lead record and creates an account, contact, or opportunity record for further follow-up.

> **Tip** Converting a lead to qualified or disqualified status does not delete the lead record; rather, it deactivates the record so it no longer appears in anyone's active leads list.

When you disqualify a lead, you can select a reason to indicate why you decided to disqualify the record. Again, your administrator can customize the disqualification reasons, but the default values include Lost, Cannot Contact, No Longer Interested, and Canceled.

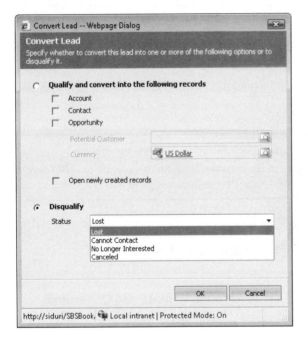

Just as recording a lead source provides valuable sales and marketing data, recording a disqualification reason also provides data that you can analyze to optimize your sales and marketing processes. Cross-referencing the lead source data with the disqualification data can provide valuable insights. For example, you could discover that your sales team disqualified 50 percent of the leads from a purchased list because of invalid contact information. Sales and marketing managers can use this information to make educated purchases of future lists or perhaps stop purchasing lists altogether. To obtain this kind of insight, it's important that each sales representative accurately records the disqualification reasons.

In this exercise, you will create a lead and disqualify it.

 BE SURE TO use the Internet Explorer Web browser to navigate to your Microsoft Dynamics CRM Web site, if necessary, before beginning this exercise.

1. In the **Sales** area, click **Leads**.

2. In the grid toolbar, click the **New Lead** button.

   A blank lead record opens.

3. In the **Topic** field, enter **Lead to Disqualify – Mike Snyder**.

4. In the **First Name** field, enter **Mike**.

5. In the **Last Name** field, enter **Snyder**.

6. In the **Company Name** field, enter **Sonoma Partners**.

7. Click the **Details** tab. In the **Lead Information** section, in the **Lead Source** list, select **Web**.

8. In the form toolbar, click **Save**, and then click the **Convert Lead** button.

   The Convert Lead dialog box opens.

9. Select **Disqualify**.

10. In the **Status** list, select **Cannot Contact**.

11. Click **OK** to update the lead's status to Disqualified and mark it inactive.

Creating an Opportunity

Opportunities represent potential sales, and many organizations carefully monitor their opportunity data to help them:

- Understand the sales pipeline.
- Evaluate the performance of individual sales representatives.
- Forecast future demand.

When you work with an opportunity, you can track all of the activities related to the potential sale, such as tasks, phone calls, and e-mail messages.

By default, you can track the potential customer's name, estimated close date, estimated revenue, probability, and rating for each sales opportunity. Many organizations customize the opportunity form to track additional data about the potential sale, depending on the products and services they provide.

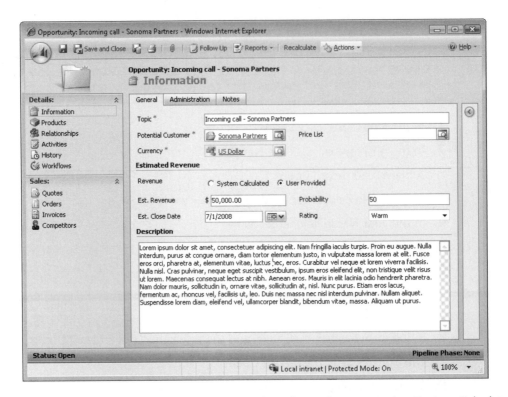

You can choose between two revenue settings for each opportunity: System Calculated and User Provided. If you select System Calculated, Microsoft Dynamics CRM automatically calculates the estimated value of the opportunity by using a combination of the products attached to the opportunity and the selected price list. If you select User Provided, you can enter the dollar amount of the opportunity value directly into the Est. Revenue field. Setting up products and price lists in Microsoft Dynamics CRM requires system administrator privileges, so the exercises in this chapter will utilize the User Provided option for revenue.

See Also If your organization wants to set up the product catalog in your deployment, your administrator can reference the Microsoft Dynamics CRM online help for additional information on the specific configuration steps.

For the Est. Close Date field, you enter the date when you expect to close the opportunity, either as a win or as a loss. The Probability field allows you to enter a percentage to indicate your confidence level that you will win the opportunity. You can enter a whole number between 0 and 100 in the Probability field. For example, entering 50 in this field means that you're 50 percent confident you will win the opportunity. Rating is another measure of the opportunity. The default values are Hot, Warm, and Cold. Some organizations use the Rating field to indicate their perception of the customer's interest, and other organizations use Rating to record how interested they are in pursuing the opportunity.

> **Tip** Many organizations use the Microsoft Dynamics CRM workflow feature to automate the Probability and Rating values based on their unique business rules. Creating and designing workflow rules is beyond the scope of this book, but you can learn more about it in *Working with Microsoft Dynamics CRM 4.0*, by Mike Snyder and Jim Steger (Microsoft Press, 2008).

Earlier in this chapter, you learned how to create an opportunity record by converting a lead. Because you will also want to create opportunities for existing accounts and contacts, you need to know how to create opportunities outside of the lead qualification process.

In this exercise, you will create an opportunity for the Sonoma Partners account record created in Chapter 3.

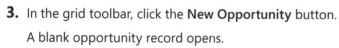

USE the Sonoma Partners account record you created in Chapter 3. If you cannot locate the Sonoma Partners record in your system, select a different account record for this exercise.

BE SURE TO use the Internet Explorer Web browser to navigate to your Microsoft Dynamics CRM Web site, if necessary, before beginning this exercise.

1. Navigate to the **Accounts** view, and open the **Sonoma Partners** account record.

2. In the left navigation pane, click **Opportunities**.

New Opportunity

3. In the grid toolbar, click the **New Opportunity** button.

A blank opportunity record opens.

4. In the **Topic** field, enter **Sonoma Partners Sample Opportunity**.

5. For the **Revenue** data field, select **User Provided**.

The Est. Revenue field becomes editable.

6. In the **Est. Revenue** field, enter **50,000.00**.

7. In the **Est. Close Date** field, enter **12/1/2008**.

8. In the **Probability** field, enter **50**.

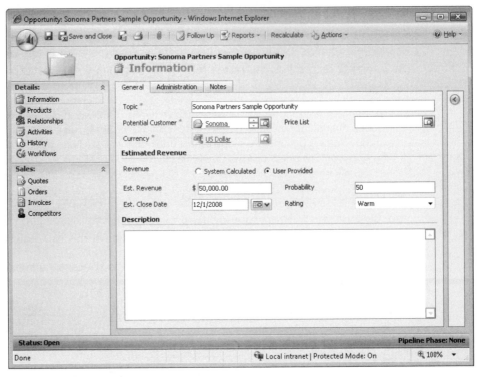

9. In the form toolbar, click **Save**.

Using Opportunities to Forecast Potential Sales

One of the main reasons that organizations track opportunities in Microsoft Dynamics CRM is to allow managers and executives to forecast upcoming and future business. As you saw in the previous section, you can record the potential customer's name, a topic name, the estimated close date, estimated revenue, and probability for each opportunity. By using these data points, sales managers can review the open opportunities to ensure orders can be fulfilled and understand which sales representatives are generating new sales pipelines.

> **Tip** To record the sales representative pursuing the opportunity, assign the sales representative as the owner of the opportunity record.

Microsoft Dynamics CRM includes several system views for opportunities, including:

- Opportunities closing next month.
- Opportunities opened last week.
- Opportunities opened this week.

You can use the Advanced Find tool to modify these views, or you can create new views to analyze your opportunity information. Refer to Chapter 15, "Using Advanced Find," for more detailed information about working with views.

In addition to opportunity views, Microsoft Dynamics CRM includes four out-of-the-box opportunity reports that you can use to analyze your sales information:

- Sales Pipeline
- Lead Source Effectiveness
- Competitor Win Loss
- Activities

If none of these reports meet your needs, you can create new reports by using the Report Wizard. Refer to Chapter 16, "Using the Report Wizard," for information about creating reports using this feature.

Lastly, you can perform ad-hoc opportunity reporting and forecasting by exporting your opportunity data into Microsoft Office Excel. Chapter 17, "Reporting with Microsoft Office Excel," explains how to create reports and perform analyses by using static and dynamic Excel worksheets.

In this exercise, you will run the Sales Pipeline report on your open opportunities.

> **Important** Your reports will appear different than the images in this exercise because your Microsoft Dynamics CRM database contains different opportunities.

BE SURE TO use the Internet Explorer Web browser to navigate to your Microsoft Dynamics CRM Web site, if necessary, before beginning this exercise.

1. In the **Sales** area, click **Opportunities**.

2. In the **View** list, select the **Open Opportunities** view.

Reports

3. In the grid toolbar, click the **Reports** button, and select **Sales Pipeline** from the submenu.

The Select Records dialog box opens. From here you can select the records to run the report against.

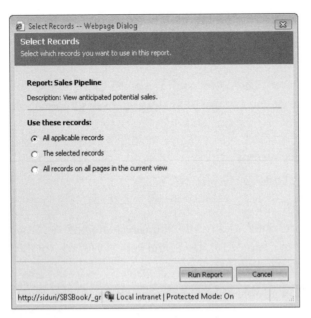

4. Select **All records on all pages in the current view**, and then click **Run Report**.

Microsoft Dynamics CRM launches the Sales Pipeline report viewer.

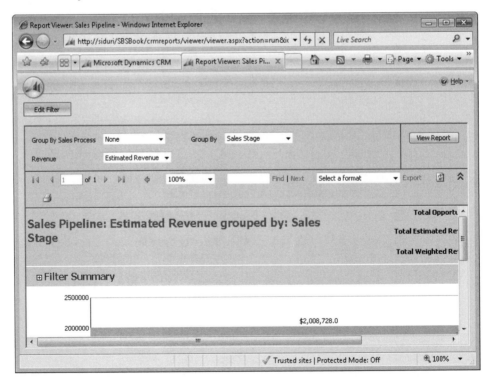

From here, you can filter and group the opportunity data to further analyze your open opportunities.

5. In the **Group By** list, select **Sales User**.

6. Click the **View Report** button.

Microsoft Dynamics CRM updates the report to show open opportunities for each sales representative.

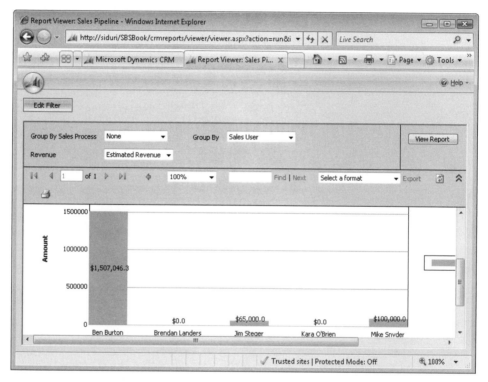

You can click on any of the columns in the report to see a list of the opportunities that make up that column's data. You can also click on the list of drill-through records to open an individual opportunity.

Closing an Opportunity

After you work with a prospect or customer to determine whether they want to purchase from your organization, you close the opportunity record to indicate what the customer decided. Closing an opportunity does not delete the record; Microsoft Dynamics CRM just deactivates the record and updates its status so it no longer appears in the active opportunities list. A *won* opportunity is one in which the customer decided to purchase from you, and a *lost* opportunity is one in which there was no purchase.

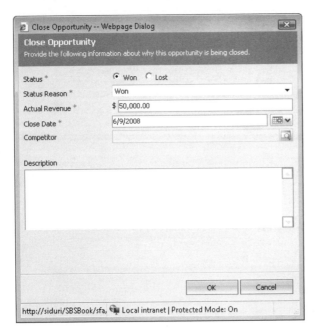

A lost opportunity does not necessarily mean that the customer purchased from someone else. You might close the opportunity as lost if the customer canceled the purchase decision or put it on indefinite hold. As with lead disqualification, your administrator can customize the reasons for marking an opportunity as lost so that you can report this type of data. Furthermore, if you lost the opportunity to a competitor, you can record which competitor you lost to for reporting and analysis.

When you close an opportunity, Microsoft Dynamics CRM automatically creates an Opportunity Close activity that stores the revenue, close date, competitor, and other notes about why the opportunity was closed. This Opportunity Close record includes date and time stamps that indicate which user created the record and when it was created. To access this information, double-click the Opportunity Close record in the History of the opportunity, and then click the Microsoft Dynamics button in the upper-left corner and select Properties to view the name of the user who created this record.

Microsoft
Dynamics

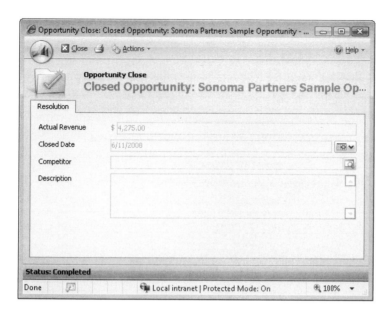

In this exercise, you will close an opportunity as Won.

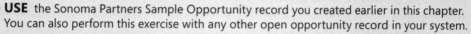

USE the Sonoma Partners Sample Opportunity record you created earlier in this chapter. You can also perform this exercise with any other open opportunity record in your system.

BE SURE TO use the Internet Explorer Web browser to navigate to your Microsoft Dynamics CRM Web site, if necessary, before beginning this exercise.

1. Open the **Sonoma Partners Sample Opportunity** record.

2. In the form toolbar, click **Actions**, and select **Close Opportunity** from the menu.

The Close Opportunity dialog box opens, with a default Status value of Won. Microsoft Dynamics CRM automatically populates the Actual Revenue field with the value from the Est. Revenue field from the opportunity. It also uses today's date as the close date by default.

3. Click **OK**.

Microsoft Dynamics CRM closes the opportunity and updates its status as Won.

> **Tip** To close an opportunity as Lost, follow a similar procedure to the one above, selecting a Status value of Lost instead of Won.

Reopening an Opportunity

The previous section mentioned that you could close an opportunity as Lost if the customer pushed off the purchase decision. If you later find out that the customer would like to reopen discussions about the potential sale, you do not need to create a new opportunity record. Instead, you can *reopen* the closed opportunity and use that record to continue tracking the sale. When you reopen a closed opportunity, you can access all of the previously created activity history and notes attached to the opportunity.

In this exercise, you will reopen a closed opportunity.

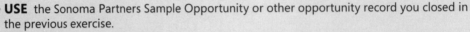

USE the Sonoma Partners Sample Opportunity or other opportunity record you closed in the previous exercise.

BE SURE TO use the Internet Explorer Web browser to navigate to your Microsoft Dynamics CRM Web site, if necessary, before beginning this exercise.

1. Navigate to the **Opportunities** view.

2. In the **View** list, select **Closed Opportunities**.

3. Find the **Sonoma Partners Sample Opportunity** record, and double-click it to open the record.

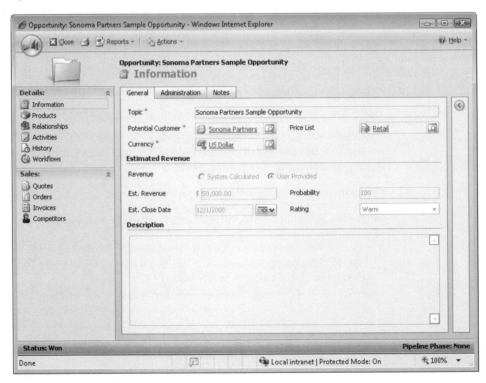

Notice that all of the fields in the opportunity are disabled; you cannot edit any of the values.

Actions

4. In the form toolbar, click the **Actions** button, and select **Reopen Opportunity**.

Microsoft Dynamics CRM prompts you with a dialog box to confirm that you want to reopen the opportunity.

5. Click **OK**.

Microsoft Dynamics CRM reopens the opportunity record so that you can edit its data fields and continue working with the record.

Converting an E-Mail Activity to a Lead

Earlier in this chapter, you learned to manually create a new lead. Another technique that you can use to create a new lead is to convert an e-mail activity into a lead. You might want to do this if you receive an e-mail message from a prospect that isn't currently recorded in your Microsoft Dynamics CRM database.

> **Tip** In addition to converting an e-mail activity into a lead, you can also convert an e-mail activity into an opportunity or a case by using the Convert Activity button on the e-mail record.

In this exercise, you will create an e-mail activity and convert it into a lead.

 BE SURE TO use the Internet Explorer Web browser to navigate to your Microsoft Dynamics CRM Web site, if necessary, before beginning this exercise.

1. In the **Workplace** area, click **Activities**.

New Activity

2. In the grid toolbar, click the **New** button.

The New Activity dialog box opens.

3. Select **E-mail**, and click **OK** to launch the **New E-mail** form.

4. In the **E-mail Subject** field, enter **Sample Lead Conversion**.

5. In the form toolbar, click **Save**.

6. In the form toolbar, select **Convert Activity**, and then select **To Lead**.

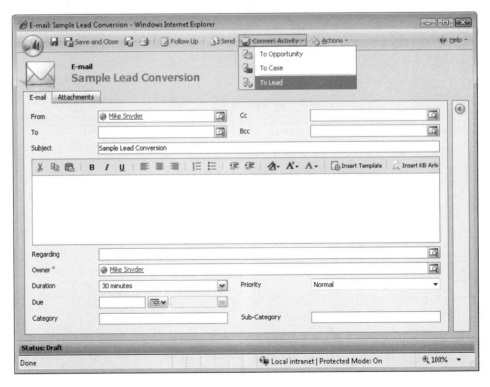

The Convert E-Mail To Lead dialog box opens. You use this dialog box to enter information about the lead, such as name, e-mail address, and company. If you want, you can also select the check boxes to open the new lead and close the e-mail form. Leave the default values checked.

7. In the **First Name** field, enter **Jim**.

8. In the **Last Name** field, enter **Steger**.

9. In the **Company** field, enter **Sonoma Partners**.

10. In the **E-mail Address** field, enter **someone@example.com**.

11. Click **OK**.

   Microsoft Dynamics CRM closes the e-mail record and creates a new lead with the values you entered.

Key Points

- Leads represent potential customers that sales representatives need to qualify or disqualify. Opportunities represent revenue-generating events such as potential sales linked to qualified prospects or existing customers.

- You can track activities such as tasks, phone calls, e-mail messages, and appointments related to leads and opportunities.

- You convert leads to mark them as qualified or disqualified.

- When you qualify a lead, you can choose to create account, contact, and opportunity records that Microsoft Dynamics CRM will populate with data from the lead record.

- When you disqualify a lead, you can choose a reason for the disqualification, which will allow you to perform reporting and analysis in the future.

- An opportunity includes data about the potential sale, such as sales representative, estimated close date, probability, and estimated revenue.

- Microsoft Dynamics CRM includes several sales forecasting tools, such as views, out-of-the-box reports, and the ability to export to Excel.

- You close an opportunity as won or lost to indicate whether or not the customer decided to purchase your products or services.

- You can reopen an opportunity after closing it.

- You can convert e-mail activity records to create new leads, cases, and opportunities.

Chapter at a Glance

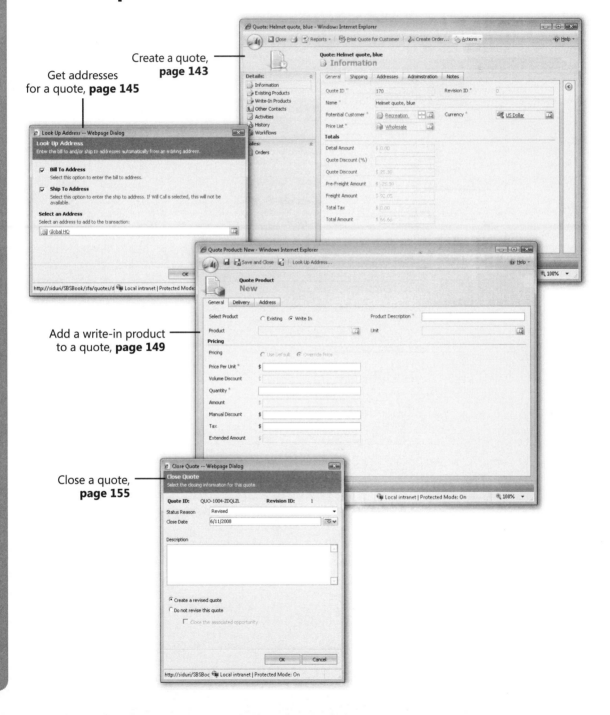

Create a quote,
page 143

Get addresses
for a quote, **page 145**

Add a write-in product
to a quote, **page 149**

Close a quote,
page 155

7 Working with Quotes

In this chapter, you will learn to:

✔ Understand quotes, orders, and invoices.

✔ Create a quote.

✔ Add bill to and ship to addresses to a quote.

✔ Add products to a quote.

✔ Activate and revise a quote.

✔ Create an order.

Many organizations provide their customers with written *quotes* of the proposed products or services that the customers are considering purchasing. Sometimes written quotes require multiple revisions, including discounting, before the customer agrees to purchase from the organization. After the sales representative receives a purchase confirmation from the customer, the representative creates an *order* to track fulfillment and payment of the purchase.

> **Tip** Sales representatives using Microsoft Dynamics CRM for Outlook with Offline Access can create quotes and orders while offline. After reconnecting to the server, Microsoft Dynamics CRM for Outlook will automatically synchronize those new records to the Microsoft Dynamics CRM server.

In this chapter, you will learn how to manage sales quotes, orders, and invoices. You will learn how to track address and product details in a quote and manage subsequent revisions. When the customer has agreed to the quote, you'll learn how to create an order.

> **Important** The exercises in this chapter require only records created in earlier chapters; none are supplied on the companion CD. For more information about practice files, see "Using the Companion CD" at the beginning of this book.

> **Troubleshooting** Graphics and operating system–related instructions in this book reflect the Windows Vista user interface. If your computer is running Windows XP and you experience trouble following the instructions as written, refer to the "Information for Readers Running Windows XP" section at the beginning of this book.

> **Important** The images used in this book reflect the default form and field names in Microsoft Dynamics CRM. Because the software offers extensive customization capabilities, it's possible that some of the record types or fields have been relabeled in your Microsoft Dynamics CRM environment. If you cannot find the forms, fields, or security roles referenced in this book, contact your system administrator for assistance.

> **Important** You must know the location of your Microsoft Dynamics CRM Web site to work the exercises in this book. Check with your system administrator to verify the Web address if you don't know it.

Understanding Quotes, Orders, and Invoices

Not every organization provides written quotes to customers before each purchase, but if your organization uses quotes, then you know the importance of quote generation. Some organizations use the term proposal instead of quote, but both quotes and proposals outline the products or services that an organization will provide to the customer, along with the related pricing and payment terms. A quote typically consists of the following:

- Customer name
- Billing address
- Shipping information for products
- Line items (each with a description, quantity, and price)
- Sales tax and discounts
- Total amount

When you first create a quote, Microsoft Dynamics CRM assigns it a Draft status. While the quote has a Draft status, you can modify anything in the quote such as the products, pricing, and shipping information. After you finish working on the quote, you will *activate the quote* and then send it to the customer. Activating the quote updates its status from Draft to Active.

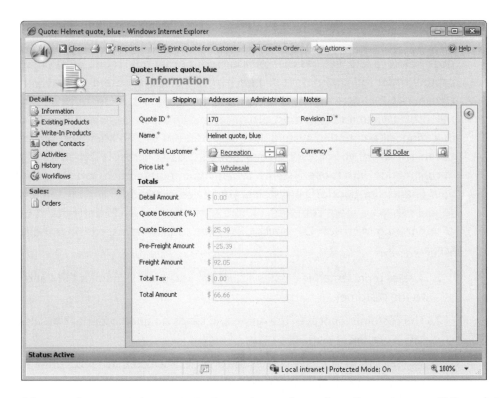

After you have sent the quote to the customer for review, the customer will then determine whether or not to move forward with the purchase. If the customer decides to purchase, you can create an order in Microsoft Dynamics CRM to record the transaction. If the customer decides not to purchase, you will either permanently close the quote or modify the quote and submit a revised quote to the customer.

In Chapter 6, "Working with Leads and Opportunities," you learned about using opportunities to forecast future sales. Reporting and analyzing your quote data also provides you with valuable information about your sales pipeline and the performance of each sales representative. Reports can be created with tools such as the Report Wizard, Advanced Find queries, and Dynamic Worksheets in Microsoft Office Excel.

See Also For more information about creating Advanced Find queries, see Chapter 15, "Using Advanced Find." For information about creating reports, see Chapter 16, "Using the Report Wizard." And for information about how to create reports and perform analyses by using static and dynamic Excel worksheets, see Chapter 17, "Reporting with Microsoft Office Excel."

After the customer has placed an order, your organization will fulfill the order with the products or services that the customer requested. Although Microsoft Dynamics CRM does include a few features that let you record order fulfillment, most organizations capture order fulfillment data in a back office software system such as Microsoft Dynamics GP, NAV, AX and SL. Likewise, although you can create new invoices in Microsoft Dynamics CRM, most organizations create invoices and receive payments in a financial accounting system. Microsoft did not design Microsoft Dynamics CRM to replace any of your back office systems; instead Microsoft Dynamics CRM works in conjunction with those systems. When you integrate Microsoft Dynamics CRM with your financial or back office systems, your sales, marketing, and customer service personnel can get a more complete picture of the customer. To understand the benefits of integrating Microsoft Dynamics CRM with other systems, consider the following scenario:

1. A sales representative creates a quote in Microsoft Dynamics CRM and presents it to the customer.

2. The customer approves the quote and sends a signed order to the sales representative (via fax or e-mail).

3. The sales representative creates the order in Microsoft Dynamics CRM. An integration process creates a corresponding order in the financial system.

4. Your organization fulfills the order via product shipment or service delivery. An integration process updates the Microsoft Dynamics CRM order record so that the sales representative knows the order was fulfilled.

5. Accounts receivable creates an invoice in the financial system. The organization's integration process creates an invoice record in Microsoft Dynamics CRM with the amount that the customer owes.

6. The customer mails a payment for the invoice. The accounts receivable team inputs the payment details in the financial system. The organization's integration process updates the corresponding invoice in Microsoft Dynamics CRM to indicate full payment.

7. The sales representative can now see the invoice payment status directly within Microsoft Dynamics CRM and sends a thank-you note to the customer.

As you can imagine, using Microsoft Dynamics CRM with this type of integration provides many benefits to both your front office and back office personnel. Contact your system administrator to determine whether your organization's Microsoft Dynamics CRM system integrates with a financial or fulfillment system.

> **Tip** Even if your Microsoft Dynamics CRM system does not automatically transfer data to and from a back office system, your organization can still improve communication with back office personnel by using the workflow feature of Microsoft Dynamics CRM. Using workflow, you can set up and create e-mail alerts in Microsoft Dynamics CRM that will automatically send new order information via e-mail to your financial team. Although setting up and creating workflows is beyond the scope of this book, you can refer to *Working with Microsoft Dynamics CRM 4.0* by Mike Snyder and Jim Steger (Microsoft Press, 2008) for more information about using workflow for e-mail alerts and notifications.

> **Important** Even though Microsoft Dynamics CRM contains information about orders and invoices, you should not attempt to replace your financial or back office software system with Microsoft Dynamics CRM. Ideally, your back office systems will integrate with Microsoft Dynamics CRM so that key data is passed between the systems. This integration provides you with a more complete view of customers and all of their sales information from your Microsoft Dynamics CRM system.

Creating a Quote

Sales representatives create quotes for customers to document the proposed products, services, and pricing. Because companies from many different industries use Microsoft Dynamics CRM, the final output of a quote can vary from one organization to another. Some quotes might be just 1 page long, whereas other companies create 50-page quotes.

Microsoft Dynamics CRM uses the term *products* to represent what your organization sells. However, if your company provides services instead of products, you can still use Microsoft Dynamics CRM to track your quotes. For example, you could set up a product in Microsoft Dynamics CRM that represents one hour of consulting service. Then, when you create the quote, you could add the consulting product to the quote with a quantity that matches the number of consulting hours that the customer requires. For example, a quote could include 50 hours of senior consulting time and 25 hours of junior consulting time.

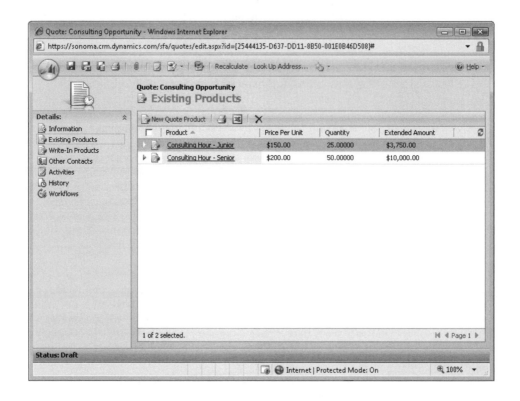

Tip Microsoft Dynamics CRM automatically assigns a number to each quote when it is first saved. Quote auto-numbering can be configured by system administrators in the Administration section of the Settings area. By default, each quote is created with a three-character prefix (*QUO*), a four-digit code, and a six-character identifier—for example, *QUO-1006-4JHFXD*.

In this exercise, you will create a quote from an existing opportunity. Microsoft Dynamics CRM does not require you to create a quote from an opportunity; however, creating a standalone quote will not populate any of the data values as it does when you create a quote from an opportunity.

Important In order to complete this exercise, you must first ensure that your system administrator has created at least one price list in your system. By default, Microsoft Dynamics CRM does not allow you to save a quote record without a price list.

1. Open the **Sonoma Partners Sample Opportunity** record.

2. In the left navigation pane, click **Quotes**.

New Quote

3. In the grid toolbar, click the **New Quote** button.

   A new window opens. Because you created the quote from the opportunity record, Microsoft Dynamics CRM populates several fields in the quote with values from the opportunity, such as the name and the customer.

4. Select a price list. (The selection will vary depending on what has been configured by your system administrator.)

Save

5. In the form toolbar, click the **Save** button.

Adding Bill to and Ship to Addresses to a Quote

Many customers (especially larger companies) will provide two different addresses—a billing address and a shipping address—when they place orders with your organization. You can enter different bill to and ship to information for each quote in Microsoft Dynamics CRM. Creating a quote for a customer does not automatically populate the bill to and ship to information; you must explicitly assign the bill to and ship to addresses to the quote.

To assign the bill to and ship to address information, you choose one of the addresses linked to the customer. However, one thing you might not expect is that you cannot select the address listed on the account or contact form. You must choose one of the *More Addresses* records linked to the account or contact. When you're adding a bill to or ship to address to a quote, ensure that the customer record includes at least one address record in the More Addresses view. You can create, view, and update the address records for an account or contact by clicking the More Addresses link in the left navigation pane of the account or contact record.

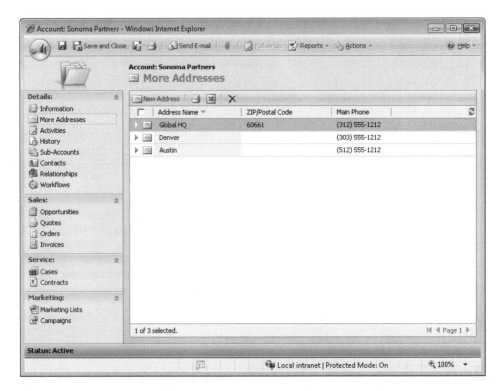

In this exercise, you will assign bill to and ship to information to the sample quote you created in the previous exercise. Because the Sonoma Partners account attached to this quote does not have any addresses in the More Addresses view, you will need to create an address record for the account first.

>
>
> **USE** the Sonoma Partners account record you created in Chapter 3. If you cannot locate the Sonoma Partners account record in your system, select a different account record for this exercise.
>
> **BE SURE TO** use the Internet Explorer Web browser to navigate to your Microsoft Dynamics CRM Web site before beginning this exercise.

1. Navigate to an account view, and open the **Sonoma Partners** account.

2. In the left navigation pane, click **More Addresses**.

3. In the grid toolbar, click the **New Address** button.

New Address

A new window opens.

4. In the address record, enter the following values:

Address Name	Global HQ
Street 1	525 W. Monroe St.
Street 2	Ste 240
City	Chicago
State/Province	IL
ZIP/Postal Code	60661
Country/Region	USA
Address Type	Primary
Main Phone	(312) 555-1212

5. For **Shipping Method**, select **DHL**. For **Freight Terms**, select **No Charge**.

6. In the **Address Contact** field, enter **Mike Snyder**.

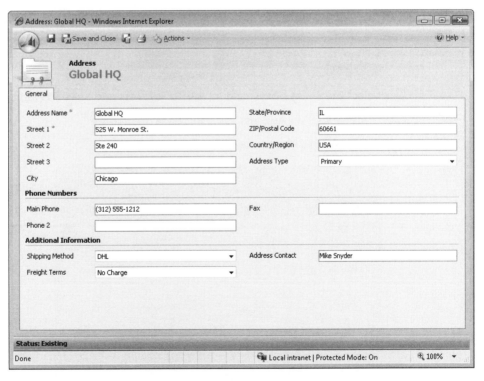

Save and Close

7. In the form toolbar, click the **Save and Close** button.

8. In the left navigation pane of the **Sonoma Partners** account, click **Quotes**, and then double-click the sample quote you created in the previous exercise.

9. Click the **Addresses** tab to confirm that the quote does not currently contain any bill to or ship to information.

10. In the quote toolbar, click the **Look Up Address** text.

    The Look Up Address dialog box opens.

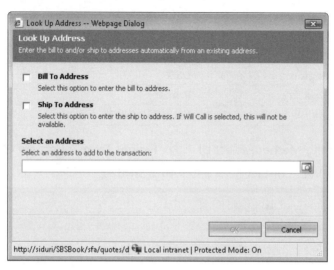

11. Select the check boxes next to **Bill To Address** and **Ship To Address**.

Look Up

12. Under **Select an Address**, click the **Look Up** button.

    The Look Up Records dialog box opens.

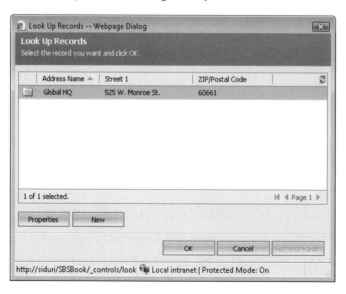

13. Select the **Global HQ** address, and click **OK**.

The Look Up Address dialog box displays the Global HQ address.

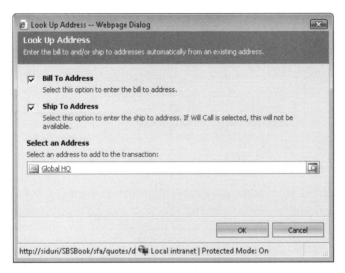

14. Click **OK**.

15. On the quote record, click the **Addresses** tab.

Microsoft Dynamics CRM populates the Bill To and Ship To data fields with data from the address you selected.

16. Click the **Shipping** tab.

Microsoft Dynamics CRM updates the Shipping Method and Freight Terms lists with the matching values from the Ship To address.

Adding Products to a Quote

Microsoft Dynamics CRM allows you to record the products and services related to a potential sale for each opportunity. When you configure price lists for your products, you also can set up Microsoft Dynamics CRM to automatically calculate the value of the potential opportunity by attaching the products to the opportunity. If you decide not to use products with opportunities, you can still track the potential value of the opportunity by simply entering a dollar amount in the estimated revenue field.

See Also For more information on tracking the value of sales opportunities, see Chapter 6, "Working with Leads and Opportunities."

However, unlike opportunities, quotes in Microsoft Dynamics CRM must have attached products so that the total value can be calculated. By default, you cannot enter a total dollar amount for a quote. Microsoft Dynamics CRM must calculate it from the attached products.

You can attach products to a quote by using one of the following techniques:

- Create a quote from an opportunity, which copies the opportunity's products to the quote.
- Get products from an existing opportunity.
- Add existing products.
- Create write-in products.

If you create a quote from an opportunity, Microsoft Dynamics CRM automatically copies the opportunity's products to the quote and populates many of the quote data fields. However, you can also add products from any active opportunity to a quote by using **Get Products**. To do this, in the quote toolbar, on the Actions menu, select Get Products. A dialog box appears, allowing you to select an existing opportunity.

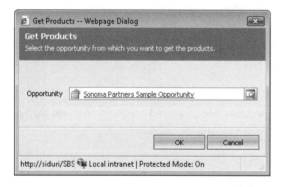

After you click OK, Microsoft Dynamics CRM copies the products from the selected opportunity to the quote record.

Tip By default, Microsoft Dynamics CRM does not check for duplicate records when copying products from an opportunity to a quote, so if you have already added some of the products from the opportunity to your quote, you might see duplicate records when using the Get Products feature.

You can also add products to a quote manually, one product at a time. When you manually add products, you can select one of the products configured in your *product catalog* (as set up by your system administrator) or you can add a *write-in product*.

> **Tip** The product catalog defines all of the details about your products and services, such as the list price, the ability to sell in fractional or whole values, the estimated cost, and the inventory requirements. If your organization wants to set up the product catalog, your administrator can refer to the Microsoft Dynamics CRM Help for additional information on the specific configuration steps.

A write-in product is a product that you add to a quote as you are creating it, without first needing to configure all of the details in the product catalog.

Whether you add an existing product or create a write-in product, you will need to specify details about the product, such as description, unit of measure, and quantity. On the quote product form, you can also enter other information about the product for the quote, such as a discount or tax. A single quote can consist of multiple products, which can be a combination of existing and write-in products.

> **Tip** Even though an order contains a ship to address, you can still specify alternate shipping addresses for the products in a quote by specifying an alternate address in the Address tab of the Quote Product record.

After you update a quote to reflect what you're offering to the customer, you're ready to send it to the customer for review. Remember that Microsoft Dynamics CRM creates a quote in Draft status, so you will need to activate the quote to indicate that you have presented the quote to the customer.

> **Tip** If you want to create a printer-friendly version of the quote, you can use the Quote For Customer Mail Merge template in Microsoft Office Word that is included in Microsoft Dynamics CRM as a starting point. However, this Quote For Customer file simply illustrates one possible quote output; you should not plan to use this quote for your customers. You can access this template by clicking the Print Quote For Customer button in the quote toolbar.

Setting up a product catalog in Microsoft Dynamics CRM takes some effort and requires administrator access. Therefore, in this exercise, you will add write-in products to the sample quote record, instead of adding a product from the product catalog. You'll then mark the quote as active to indicate that it's ready for the customer to review.

BE SURE TO use the Internet Explorer Web browser to navigate to your Microsoft Dynamics CRM Web site before beginning this exercise.

1. Open the quote record you created in the previous exercise.

2. In the navigation pane, click **Write-In Products**.

3. In the grid toolbar, click **New Quote Product**.

   The New Quote Product window opens.

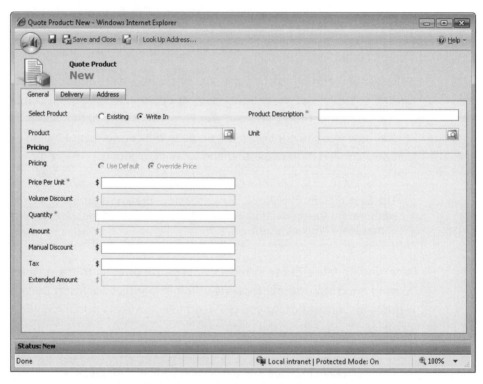

4. In the **Product Description** field, enter **Microsoft Dynamics CRM User License**.

5. In the **Price Per Unit** field, enter **500.00**.

6. In the **Quantity** field, enter **5**.

Save and New

7. In the toolbar, click the **Save and New** button.

8. In the description field, enter **Microsoft Dynamics CRM Server License**.

9. In the **Price Per Unit** field, enter **2000.00**.

10. In the **Quantity** field, enter **1**.

11. In the toolbar, click **Save and Close**.

Microsoft Dynamics CRM closes the quote product window and returns to the quote record. On the Write-In Products link of the quote, you can see the two products that you just added to the quote.

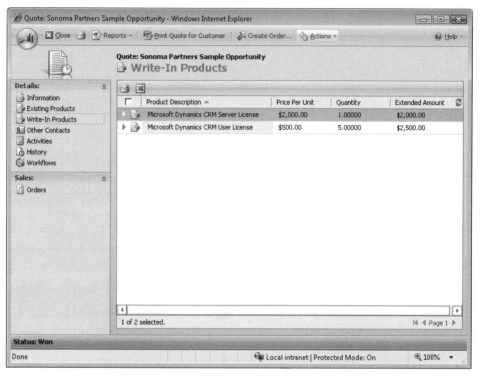

12. In the left navigation pane of the quote record, click the **Information** link.

Microsoft Dynamics CRM did not update the amount of the quote yet. It still lists $0.00 for the total amount.

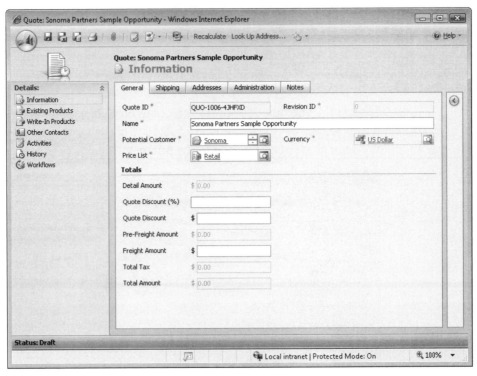

13. In the quote toolbar, click the **Recalculate** button.

Microsoft Dynamics CRM automatically calculates the total amount of the quote as $4,500.00 by summing the cost of the products attached to the quote.

14. In the quote toolbar, on the **Actions** menu, select **Activate Quote**.

Microsoft Dynamics CRM updates the quote status to Active and disables all fields on the quote form so that it can no longer be edited.

> **Tip** You can provide discounts on your quotes by discounting an individual product attached to the quote or by providing a blanket discount to the quote. You can assign quote discounts as a percentage of the price or as a fixed dollar amount. At the product level, you can only apply fixed dollar discounts.

Revising a Quote

By marking the quote as active, you lock down the product selections, pricing, and other values on the quote and can print it to provide to the customer for review. After the customer has reviewed your quote and given you feedback, you can:

- Close the quote as lost (if the customer purchased from someone else).
- Close the quote as canceled (if the customer did not purchase from anyone).
- Revise the quote.
- Create an order.

When you close the quote or create an order, Microsoft Dynamics CRM also gives you the option to close the opportunity associated with the quote. By doing so, you can save yourself a few clicks, because you won't need to go back and update the opportunity record as won or lost.

If you revise a quote, Microsoft Dynamics CRM automatically creates a new quote record with a Draft status and a revision ID of 1 (instead of a revision ID of 0, as on the original quote). It also automatically updates the status of the original quote from Active to Closed.

In this exercise, you will revise a quote to add a discount, and then you will reactivate the quote.

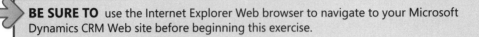

BE SURE TO use the Internet Explorer Web browser to navigate to your Microsoft Dynamics CRM Web site before beginning this exercise.

1. Open the quote record from the previous example.

2. In the quote toolbar, click **Actions**, and then click **Revise**.

Microsoft Dynamics CRM deactivates the current revision of the quote and opens a new quote record with a revision ID of 1.

3. In the **Quote Discount (%)** field, enter 5.

4. Click **Save**.

Microsoft Dynamics CRM updates the total amount of the quote to reflect the 5 percent discount you just added.

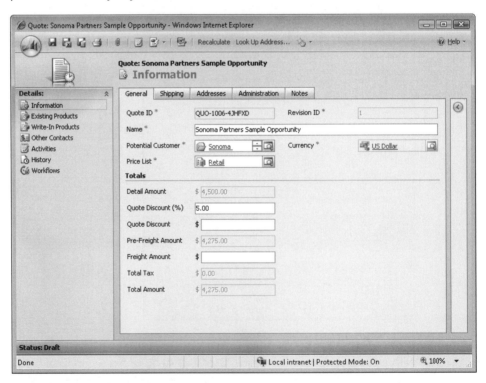

5. In the quote toolbar, click **Actions**, and then click **Activate Quote**.

Microsoft Dynamics CRM updates the quote status to Active and disables all fields on the quote form.

Creating an Order

Suppose that the customer agreed to the discount you offered and would like to move forward with the purchase. Creating an order in Microsoft Dynamics CRM from a quote is a very simple process; you just click the Create Order button in the quote toolbar. When the Create Order dialog box opens, you enter the order date, a short description, the dollar amount of the order, and any other necessary information.

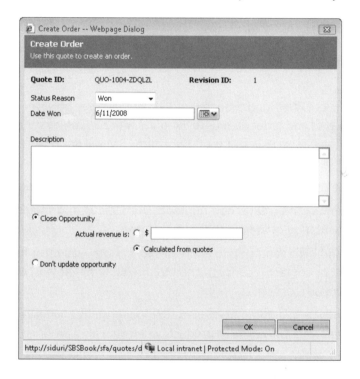

> **Tip** The Create Order button will not appear on the quote toolbar if the quote is still in Draft status; you can only create orders from quotes in Active status.

In this exercise, you will create an order from an active quote.

 BE SURE TO use the Internet Explorer Web browser to navigate to your Microsoft Dynamics CRM Web site before beginning this exercise.

1. Open the quote record from the previous example.

Create Order

2. In the quote toolbar, click the **Create Order** button.

> **Troubleshooting**   If the Create Order button does not appear in your quote toolbar, make sure your quote is in Active status.

3. Click **OK**.

Microsoft Dynamics CRM updates the quote status to Won and creates a new order record.

Key Points

- Microsoft Dynamics CRM includes quotes, orders, and invoices; however, Microsoft designed the invoice and order records to integrate with back office systems. The invoice and order functionality in Microsoft Dynamics CRM will not replace a financial system with out-of-the-box functionality.

- You can link one or more quotes to an opportunity or create a standalone quote.

- Microsoft Dynamics CRM creates new quotes in Draft status. You should activate them upon presentation of the quote to the customer.

- If you want to add bill to and ship to addresses to a quote, you must first ensure that the account or contact record attached to the quote has at least one record in its More Addresses section.

- You can add products to a quote from an existing opportunity, manually add existing products, or create your own write-in products when attaching products to a quote.

- The quote total amount is the sum of the products attached to the quote minus any discounts, taxes, and other charges.

- After activating a quote, you can close it, revise it, or create an order.

- Microsoft Dynamics CRM includes a Quote For Customer Mail Merge template that you can use as a starting point to create your own printer-friendly quote.

- When you close a quote or create an order, Microsoft Dynamics CRM can automatically close the related opportunity at the same time, if applicable.

Part III

Marketing

Chapter at a Glance

Create a marketing list, **page 162**

Manage list members, **pages 165, 168, 171, and 173**

Use mail merge to generate a Word document that includes list member information, **page 181**

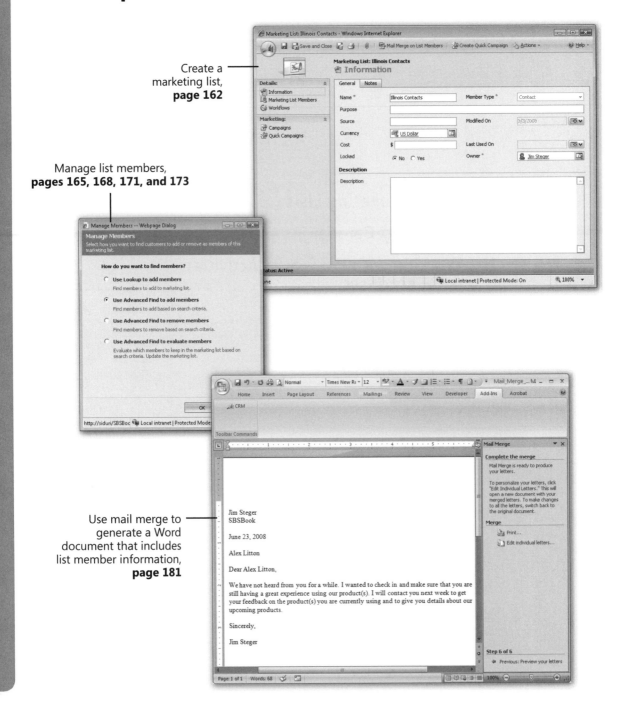

8 Using Marketing Lists

In this chapter, you will learn to

✔ Create a marketing list.

✔ Add members to a list by using a lookup.

✔ Add members to a list by using Advanced Find.

✔ Remove members from a list by using Advanced Find.

✔ Evaluate members included in a list by using Advanced Find.

✔ Remove selected members from a list.

✔ Copy members to another marketing list.

✔ Create opportunities for list members.

✔ Use mail merge to generate a Word document that includes list member information.

Organizations rely on proper communication with their customers and prospects. Marketing is often described as a process by which an organization creates the communication and mechanisms to convince customers to purchase its products or services. Marketing typically uses numerous communication channels—direct mail, e-mail, seminars, on-site visits, outreach programs, and phone calls, for example—to communicate with customers and prospects. Firms leverage lists of customers and prospects to properly articulate the benefits of their products and services to their target audience. For example, a company might e-mail all prospects within a city about an exciting promotion occurring at a local store. Or a firm might send a renewal notice to all customers whose contracts expire in the next 30 days.

Marketing professionals can use Microsoft Dynamics CRM to execute marketing strategies and segment customer lists. *Marketing lists* are groups of accounts, contacts, and leads that can be used in marketing campaigns and for various other business purposes. For example, a sales representative can create a marketing list of her new accounts to quickly send proposal letters and create new sales opportunities in Microsoft Dynamics CRM.

In this chapter, you will learn how to use Microsoft Dynamics CRM to create a marketing list, manage list members, and create a mail merge document that includes marketing list member data.

> **Important** There are no practice files for this chapter.

> **Troubleshooting** Graphics and operating system–related instructions in this book reflect the Windows Vista user interface. If your computer is running Windows XP and you experience trouble following the instructions as written, refer to the "Information for Readers Running Windows XP" section at the beginning of this book.

> **Important** The images used in this book reflect the default form and field names in Microsoft Dynamics CRM. Because the software offers extensive customization capabilities, it's possible that some of the record types or fields have been relabeled in your Microsoft Dynamics CRM environment. If you cannot find the forms, fields, or security roles referenced in this book, contact your system administrator for assistance.

> **Important** You must know the location of your Microsoft Dynamics CRM Web site to work the exercises in this book. Check with your system administrator to verify the Web address if you don't know it.

Creating a Marketing List

The true value of a customer relationship management system lies in the quality of its data. Marketing lists provide a convenient mechanism for grouping account, contact, and lead records. Before you select the members of a list, you must first define the list itself. By default, Microsoft Dynamics CRM requires you to enter a name for the list and choose a member type. The member type must be either Account, Contact, or Lead; each list can have only one member type. Additional information can be captured, such as the source, cost, and purpose of the list. You can also configure custom attributes to further define your list.

See Also Microsoft Dynamics CRM provides the ability to import marketing lists, allowing you to quickly create multiple marketing lists by using a simple import wizard. Although you can use Microsoft Dynamics CRM to import marketing lists, you will still need to add members by using the techniques described in this chapter. For more information on importing data into Microsoft Dynamics CRM, see Chapter 18, "Importing Data."

In this exercise, you will create a marketing list of customer contacts who reside in the state of Illinois.

USE a user account that has the Marketing Manager security role or another role with privileges to create marketing lists.

BE SURE TO use the Windows Internet Explorer Web browser to navigate to your Microsoft Dynamics CRM Web site before beginning this exercise.

1. In the **Marketing** area, click **Marketing Lists**.

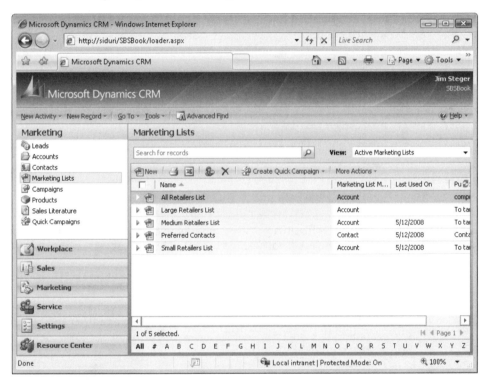

New Marketing
LIst

2. Click the **New** button.

The Marketing List form opens.

3. In the **Name** field, enter **Illinois Contacts**. In the **Member Type** field, select **Contact**.

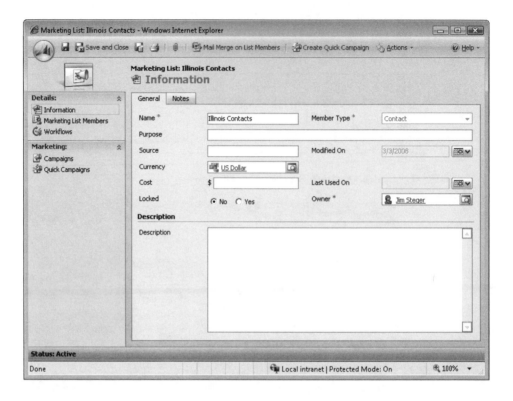

Troubleshooting The member type cannot be changed after you save the marketing list. If you want to market to both prospects and customers, you should create multiple marketing lists.

Important The Locked attribute prevents anyone from adding members to or removing them from your list. Leave this attribute set to No until you have added the desired members to your list.

Save and Close

4. Click the **Save and Close** button.

Adding Members to a List by Using a Lookup

The primary purpose of a marketing list is to associate multiple *list members* for use in one or more marketing campaigns. For example, you might want to have a list that contains all prospects you plan to invite to a seminar and another that contains all preferred customers. After you have saved a marketing list, you need to add list members to it. Microsoft Dynamics CRM provides a few ways to add members to a marketing list. You can add members individually or use the Microsoft Dynamics CRM Advanced Find feature to add multiple list members who share a common interest or attribute.

Adding members individually by using a lookup is the most straightforward approach to adding members to a list. Because you specifically select each member, you retain the greatest level of control of your list. Further, unlike using Advanced Find, using lookup allows you to create a list of records that do not share common data. For instance, imagine you have a pre-existing group of registrants for an upcoming seminar. You can create a new marketing list to track all the confirmed registrants. After a customer confirms his or her registration for the event, you can manually select the registrant's contact record and add it as a member to your seminar's confirmation list.

In this exercise, you will add members to an existing marketing list one at a time by using the standard lookup approach.

USE a user account that has the Marketing Manager security role or another role with privileges to add members to a marketing list.

BE SURE TO use the Internet Explorer Web browser to navigate to your Microsoft Dynamics CRM Web site before beginning this exercise.

1. In the **Marketing** area, click **Marketing Lists**.

2. Double-click the Illinois Contacts marketing list created in the previous section.

3. In the left navigation area, click **Marketing List Members** to add members to the list.

Manage
Members

4. Click the **Manage Members** button.

The Manage Members dialog box opens.

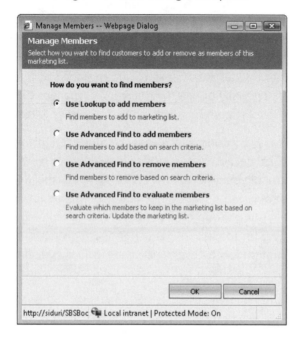

> **Tip** If you do not see the Manage Members button, check to ensure that you have not locked the list. Locking a marketing list prevents any members from being added or removed.

5. Click **Use Lookup to add members**, and click **OK**.

The Look Up Records dialog box opens. The Look For field is automatically set to the member type specified on the marketing list.

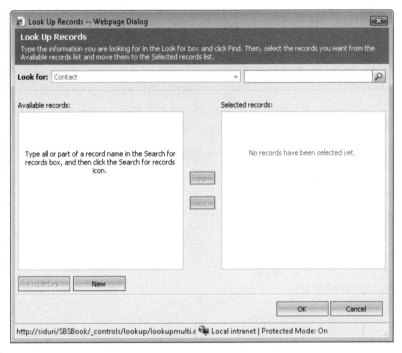

6. Search for one or more records and add them to the **Selected** records list.

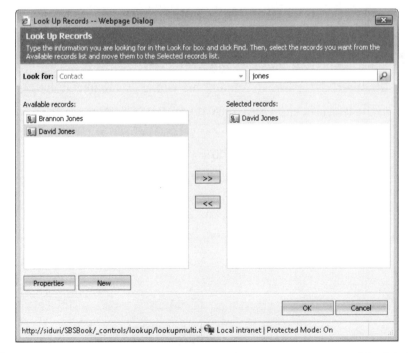

7. When you have finished selecting the records you want to add, click **OK**.

Adding Members to a List by Using Advanced Find

Most lists have something that relates the records to each other—for example, a list might contain only those contacts who reside in the state of Illinois or all accounts with a preferred customer status. The Advanced Find feature allows you to easily search for records that share a specified attribute and add either all of them or a selected set from the query results as members to your marketing list.

See Also For more information on searching for data with the Advanced Find feature, see Chapter 15, "Using Advanced Find."

In this exercise, you will add all active contacts with an Illinois address as members to the Illinois Contacts marketing list created in the previous section.

> **Tip** Microsoft Dynamics CRM will not add duplicate members to a list. If your query results contain a record that already exists in the marketing list, Microsoft Dynamics CRM ignores the duplicate record.

USE a user account that has the Marketing Manager security role or another role with privileges to add members to a marketing list.

BE SURE TO use the Internet Explorer Web browser to navigate to your Microsoft Dynamics CRM Web site before beginning this exercise.

1. In the **Marketing** area, click **Marketing Lists**.

2. Double-click the Illinois Contacts marketing list created in the previous exercise.

3. In the left navigation area, click **Marketing List Members** to view the members of the list.

4. Click the **Manage Members** button.

5. In the **Manage Members** dialog box, click **Use Advanced Find to add members**.

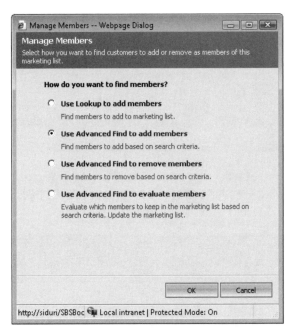

6. Click **OK**. In the **Add Members** dialog box, create your query conditions where the Status field equals Active and the Address1:State/Province field equals IL.

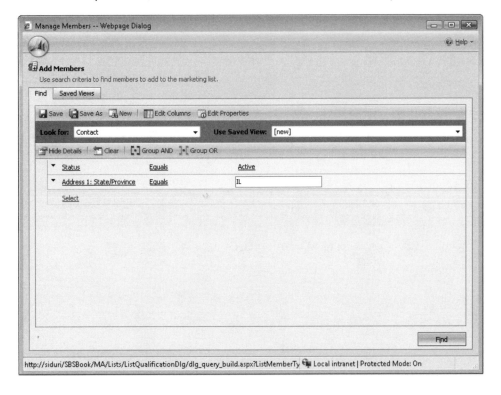

> **Important** If your organization typically enters the full state name instead of an abbreviation or does not have any contact records with an IL address, enter a different state or other criterion instead to ensure that results are returned in your search.

> **Tip** Save your Advanced Find query to quickly add additional member records in the future.

7. Click **Find**. Verify that at least one contact is returned in the results. Then, below the results view, click **Add all the members returned by the search to the marketing list**.

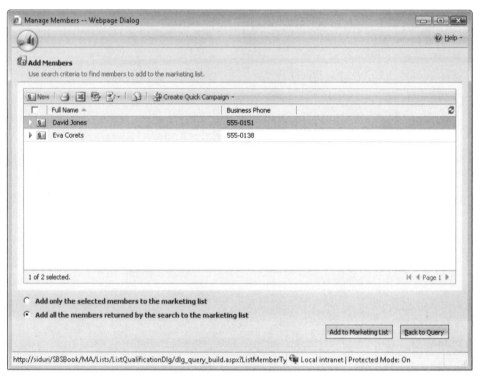

8. Click **Add to Marketing List**.

Removing Members from a List by Using Advanced Find

Members added to a marketing list will remain on the list until you manually remove them. As when you add members to a list, you can remove members individually or use the Advanced Find feature to remove a group of members. Using an Advanced Find query allows you to quickly remove multiple members based on common selection criteria.

In this exercise, you will use an Advanced Find query to remove contacts that do not have a city populated from your Illinois Contacts marketing list.

> **Important** This action only removes records from the list. It does not delete the actual record. To undo this change, you will need to re-add the members to your list.

USE a user account that has the Marketing Manager security role or another role with privileges to manage marketing lists.

BE SURE TO use the Internet Explorer Web browser to navigate to your Microsoft Dynamics CRM Web site before beginning this exercise.

1. In the **Marketing** area, click **Marketing Lists**.

2. Double-click the Illinois Contacts marketing list created earlier in this chapter section.

3. In the left navigation area, click **Marketing List Members**.

4. Click the **Manage Members** button to launch the **Manage Members** dialog box.

5. Click **Use Advanced Find to remove members**.

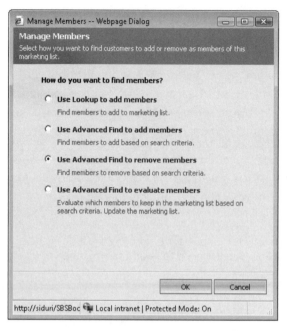

6. Click **OK**. In the **Remove Members** dialog box, create a query that checks to see if **Address1:City** does not contain data.

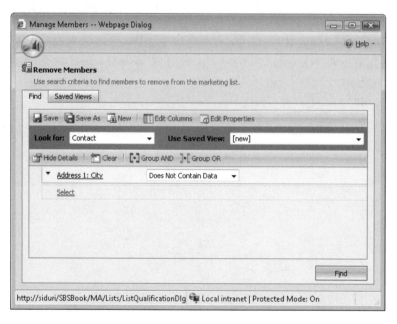

> **Important** If your list does not return any contacts, use different search criteria to ensure that your query returns at least one contact record in the results. If no records are returned and you click the Remove From Marketing List button, you will receive an error.

7. Click **Find** to execute the search.

8. Verify that at least one contact is returned in the results. Then, below the results view, click **Remove all the members returned by the search from the marketing list**.

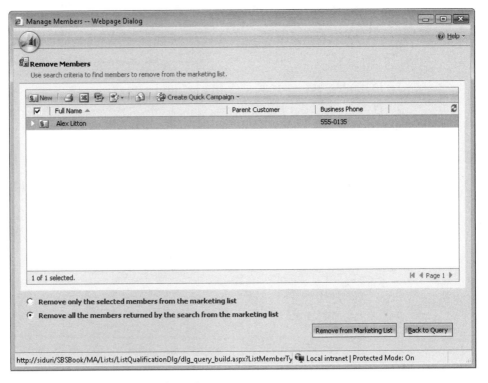

9. Click **Remove from Marketing List**.

Evaluating Members Included in a List by Using Advanced Find

Just as you can add and remove multiple members to a list by using an Advanced Find query, you can also use this same technique to evaluate which members should be kept on a list. The evaluation option provides you with the ability to easily update a marketing list based on a query. This option does not add new members based on the results, but it does remove any members from the list that don't match the search criteria.

For instance, let's assume you have a list of all contacts who reside in the state of Illinois. If some of the members added previously have moved and no longer live in Illinois, you will need to remove them from the list manually.

In this exercise, you'll evaluate the marketing list members for the Illinois Contacts list used in the previous section to ensure that only those contacts with an Illinois address are included in the list.

USE a user account that has the Marketing Manager security role or another role with privileges to manage marketing lists.

BE SURE TO use the Internet Explorer Web browser to navigate to your Microsoft Dynamics CRM Web site before beginning this exercise.

1. In the **Marketing** area, click **Marketing Lists**.

2. Double-click the Illinois Contacts marketing list created earlier in this chapter.

3. In the left navigation area, click **Marketing List Members**.

4. Click the **Manage Members** button.

5. In the **Manage Members** dialog box, click **Use Advanced Find to evaluate members**.

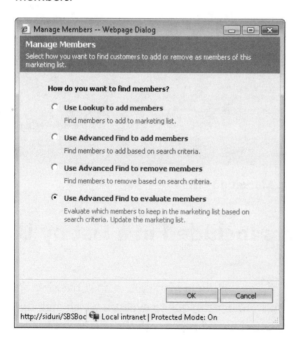

6. Click **OK**. In the **Evaluate Members and Update Marketing List** dialog box, create the same query used in a previous section to find all active contacts who reside in Illinois.

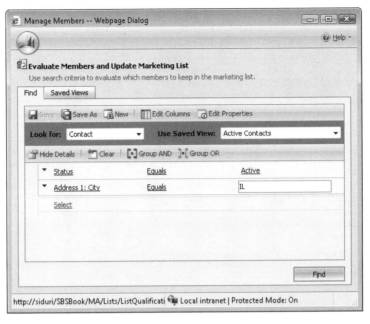

7. Click **Find** to execute your search.

8. Verify that at least one contact is returned in the results. Then, below the results view, click **Keep all the members returned by the search from the marketing list**, and click **Update Marketing List**.

Removing Selected Members from a List

As mentioned previously, marketing list members do not update dynamically the same way that lead, contact, and account records are updated in the system; members stay on the list until you manually remove them. In addition to removing records with the options discussed earlier, Microsoft Dynamics CRM allows you to remove members from a list individually by using the Remove From Marketing List command.

In this exercise, you will remove individual members from your Illinois Contact list.

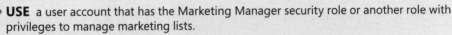

USE a user account that has the Marketing Manager security role or another role with privileges to manage marketing lists.

BE SURE TO use the Internet Explorer Web browser to navigate to your Microsoft Dynamics CRM Web site before beginning this exercise.

1. In the **Marketing** area, click **Marketing Lists**.

2. Double-click the Illinois Contacts marketing list used in the previous exercise.

3. In the left navigation area, click **Marketing List Members**.

4. Without opening the marketing list member record, select at least one member that you want to remove from the list.

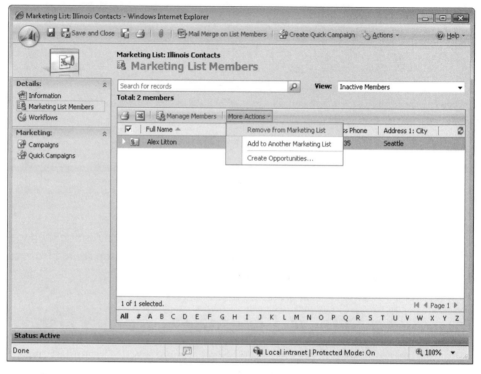

5. In the grid toolbar, click the **More Actions** button. In the menu that opens, click **Remove from Marketing List**.

A confirmation page appears.

6. In the **Remove Members** dialog box, click **OK** to remove the selected member from the list.

> **Important** This action permanently removes the member from the list. If you want to undo the change, you will need to re-add the member to your list.

Copying Members to Another Marketing List

You might sometimes want to quickly copy list members from one list to another. For example, let's assume you have a list of leads who confirmed that they would attend your recent sales event. You decide to lock this particular list to ensure that you have a history of the individuals who responded prior to the event. However, you need to create another list of prospects who actually attended the event so that your sales team can follow up with them. This new list of attendees will contain many of the same members as the RSVP list, but it will also contain some individuals who did not confirm ahead of time and exclude those prospects who registered but did not attend the event. Microsoft Dynamics CRM provides a simple mechanism to add marketing list members from one list to another.

In this exercise, you will copy the Illinois Contacts marketing list used in the previous section to a new marketing list called Illinois Seminar Invites.

> **Tip** Microsoft Dynamics CRM limits your selection to the maximum number of records displayed in the view. For information about changing the number of records returned per page, see Chapter 2, "Getting Around in Microsoft Dynamics CRM."

USE a user account that has the Marketing Manager security role or another role with privileges to manage marketing lists.

BE SURE TO use the Internet Explorer Web browser to navigate to your Microsoft Dynamics CRM Web site before beginning this exercise.

1. In the **Marketing** area, click **Marketing Lists**.

2. Double-click the Illinois Contacts marketing list used in the previous section.

3. In the left navigation area, click **Marketing List Members** to view the members of the list.

4. Without opening a list member record, select at least one member that you want to copy to your new list.

5. In the grid toolbar, click the **More Actions** button, and then select **Add to Another Marketing List** from the menu.

In the Look Up Records dialog box, the Look for field is automatically set to Marketing List and displays any available marketing lists with the same member type.

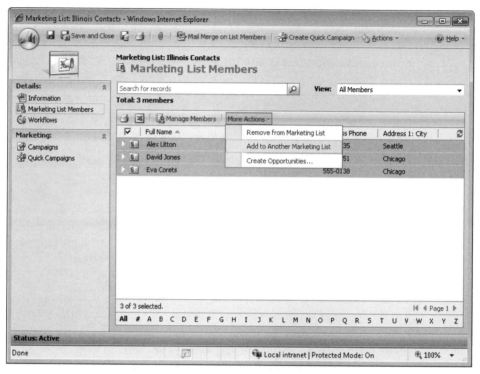

6. Click **New** to create a new marketing list.

7. In the **New Marketing List** form, in the **Name** field, enter **Illinois Seminar Invites**. In the **Member Type** field, select **Contact**.

8. Click the **Save and Close** button to create the marketing list.

   The Look Up Records dialog box opens, displaying the Illinois Seminar Invites marketing list.

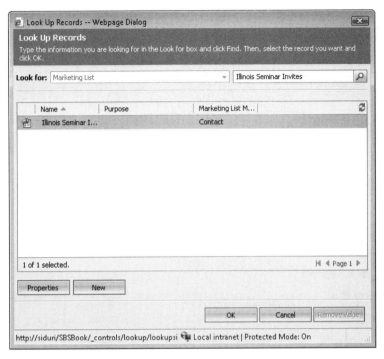

9. Select the Illinois Seminar Invites marketing list, and then click **OK** to add the selected members to the new list.

Creating Opportunities for List Members

Microsoft Dynamics CRM also allows you to easily create new opportunities directly from the members' grid of a marketing list that has account or contact members. You can select up to the number of records displayed in the grid, but each opportunity created using this approach will have the same entered values (such as Topic). For lists that contain lead members, you can convert leads to opportunities by using the Convert Lead action.

Continuing the example from the previous section, a marketing manager could use this feature to create opportunities for the sales team to track each prospect that attended the sales event.

In this exercise, you will create new opportunities for selected members of a marketing list.

USE a user account that has the Marketing Manager security role or another role with privileges to create opportunities.

BE SURE TO use the Internet Explorer Web browser to navigate to your Microsoft Dynamics CRM Web site before beginning this exercise.

1. In the **Marketing** area, click **Marketing Lists**.

2. Double-click the Illinois Seminar Invites marketing list created in the previous section.

3. In the left navigation area, click **Marketing List Members**.

4. In the grid, manually select the individual members for which you will create new opportunities.

5. In the grid toolbar, click the **More Actions** button, and then click **Create Opportunities** on the menu.

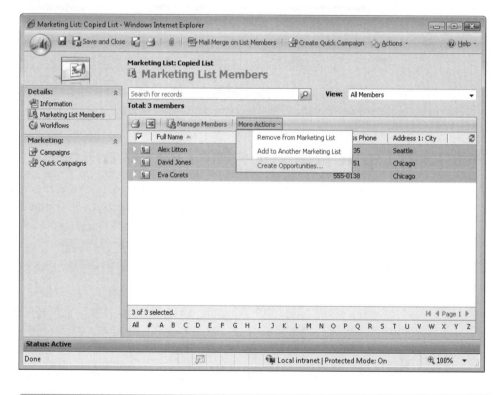

Tip The Create Opportunities menu option appears only for lists that contain account or contact members. Lists that contain lead members shows the Convert Lead menu option.

6. In the **Create New Opportunities** dialog box, complete all required fields.

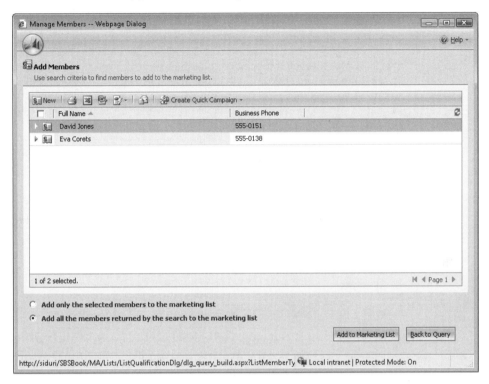

7. Click **Create**.

> **Tip** Just as when you bulk edit records, all values entered in the Create New Opportunities dialog box will be the same across all the newly created opportunities. The Potential Customer field will automatically populate with each account or contact selected in the marketing list.

Using Mail Merge to Generate a Word Document That Includes List Member Information

Marketing and service organizations often utilize direct mail as a critical communication strategy with their customers and prospects. They might send a special offer letter to all prospects, encouraging them to purchase a product; or they might distribute a customer service notification to all existing customers. The mail merge capabilities of Microsoft Dynamics CRM provide a convenient way to quickly generate these documents with personalized data directly from a marketing list.

In this exercise, you will create a mail merge letter with data from a marketing list.

> **Important** To complete this exercise, you must have access to the Reconnect With Contacts template for Microsoft Office Word that is included in every Microsoft Dynamics CRM installation. To verify that you have access to this template, in the Settings area, click Templates, and then click Mail Merge Templates. Change the view to Active Mail Merge Templates and check to see if the Reconnect With Contacts template appears in the list. If you cannot locate the template, you can select another template or contact your system administrator.

USE a user account that has the Marketing Manager security role or another role with privileges to manage marketing lists and mail merge templates.

BE SURE TO use the Internet Explorer Web browser to navigate to your Microsoft Dynamics CRM Web site before beginning this exercise.

1. In the **Marketing** area, click **Marketing Lists**.

2. Double-click the Illinois Seminar Invites marketing list used in the previous exercise.

Mail Merge on
List Members

3. In the form toolbar, click the **Mail Merge on List Members** button.

4. In the **Microsoft Dynamics CRM Mail Merge for Microsoft Office Word** dialog box, select **Letter** for the mail merge type. Then click the **Organization** mail merge template option, and click the now-enabled **Look Up** button.

Look Up

5. The **Look Up Records** dialog box opens, displaying the available mail merge templates. Select the **Reconnect with Contacts** template, and then click **OK**.

> **Tip** Microsoft Dynamics CRM includes numerous mail merge templates. You can edit these templates or create your own.

6. Back in the **Microsoft Dynamics CRM Mail Merge for Microsoft Office Word** dialog box, click **OK**.

7. In the **File Download** dialog box, click **Open** to view the file in Word. If you want, you can select **Save** instead to save the mail merge to your computer.

8. You might receive a warning from Word informing you that opening the document will run a SQL command and asking you if you want to continue. Because you already have the data you need, click **No** to continue.

> **Important** The next steps assume that you use Microsoft Office Word 2007 and have the Microsoft Dynamics CRM for Outlook client installed. The CRM button on the Add-Ins tab will appear only if the Microsoft Dynamics CRM for Outlook client is installed on your computer.

9. In Word, click the **Add-Ins** tab, and then click the **CRM** button.

10. At the bottom of the **Mail Merge** pane on the right side of the Word document, click **Next: Write your letter**.

11. You can update the text of the letter and add information. After you have completed your edits, click **Next: Preview your letters** in the **Mail Merge** pane.

12. Preview the final information for each recipient and update the recipient list as necessary. When finished, click **Next: Complete the merge**.

13. In the final step, you can print the resulting letters or edit each individual letter.

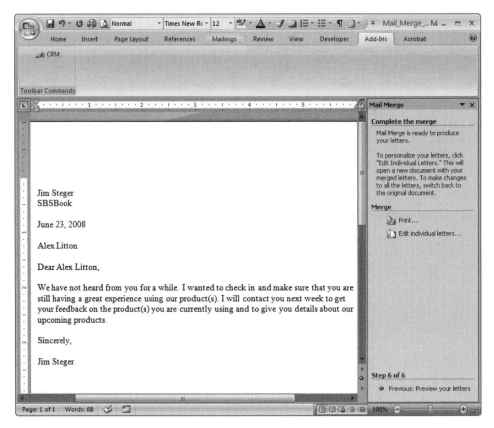

Key Points

- Marketing lists provide a convenient way to group accounts, contacts, or leads for use in marketing or outreach campaigns. Marketing lists can help you keep track of key customers, prospects invited to an event, all companies located in a particular geographic region, and more.

- Microsoft Dynamics CRM restricts marketing lists members to accounts, contacts, or leads.

- Because attributes can vary between accounts, contacts, and leads, each marketing list can contain only one member type. If you want to send a letter to both customers and prospects, you will need to create multiple lists.

- You must manually keep your marketing list members current.

- You can add, remove, or update members from a list by using an Advanced Find query.

- Locking a marketing list prevents members from being added to or removed from the list.

- You can use the members of a marketing list to quickly create opportunities or targeted distribution lists for mail merge documents.

Chapter at a Glance

Create a marketing or outreach campaign, **page 189**

Manage your campaign's planning tasks, **page 191**

Easily distribute campaign activities, **page 201**

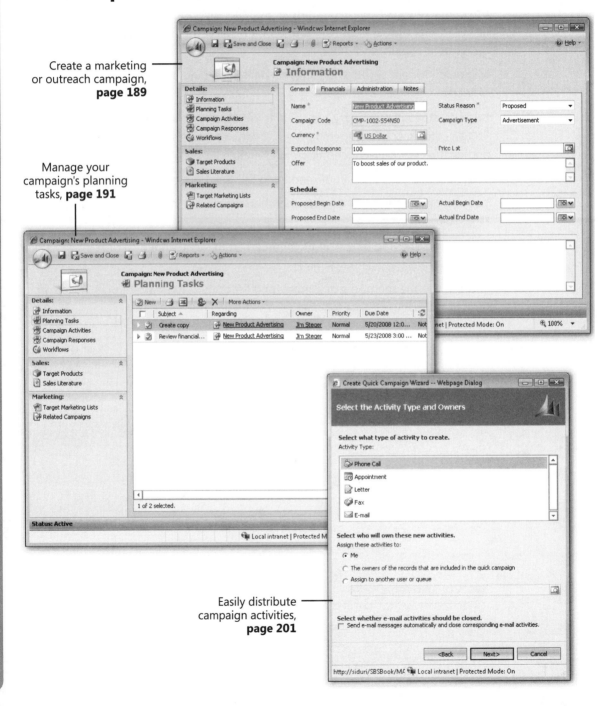

9 Managing Campaigns and Quick Campaigns

In this chapter, you will learn to

✔ Create a campaign.

✔ Add planning tasks.

✔ Select target marketing lists.

✔ Add target products and sales literature.

✔ Relate campaigns.

✔ Create campaign templates.

✔ Copy campaign records.

✔ Use quick campaigns.

In Chapter 8, "Using Marketing Lists," you learned how to use marketing lists to group your customers and prospects into lists. However, marketing lists make up just a small piece of a marketing strategy. After you've defined your customer or prospect groups, you can use marketing campaigns in Microsoft Dynamics CRM to communicate with each group and track the responses.

See Also Chapter 10, "Working with Campaign Activities and Responses," discusses how to execute a campaign and track the results with campaign activities and responses, including several reports to measure campaign performance, compare campaigns, and track campaign activities.

A *marketing campaign* is a series of activities intended to increase awareness of your company, products, or services. As any marketer knows, a properly executed marketing campaign requires coordination of many parties, collateral, and tasks. Microsoft Dynamics CRM provides a convenient way to manage marketing campaigns and their associated activities, tasks, and information.

For instance, suppose you want to launch a new customer loyalty program. This program will reward customers for repeat purchases of your product and entitle them to special discounts and promotions. To initiate the campaign, you plan to send a welcome letter and follow-up e-mail to all qualifying customers, informing them of the program. Some of your tasks might include:

- Determining the anticipated costs and expected results of the campaign.
- Creating and approving the copy for the welcome letter and e-mail message.
- Defining customers to be included in the loyalty program.
- Coordinating the graphics and delivery of the letters and e-mail messages with vendors or your IT staff.
- Actually sending the campaign-related content to your customers.
- Tracking the responses for follow-up activities and analysis.

In this chapter, you will learn how to create a campaign and then associate planning tasks, customer lists, products, and sales literature to it. Further, you will create campaign templates that can be reused in future campaigns. Finally, you will learn how to use the Quick Campaign Wizard in Microsoft Dynamics CRM to quickly create campaign activities for a selected set of leads, contacts, or accounts.

Important There are no practice files for this chapter.

Troubleshooting Graphics and operating system–related instructions in this book reflect the Windows Vista user interface. If your computer is running Windows XP and you experience trouble following the instructions as written, refer to the "Information for Readers Running Windows XP" section at the beginning of this book.

Important The images used in this book reflect the default form and field names in Microsoft Dynamics CRM. Because the software offers extensive customization capabilities, it's possible that some of the record types or fields have been relabeled in your Microsoft Dynamics CRM environment. If you cannot find the forms, fields, or security roles referenced in this book, contact your system administrator for assistance.

Important You must know the location of your Microsoft Dynamics CRM Web site to work the exercises in this book. Check with your system administrator to verify the Web address if you don't know it.

Creating a Campaign

Microsoft Dynamics CRM allows you to track marketing or outreach program information on a campaign record. You can track the offer, type, schedule, and financial information about the campaign. For instance, you might have a campaign that coordinates the advertising activities planned for the launch of a new product.

By default, the fields in the following table are tracked on campaigns and campaign templates in Microsoft Dynamics CRM.

Field	Description
Name	This field contains the title of the campaign.
Status Reason	This denotes the status of the campaign for reporting purposes. The default statuses are Proposed, Ready To Launch, Launched, Completed, Canceled, and Suspended.
Campaign Code	This can be either a user-entered or system-generated code for the campaign.
Campaign Type	This provides a category for the campaign, such as Advertisement, Direct Marketing, Event, or Co-branding. This field is useful in reporting.
Expected Response	This allows you to record the expected response for a campaign as a percentage from 0 through 100.
Total Cost of Campaign Activities	In this field, Microsoft Dynamics CRM automatically totals the costs of all campaign activities.
Miscellaneous Costs	This field records miscellaneous costs associated with the campaign.
Total Cost of Campaign	This field contains the sum of the total cost of campaign activities and miscellaneous costs.

In this exercise, you will create the campaign record that will be used to coordinate the advertising activities of your new product launch.

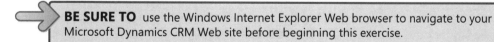

BE SURE TO use the Windows Internet Explorer Web browser to navigate to your Microsoft Dynamics CRM Web site before beginning this exercise.

1. In the **Marketing** area, click **Campaigns**.

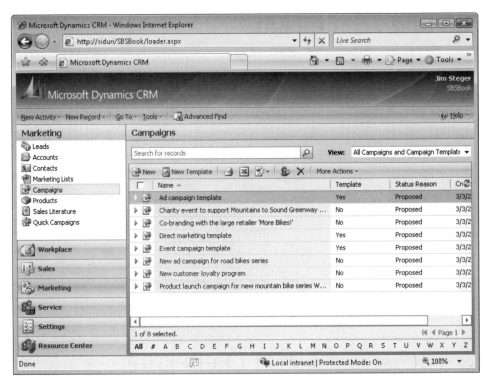

New Campaign

2. In the grid toolbar, click the **New** button.

   The New Campaign form opens.

3. In the **Name** field, enter **New Product Advertising**. In the **Status Reason** field, select **Proposed** and in the **Campaign Type** field, select **Advertisement**. In the **Expected Response** field, enter **100** and in the **Offer** field, enter **To boost sales of our product**.

> **Tip** The campaign code will be completed automatically by Microsoft Dynamics CRM if you do not enter a value. The campaign code cannot be changed after you save the record.

Save

4. Click the **Save** button to create the campaign.

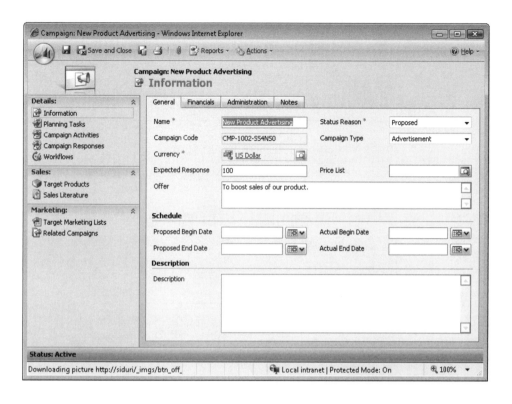

Adding Planning Tasks

For each campaign, you can track the to-do list of activities that need to be completed to execute the campaign. These activities might include:

- Contacting your direct mail vendor.
- Creating and approving copy.
- Creating a target list.
- Printing collateral.
- Approving the offer.

With Microsoft Dynamics CRM, you can manage these activities by using the planning tasks area of a campaign. Planning tasks are standard Microsoft Dynamics CRM task activities that are associated with a campaign.

In this example, you will create a planning task to approve the offer for the new product advertising campaign created in the previous section.

BE SURE TO use the Internet Explorer Web browser to navigate to your Microsoft Dynamics CRM Web site, if necessary, before beginning this exercise.

1. In the **Marketing** area, click **Campaigns**.

2. Open the New Product Advertising campaign you created in the previous exercise, if it is not already open.

3. In the left navigation area, click **Planning Tasks**.

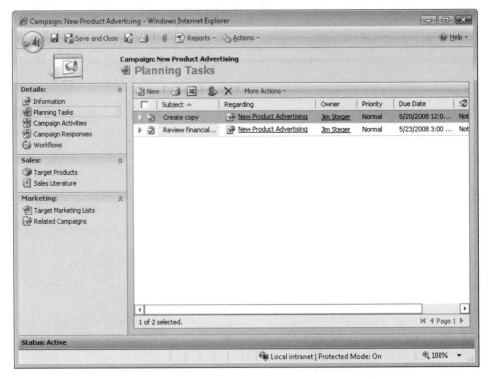

New Planning Task

4. In the grid toolbar, click the **New** button to launch the **New Task** form.

5. In the **Subject** field, enter **Approve Offer**. In the **Due** field, enter a date two weeks from today. In the **Duration** and **Priority** fields, leave the default values of **30 minutes** and **Normal** selected.

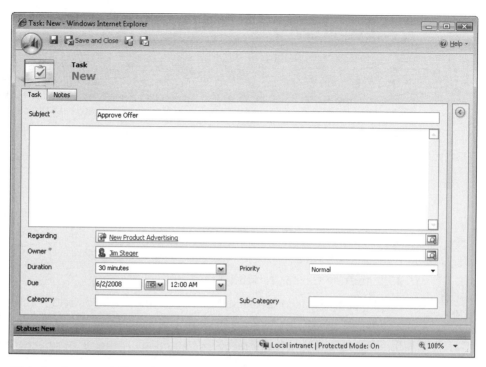

Save and Close

6. Click the **Save and Close** button to create the planning task.

See Also For more information about working with task activities, see Chapter 4, "Working with Activities and Notes."

Selecting Target Marketing Lists

You can use marketing lists to group accounts, contacts, and leads in Microsoft Dynamics CRM and then associate one or more of the lists with each campaign.

Marketing lists link your customers or prospects to your campaign, which is critical when working with and distributing *campaign activities*. Campaign activities are special activities—such as letters, faxes, and phone calls—within Microsoft Dynamics CRM that are created and associated with campaigns. Campaign activities contain campaign-specific information and must be distributed to create the individual activities for users to perform.

See Also For more information about working with campaign activities, see Chapter 10.

In this exercise, you will add the Illinois Contacts marketing list from Chapter 8 to the New Product Advertising campaign.

> **USE** the Illinois Contacts marketing list you created in Chapter 8. If you cannot locate the Illinois Contacts marketing list in your system, select a different marketing list for this exercise. You must have at least one marketing list available to associate with the campaign.
>
> **BE SURE TO** use the Internet Explorer Web browser to navigate to your Microsoft Dynamics CRM Web site, if necessary, before beginning this exercise.

1. In the **Marketing** area, click **Campaigns**.

2. Open the New Product Advertising campaign record you created in the previous exercise, if it is not already open.

3. In the left navigation area, click **Target Marketing Lists**.

Add Marketing List

4. In the grid toolbar, click the **Add** button.

   The Look Up Records dialog box opens. The Look For field is automatically set to Marketing List.

5. Look for the Illinois Contacts list created in Chapter 8, or select another marketing list to add to your campaign.

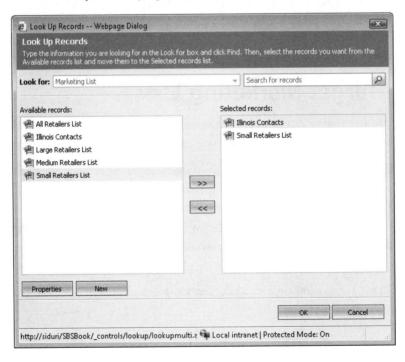

> **Tip** You can create a new marketing list directly from the Look Up Records dialog box by clicking the New button. To view additional details about a selected available record, click the Properties button.

See Also For more information about creating marketing lists, see Chapter 8.

6. When you have finished selecting the marketing lists you want to add to your campaign, click **OK**.

7. You will be prompted to specify whether you want to add the marketing lists to undistributed campaign activities. If you want to add the members of these lists to your campaign activities, leave the box selected.

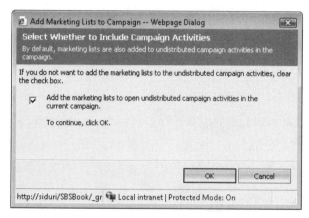

8. Click **OK** to add the selected marketing lists to your campaign.

Adding Target Products and Sales Literature

Campaigns can be used to promote your organization's products or services or to create awareness of a new program or outreach effort. For campaigns involving products or services, you can specify the target products or services within the campaign.

> **Tip** Products and services are configured by using the Products feature of Microsoft Dynamics CRM, located in the Settings area. Consult with your system administrator to properly set up a product or service.

In addition to tracking products and services, you can also relate sales and marketing collateral to a campaign. These documents might include presentations, product and pricing sheets, marketing collateral, and company manuals. Microsoft Dynamics CRM uses *Sales Literature* to store one or more documents for use with marketing campaigns and products.

In this exercise, you will attach a product and sales literature about the product to your campaign.

 BE SURE TO use the Internet Explorer Web browser to navigate to your Microsoft Dynamics CRM Web site, if necessary, and have at least one product created before beginning this exercise.

1. In the **Marketing** area, click **Campaigns**.

2. Open the New Product Advertising campaign record you created in the previous exercise, if it is not already open.

3. In the left navigation area, click **Target Products**.

Add Existing Product

4. In the grid toolbar, click the **Add Existing** button.

   The Look Up Records dialog box opens, with the Look For field automatically set to Product.

5. Select one or more products to associate with your campaign, and then click **OK**.

   The Target Products grid on the New Product Advertising campaign shows the product you selected.

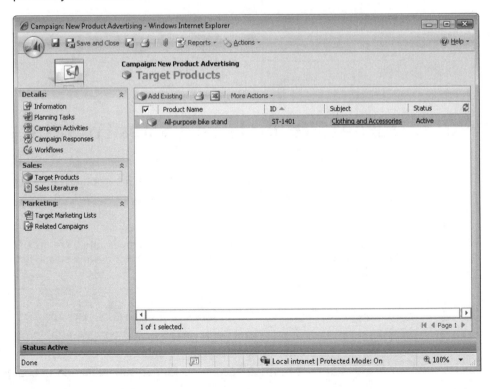

6. In the left navigation area, click **Sales Literature**.

Add Existing
Sales Literature

7. In the grid toolbar, click the **Add Existing** button.

The Look Up Records dialog box opens.

8. Click **New** to create a new sales literature record.

> **Tip** You will create a basic sales literature record for the purposes of this exercise. You can also upload one or more documents and associate specific products with a sales literature record.

9. In the **Title** field, enter **Product pricing**, and select a subject from the **Subject** field. Then, in the **Type** field, select **Price Sheets.**

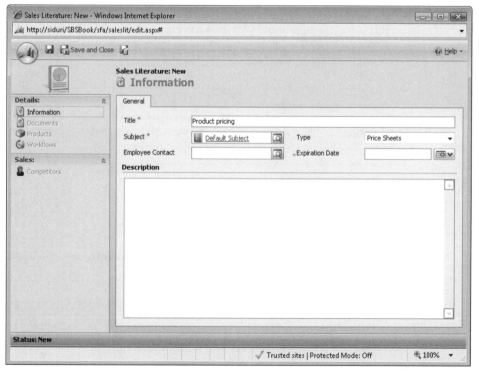

10. Click the **Save and Close** button.

The Product Pricing sales literature record now appears in the Look Up Records dialog box.

11. Double-click the Product Pricing sales literature record to associate it with your campaign, and then click **OK**.

Relating Campaigns

You can relate your marketing campaign to other campaigns for reporting and tracking purposes. For instance, assume you have a global branding campaign. The initial branding campaign is comprised of multiple child campaigns, such as a direct mail campaign, an e-mail campaign, and radio and television spots. In Microsoft Dynamics CRM, you can create a campaign record for each and relate all of them to a parent campaign. This allows you to track results for each campaign channel and aggregate multiple campaigns to measure the effectiveness of the entire branding effort.

In this exercise, you will create a related campaign to track co-branding efforts with a partner retailer as part of your new product advertising campaign.

> **Tip** When you relate two campaigns, Microsoft Dynamics CRM creates a one-way relationship. For instance, suppose you have campaigns A and B. With campaign B as the active campaign, you relate campaign A to campaign B. When you open campaign A, you will *not* see a relationship to campaign B, but you will see campaign A listed as a related campaign in campaign B.

 BE SURE TO use the Internet Explorer Web browser to navigate to your Microsoft Dynamics CRM Web site, if necessary, before beginning this exercise.

1. In the **Marketing** area, click **Campaigns**.

2. Open the New Product Advertising campaign you created earlier in this chapter, if it is not already open.

3. In the left navigation area, click **Related Campaigns**.

4. In the grid toolbar, click the **Add Existing** button.

   Add Existing Campaign

   The Look Up Records dialog box opens, with the Look For field automatically set to Campaign.

5. Click the **New** button to create a new campaign.

6. On the **New Campaign** form, in the **Name** field, enter **Co-branding with the large retailer 'More Bikes!'**.

7. Click **Save and Close** to create the new campaign.

8. Back in the **Look Up Records** dialog box, select the new **Co-branding with the large retailer 'More Bikes!'** campaign, and click **OK** to relate it to the parent campaign.

The related campaign is displayed in the Related Campaigns area of the parent campaign.

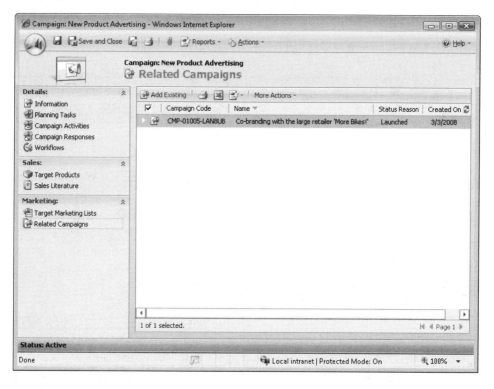

 CLOSE the campaign record.

Creating Campaign Templates

Suppose you are the marketing manager for your company's monthly product catalog. Most of the planning tasks and activities for the catalog are the same each month. Rather than leaving you to recreate all of the common information for your campaign each month, Microsoft Dynamics CRM lets you create a campaign template that can be used as the starting point for your new campaign.

The campaign template stores core details and related information about the campaign and can be used to quickly launch a similar campaign. In Microsoft Dynamics CRM, campaign templates work just like campaigns.

In this example, you will create a campaign template.

> **BE SURE TO** use the Internet Explorer Web browser to navigate to your Microsoft Dynamics CRM Web site, if necessary, before beginning this exercise.

New Campaign Template

1. In the **Marketing** area, click **Campaigns**.

2. In the grid toolbar, click the **New Template** button to launch the **New Campaign (Template)** form.

3. In the **Name** field, enter **TEMPLATE: Product Advertising**.

4. Click **Save**.

Copying Campaign Records

Marketing campaigns can be very involved, and for complex campaigns, it can take considerable effort to enter the correct information in Microsoft Dynamics CRM. Campaign templates provide a common starting point for future campaigns and can save you time and duplication of effort when you are creating campaigns. Microsoft Dynamics CRM also provides two actions, Copy As Campaign and Copy As Template, to quickly duplicate information from an existing campaign or template. The copy action replicates all of the planning tasks, campaign activities, marketing lists, and products to your new campaign or template.

The Copy As Campaign and Copy As Template actions work similarly and can be used from either a campaign or campaign template. The key difference is the resulting output. When you use Copy As Campaign, the output will be a campaign ready for use. The Copy As Template action will produce a campaign template that can be used to create a campaign in the future. The following table can help you decide which copy action is appropriate.

Scenario	Appropriate copy action
You have an existing campaign that you want to preserve for future use.	From the campaign record, use Copy As Template to create a template record that can be used for a later campaign.
You want to create a campaign that's similar to an existing campaign for immediate use.	From the campaign record, use Copy As Campaign to create a new campaign record that can be used immediately.
You want to create a new campaign from an existing campaign template.	Open the campaign template and use Copy As Campaign to create the new campaign record.
You want to create a similar campaign template from an existing template.	Open the campaign template and use Copy As Template to create a new template record.

In this exercise, you will create a new campaign from the campaign template created in the previous section.

 BE SURE TO use the Internet Explorer Web browser to navigate to your Microsoft Dynamics CRM Web site, if necessary, before beginning this exercise.

1. In the **Marketing** area, click **Campaigns**.

2. Open the TEMPLATE: Product Advertising campaign template you created in the previous exercise.

Actions

3. In the grid toolbar, click the **Actions** button, and then select **Copy as Campaign** from the menu.

A campaign record opens, with a copy of all of the information from the originating campaign.

> **Troubleshooting** Microsoft Dynamics CRM allows campaign and campaign template records to have the same name. Be sure to rename your new campaign (or campaign template) to avoid confusion.

Using Quick Campaigns

As you have seen, you can plan and track your marketing efforts with campaigns in Microsoft Dynamics CRM. But sometimes you might want to simply distribute a campaign activity (such as a letter, phone call, or e-mail) to an ad-hoc list without the extra overhead and tracking of a full campaign. A *quick campaign* is a simplified version of a campaign in Microsoft Dynamics CRM that allows you to distribute a single campaign activity to a group of accounts, contacts, leads, or marketing lists.

In this exercise, you will create a quick campaign to track follow-up tasks for a group of leads.

BE SURE TO use the Internet Explorer Web browser to navigate to your Microsoft Dynamics CRM Web site, if necessary, and have multiple lead records already created and available before beginning this exercise.

1. In the **Marketing** area, click **Leads**.

2. Select a few lead records.

> **Tip** You can select multiple records by holding the Ctrl key while clicking the records.

Create Quick Campaign

3. In the grid toolbar, click the **Create Quick Campaign** button, and then select **For Selected Records** from the submenu.

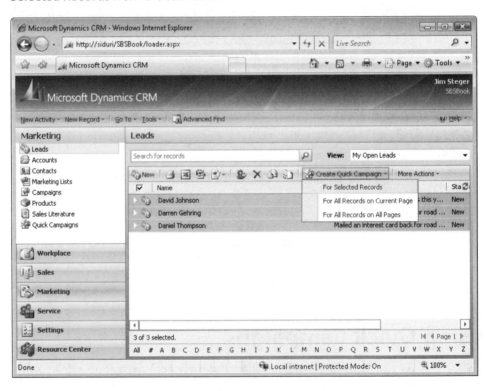

The Create Quick Campaign Wizard form opens. The first step of the Create Quick Campaign Wizard describes the steps you are about to take.

4. Click **Next** to continue.

The next step asks you to enter a name for the quick campaign.

5. In the **Name** field, enter **Our First Lead Quick Campaign**, and then click **Next**.

Now you will need to choose an activity type and user to whom the resulting activities should be assigned. If you choose to do an e-mail activity, you also have the option of automatically sending and closing the e-mail activity.

6. In the **Activity Type** box, select **Phone Call**, and for the **Assign these activities to** option, select **Me**.

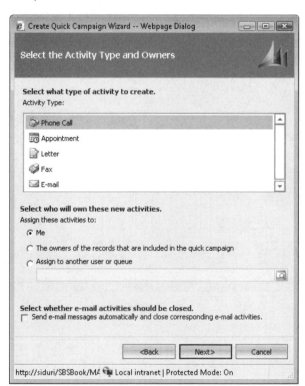

7. Click **Next**.

The next step allows you to enter the content for the activity chosen in the previous step. Since you chose Phone Call, you will see the Phone Call form displayed.

8. In the **Subject** and **Description** fields, enter **Follow up call on leads**. In the **Due** field, select the date you want the activity to be completed.

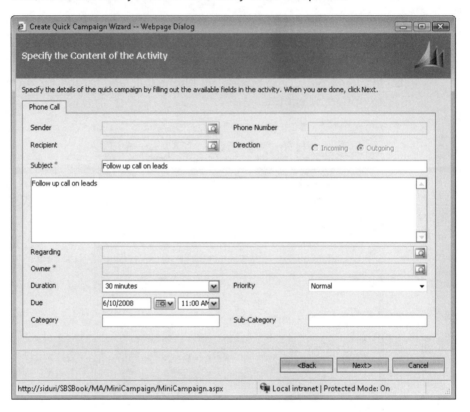

9. Click **Next**.

The final step summarizes the choices made in the previous steps.

10. If everything is correct, click **Create** to complete the quick campaign.

11. After completion, view your new quick campaign by clicking **Quick Campaigns** in the **Marketing** area.

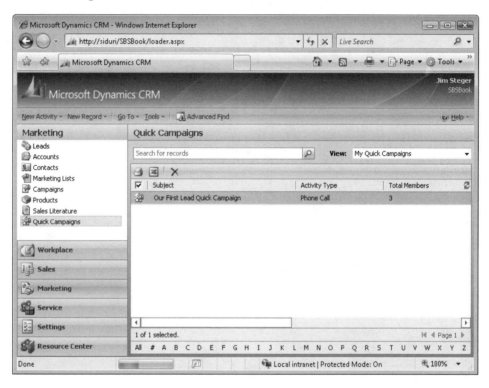

12. Double-click the Our First Lead Quick Campaign record to see your quick campaign details, including the phone call activities created.

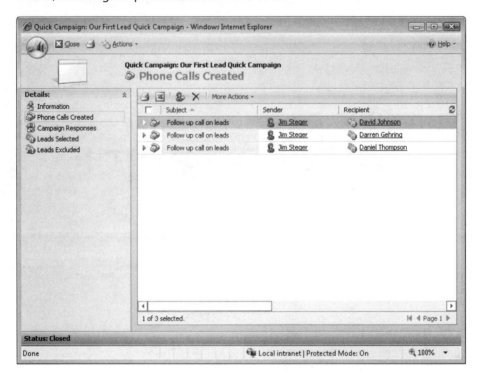

Key Points

- Campaigns allow you to track and communicate the schedules, costs, tasks, lists, and responses related to your marketing and outreach efforts.

- Planning tasks are common Microsoft Dynamics CRM task activities in a campaign or quick campaign.

- Marketing lists associated with a campaign provide the names of customers targeted for campaign activities.

- You can track related products and sales collateral to campaigns.

- You can copy a campaign and all of its related information to a campaign template or another campaign.

- You can quickly distribute campaign activities to ad-hoc lists of accounts, leads, contacts, or marketing lists by using the Quick Campaign Wizard.

Chapter at a Glance

Create campaign activities, **page 210**

Distribute campaign activities, **page 218**

Capture campaign responses, **page 223**

Run campaign analysis reports, **page 230**

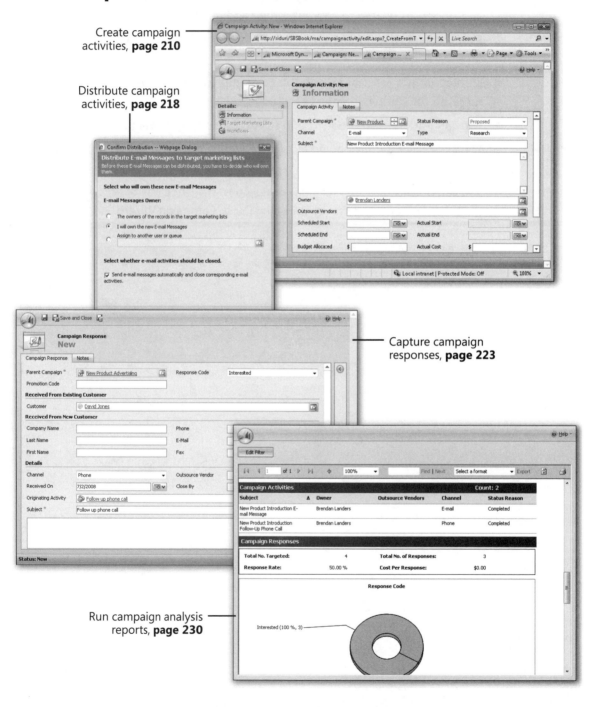

10 Working with Campaign Activities and Responses

In this chapter, you will learn to

✔ Create campaign activities.

✔ Associate marketing lists with campaign activities.

✔ Distribute campaign activities.

✔ Record campaign responses.

✔ Convert campaign responses to other record types.

✔ View campaign results.

In Chapter 9, "Managing Campaigns and Quick Campaigns," you learned how to use Microsoft Dynamics CRM to plan and prepare for a marketing campaign. Proper planning and setup of your campaign helps ensure successful execution and tracking. In addition to helping you prepare for a marketing campaign, Microsoft Dynamics CRM simplifies the execution of your marketing campaign by using *campaign activities* and *campaign responses*. This chapter introduces the concepts of campaign execution and tracking to help you successfully complete a marketing campaign.

A marketing campaign typically includes one or more communications to your target marketing list. For instance, assume that your marketing manager wants to send an e-mail message that introduces a new product to all of the members in a marketing list. You would like your sales team to follow up on the e-mail message with a phone call seven days later. When recipients of the communication respond to the campaign, you would like to record the responses and take additional actions that will vary depending on the character of each response. In Microsoft Dynamics CRM, campaign communications are recorded as campaign activities and member responses are recorded as campaign responses.

In this chapter, you will learn how to set up and *distribute* campaign activities. Additionally, you will learn how to record campaign responses and how to convert them to other record types. Finally, you will learn how to view the results of a marketing campaign to understand its effectiveness.

> **Important** The exercises in this chapter require only records created in earlier chapters; none are supplied on the companion CD. For more information about practice files, see "Using the Companion CD" at the beginning of this book.

> **Troubleshooting** Graphics and operating system–related instructions in this book reflect the Windows Vista user interface. If your computer is running Windows XP and you experience trouble following the instructions as written, refer to the "Information for Readers Running Windows XP" section at the beginning of this book.

> **Important** The images used in this book reflect the default form and field names in Microsoft Dynamics CRM. Because the software offers extensive customization capabilities, it's possible that some of the record types or fields have been relabeled in your Microsoft Dynamics CRM environment. If you cannot find the forms, fields, or security roles referenced in this book, contact your system administrator for assistance.

> **Important** You must know the location of your Microsoft Dynamics CRM Web site to work the exercises in this book. Check with your system administrator to verify the Web address if you don't know it.

Creating a Campaign Activity

In the example introduced at the beginning of this chapter, we discussed a simple campaign with two communication points: an e-mail message followed by a phone call. Microsoft Dynamics CRM allows you to set up these communication points as campaign activities. You can record information about a campaign activity for tracking and analysis across one or many campaigns. The following table describes the fields that are most often tracked for a campaign activity.

Field	Description
Channel	The communication method for the activity
Type	A way to categorize the activity
Subject	A high-level description of the activity
Owner	The user who has been assigned to the activity
Outsource Vendors	Any accounts or contacts related to the activity from an execution standpoint (not targets of the campaign)
Scheduled Start	The target start date for the activity
Scheduled End	The target end date for the activity
Actual Start	The actual start date for the activity
Actual End	The actual end date for the activity
Budget Allocated	The amount of budget allocated for the activity
Actual Cost	The actual cost of the activity
Priority	Prioritization of the activity
No. of Days	An anti-spam setting that lets you prevent too-frequent communication from a campaign

In this exercise, you will create two campaign activities to be distributed to your team to support your marketing campaign.

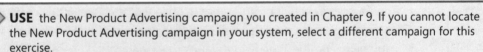

USE the New Product Advertising campaign you created in Chapter 9. If you cannot locate the New Product Advertising campaign in your system, select a different campaign for this exercise.

BE SURE TO use the Windows Internet Explorer Web browser to navigate to your Microsoft Dynamics CRM Web site before beginning this exercise.

1. In the **Marketing** area, click **Campaigns**.

2. Open the **New Product Advertising** campaign.

3. In the left navigation area, click **Campaign Activities**.

   A list of campaign activities associated with this campaign appears. This list will be empty at this point.

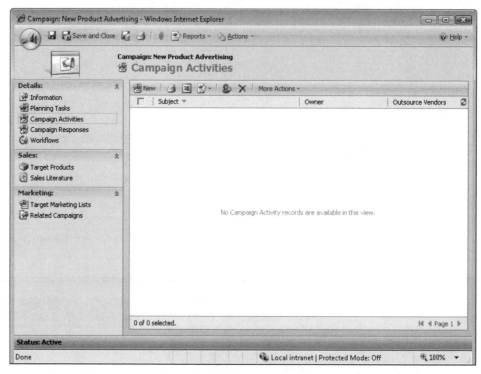

New Campaign
Activity

4. In the grid toolbar, click the **New** button.

The Campaign Activity form opens. Notice that the Owner field defaults to your name, the Parent Campaign field is populated with the New Product Advertising campaign, and the Type field defaults to Research.

5. In the **Subject** field, enter **New Product Introduction E-mail Message**.

6. In the **Channel** field, select **E-mail**.

This selection affects how an activity will be distributed. By selecting E-Mail, you are choosing to send an e-mail message to the recipients.

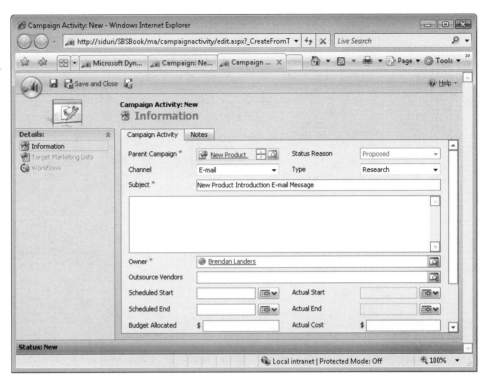

Save and Close

7. In the form toolbar, click the **Save and Close** button to create the campaign activity.

8. In the grid toolbar, click the **New** button.

9. In the **New Campaign Activity** form, enter **New Product Introduction Follow-Up Phone Call** in the **Subject** field.

10. In the **Channel** field, select **Phone**.

11. Click **Save and Close**.

Two campaign activities now appear in the list.

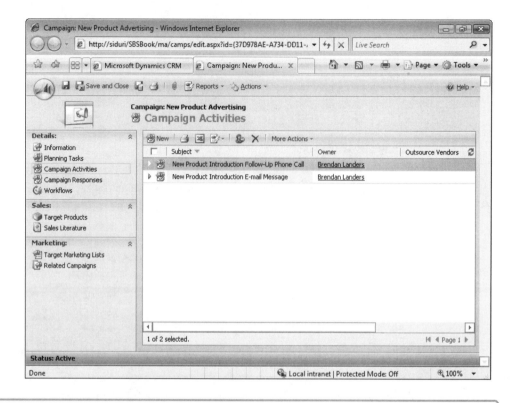

Tip The channels available for the campaign activity directly relate to the activity types in Microsoft Dynamics CRM. The only exception is the Other channel, which exists to handle custom campaign activities that do not align with the native activity types. A campaign activity designated as Other serves as a record of the activity for scheduling and budgeting purposes only and cannot be distributed to list members.

See Also The Letter, Fax, and E-mail channels let you leverage the Microsoft Office Word mail merge feature. For more information about mail merge, see "Using Mail Merge to Generate a Word Document That Includes List Member Information" in Chapter 8, "Using Marketing Lists."

Associating a Marketing List to a Campaign Activity

In Chapter 9, you created marketing lists and associated them with your campaign. As you might expect, when you create a campaign activity, the marketing lists associated with the campaign are automatically associated with the activity. As things change over the course of the campaign, you might decide that you do not want to distribute a campaign activity to all marketing lists. For example, suppose you have different activity templates for different industries, so that you can emphasize different benefits of your new product to different audiences. In this case, you could create specific campaign activities for each vertical. Or consider the case in which you need to add another marketing list after a campaign activity has been set up. If you have additional marketing lists you would like to add to the campaign, you can automatically add the list to all pending campaign activities or manually add the list to specific campaign activities if you don't want to associate the list to all open activities.

In this exercise, you will add and remove marketing lists from a campaign activity.

USE the New Product Advertising campaign you created in Chapter 9. If you cannot locate the New Product Advertising campaign in your system, select a different campaign for this exercise.

BE SURE TO use the Internet Explorer Web browser to navigate to your Microsoft Dynamics CRM Web site, if necessary, before beginning this exercise.

1. In the **Marketing** area, click **Campaigns**.

2. Open the **New Product Advertising** campaign.

3. In the left navigation area, click **Target Marketing Lists**.

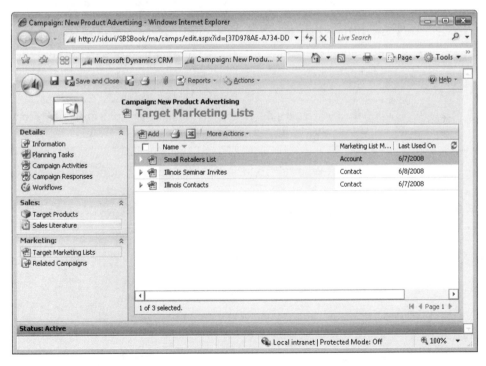

Add

4. Click the **Add** button.

The Look Up Records dialog box opens.

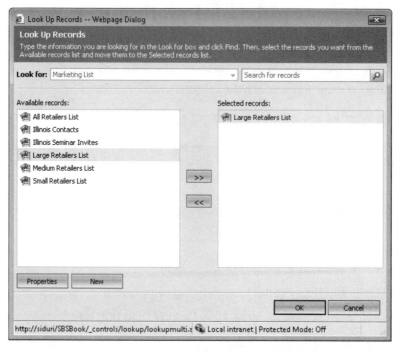

5. In the **Look Up Records** dialog box, select an additional marketing list. If no additional marketing lists exist, create a new one by clicking the **New** button. Click **OK**.

> **Tip** If you need a refresher on creating a marketing list, see "Creating a Marketing List" in Chapter 8.

The Select Whether To Include Campaign Activities dialog box opens.

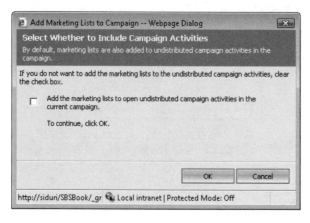

6. In the dialog box, clear the check box, and then click **OK** to indicate that you do not want to associate the marketing list to the open campaign activities.

7. In the left navigation area, click **Campaign Activities**.

8. Open the **New Product Introduction E-mail Message** campaign activity.

9. In the left navigation area, click **Target Marketing Lists**.

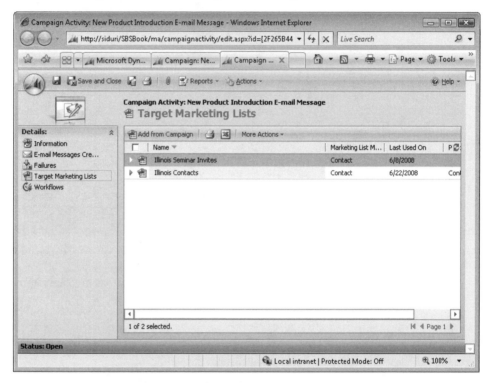

Add from
Campaign

10. In the grid toolbar, click the **Add from Campaign** button.

11. Select the new marketing list that you added to the campaign, and then click **OK**.

The additional marketing list has now been added to the campaign activity. When you distribute this campaign activity, the additional marketing list members will also be included in the activity.

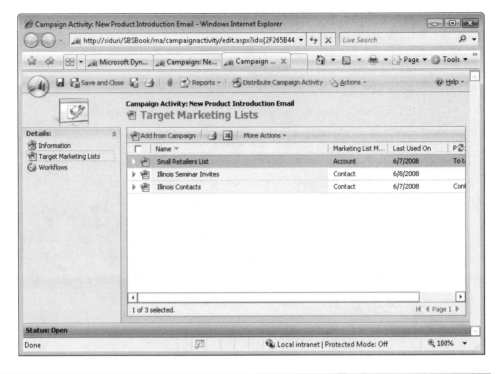

Tip Just as you can add a marketing list to a campaign activity, you can also remove a marketing list. To do so, select the marketing list, and then select Remove from the More Actions menu in the grid toolbar.

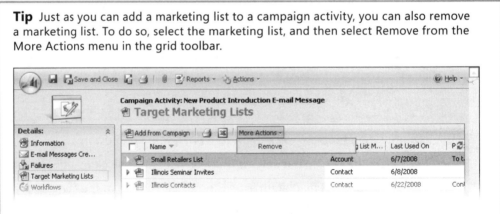

Distributing a Campaign Activity

When you have created and associated the appropriate marketing lists with your campaign activities, you have taken the necessary steps to prepare for the execution of the activity. Then, when you are ready to execute the campaign activity, you will *distribute* the activity. This action will create Microsoft Dynamics CRM activity records that will exist under the account, contact, or lead records specified in the target marketing lists.

> **Tip** Most distributed campaign activities are distributed as open activities that need to be completed. The only exceptions to this rule are e-mail campaign activities, because you can choose to automatically send an e-mail when you distribute the e-mail campaign activity.

In this exercise, you will distribute the e-mail and phone call campaign activities you created earlier in this chapter.

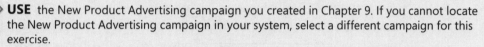

USE the New Product Advertising campaign you created in Chapter 9. If you cannot locate the New Product Advertising campaign in your system, select a different campaign for this exercise.

BE SURE TO use the Internet Explorer Web browser to navigate to your Microsoft Dynamics CRM Web site, if necessary, before beginning this exercise.

1. In the **Marketing** area, click **Campaigns**.

2. Open the **New Product Advertising** campaign.

3. In the left navigation area, click **Campaign Activities**.

4. Open the **New Product Introduction E-mail Message** campaign activity.

Distribute
Campaign
Activity

5. Click the **Distribute Campaign Activity** button to open the **New E-mails** dialog box.

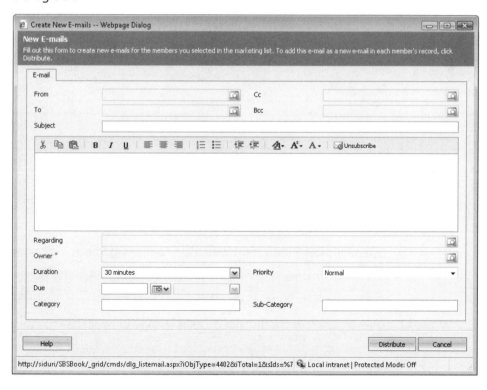

> **Important** The following steps will send an e-mail message to the e-mail addresses of all members included in the target marketing lists for this campaign activity. Make sure that your marketing lists do not include any customer e-mail addresses, so that you do not send a test message to them!

6. Enter a subject and body for your e-mail message. You can also choose to fill in the additional fields of the e-mail activity. Then click **Distribute**.

The Distribute E-Mail Messages To Target Marketing Lists dialog box opens. In this dialog box, you can select who will own the activity by choosing either the record owners, yourself, or another user or queue. You can also specify whether the e-mail message should automatically be sent and closed when the activity is distributed.

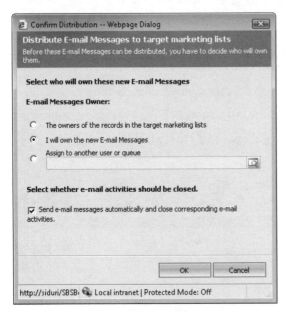

7. Leave the **Send e-mail messages automatically and close corresponding e-mail activities** check box selected, and click **OK**.

The e-mail messages are now sent.

8. In the campaign activity, click **Save and Close**.

9. Open the **New Product Introduction Follow-Up Phone Call** campaign activity.

10. In the form toolbar, click the **Distribute Campaign Activity** button.

The Create New Phone Calls dialog box opens.

11. Enter a subject and a description, and change the due date to one week in the future.

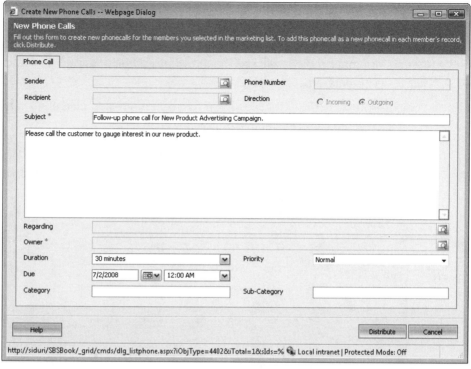

12. Click **Distribute**.

The Distribute Phone Calls To Target Marketing Lists dialog box opens.

13. Under **Phone Calls Owner**, select **The owners of the records in the target marketing lists**, and then click **OK**.

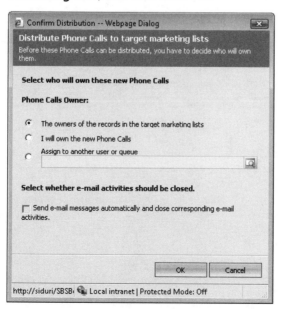

You have successfully distributed your campaign activities. The New Product Introduction e-mail message has been sent, and the New Product Introduction Follow-Up Phone Call activity has been created. Owners of the marketing list member records will see the activities in their activity lists with the due date you entered.

Microsoft Dynamics CRM allows you to create multi-step marketing campaigns and allows you to record campaign activities in many channels.

When you have distributed the activities, you can view the activities you created (both the successes and the failures) in the left navigation area of the campaign activity.

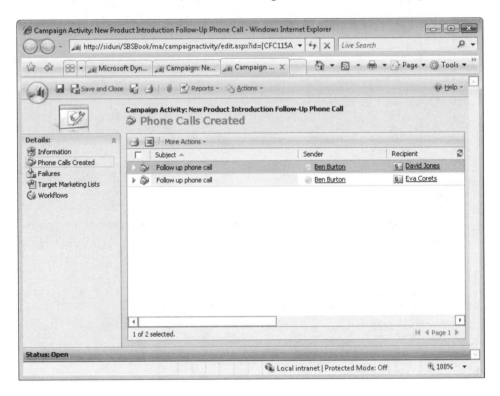

Recording a Campaign Response

After your campaign activities have been distributed and your target marketing list members have received the communication, you can record the responses you receive, both positive and negative. By tracking responses, you can take additional action to pursue the customer or prospect. For positive responses, you might schedule a follow-up phone call or other activity. For negative responses, you might remove members from a certain marketing list. Recording both positive and negative responses provides marketing managers with an overall understanding of the total response rate along with the positive response rate. You can record campaign responses in Microsoft Dynamics CRM in the following ways:

- Manually create a campaign response record.
- Close a campaign activity as a response.
- Automatically create a campaign response for e-mail replies.
- Import campaign responses.

See Also **For more information about importing campaign responses and other record types, refer to Chapter 18, "Importing Data."**

In this exercise, you will manually create a campaign response.

USE the New Product Advertising campaign you created in Chapter 9. If you cannot locate the New Product Advertising campaign in your system, select a different campaign for this exercise.

BE SURE TO use the Internet Explorer Web browser to navigate to your Microsoft Dynamics CRM Web site, if necessary, before beginning this exercise.

1. In the **Marketing** area, click **Campaigns**.

2. Open the **New Product Advertising** campaign.

3. In the left navigation area, click **Campaign Responses**.

4. Click the **New** button.

New Campaign
Response

The Campaign Response activity form opens. Many fields are available for capture in a campaign response, including the response code, who the response was received from, and other details about the response.

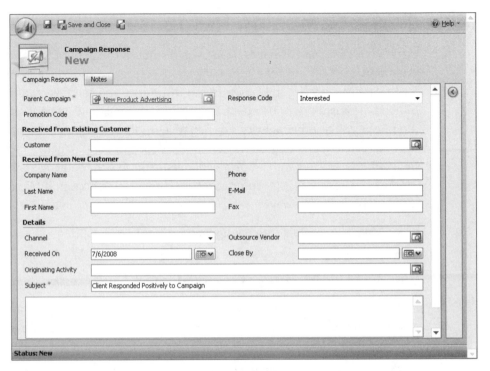

Save

5. Enter a subject, and then click the **Save** button.

Promoting a Campaign Activity to a Campaign Response

You might have noticed that one of the fields in the Campaign Response form, Originating Activity, lets you associate the campaign response with the original campaign activity. Microsoft Dynamics CRM also lets you create the campaign response from the original campaign activity, so you can track the effectiveness of each campaign activity in addition to understanding the effectiveness of the overall campaign.

In this exercise, you will promote a campaign activity to a campaign response.

USE the New Product Advertising campaign you created in Chapter 9. If you cannot locate the New Product Advertising campaign in your system, select a different campaign for this exercise.

BE SURE TO use the Internet Explorer Web browser to navigate to your Microsoft Dynamics CRM Web site, if necessary, before beginning this exercise.

1. In the **Marketing** area, click **Campaigns**.

2. Open the **New Product Advertising** campaign.

3. In the left navigation area, click **Campaign Activities**.

4. Open the **New Product Introduction Follow-Up Phone Call** activity.

5. In the left navigation area, click **Phone Calls Created**.

The Phone Calls Created list opens.

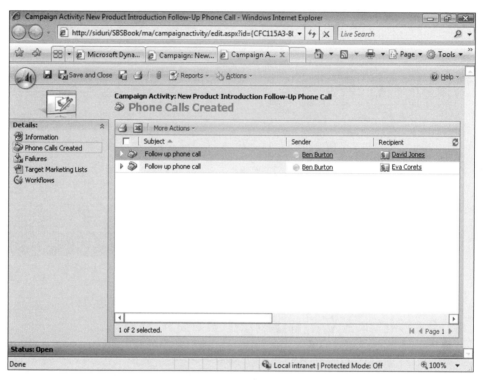

6. Open one of the phone call activities in the list.

7. In the activity form toolbar, on the **Actions** menu, select **Promote to Response**.

The campaign activity is closed, and the Campaign Response form opens. Notice that many of the fields are populated based on the campaign activity you just closed.

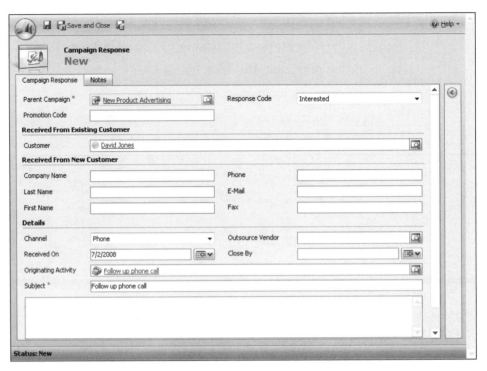

8. Enter a subject, and then click the **Save** button.

Converting a Campaign Response

When you receive a positive response from a target marketing list member, you will probably want to pursue the customer or prospect further. Microsoft Dynamics CRM lets you close the campaign response and convert it into one of several different record types. The following table describes the converted record types.

Converted record option	Reason for use
Create New Lead	The target member responds with interest in learning more, but the potential customer has not been qualified yet.
Convert An Existing Lead	The target member currently exists as a lead. As a result of the campaign response, the lead is qualified and therefore will be converted.
Create New Record For A Customer	The target member is an existing customer targeted for potential up-sale or cross-sale. You would like to create a new quote, order, or opportunity for the existing customer.

In this exercise, you will convert a campaign response into a new lead.

> **USE** the New Product Advertising campaign you created in Chapter 9. If you cannot locate the New Product Advertising campaign in your system, select a different campaign for this exercise.
>
> **BE SURE TO** use the Internet Explorer Web browser to navigate to your Microsoft Dynamics CRM Web site, if necessary, before beginning this exercise.

1. In the **Marketing** area, click **Campaigns**.

2. Open the **New Product Advertising** campaign.

3. In the left navigation area, click **Campaign Responses**.

   A list of all responses associated with the campaign appears.

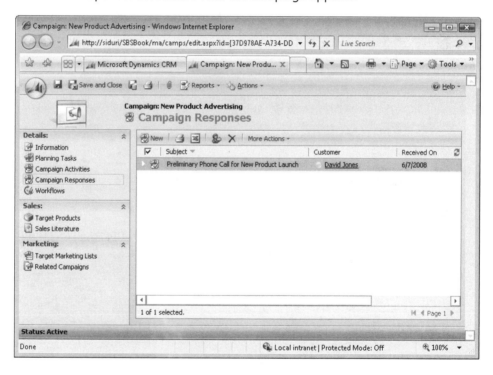

4. Open any open campaign response record.

5. In the form toolbar, click the **Convert Campaign Response** button.

Convert
Campaign
Response

The Close And Convert The Response dialog box opens.

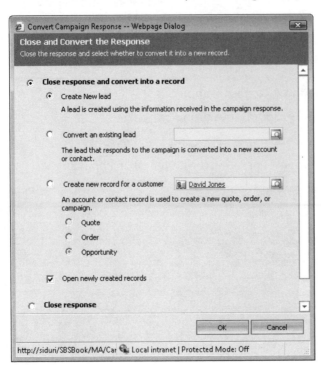

6. Leave **Create New lead** selected, and click **OK**.

This action closes the campaign response and opens a New Lead form with the Topic populated from the campaign response.

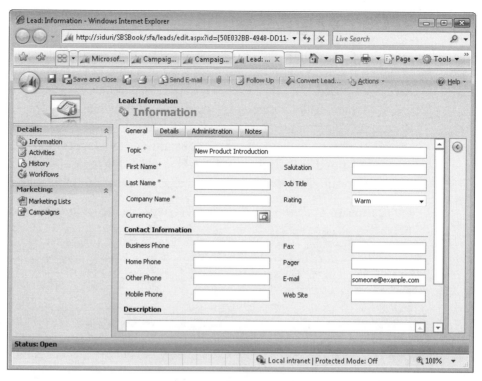

You have successfully converted the campaign response to a lead record. From here, you can follow your normal sales processes to further pursue the record. If the lead record already existed when you chose to convert the lead, you would have been presented with the standard lead conversion dialog box. If you chose to create a new record for a customer, the specified record would be created with information populated from the campaign response (as when you converted the lead). Alternatively, you could select to close the response with a status of Completed or Canceled, without creating new records.

Viewing Campaign Results

While the campaign is being executed, you'll want to have visibility into the campaign activities and understand the results of the campaign. The speed with which activities have been closed, the activities that are still open, and the number of responses received are all very important data points. You might want to take additional actions based on these data points. For example, you could create an additional campaign activity for target members who have not responded, or you could follow up with the marketing team to ensure that the activities are taking place. Microsoft Dynamics CRM provides you with several reports you can use to view the results of marketing campaigns.

In this exercise, you will view the overall results of a marketing campaign by using the default campaign reports.

> **USE** the New Product Advertising campaign you created in Chapter 9. If you cannot locate the New Product Advertising campaign in your system, select a different campaign for this exercise.
>
> **BE SURE TO** use the Internet Explorer Web browser to navigate to your Microsoft Dynamics CRM Web site, if necessary, before beginning this exercise.

1. In the **Marketing** area, click **Campaigns**.

2. Open the **New Product Advertising** campaign.

Reports

3. In the form toolbar, click the **Reports** button, and select **Campaign Performance** from the menu.

The Campaign Performance report is run. This report includes a view that combines information across the campaign record, including the target marketing lists, sales literature, related campaigns, planning tasks, campaign activities, campaign responses, and campaign financials.

> **Tip** The data in the following examples will reflect the campaign you have created and will vary depending on the size of the marketing lists selected. Therefore, you will probably see different data than in the example.

In this example, four campaign activities have been created and three campaign responses have been received. The response rate is 50 percent.

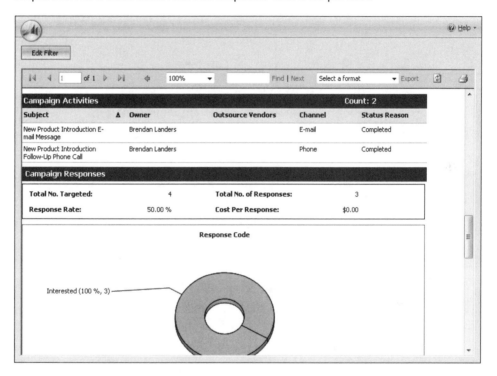

 CLOSE the Campaign Performance report.

Viewing Specific Campaign Information

In addition to viewing the results of a marketing campaign, you might want to view specific information about the status of campaign activities. The Campaign Activity Status report provides information related to the status of campaign activities.

In this exercise, you will view the status of a campaign activity by using the Campaign Activity Status report.

USE the New Product Advertising campaign you created in Chapter 9. If you cannot locate the New Product Advertising campaign in your system, select a different campaign for this exercise.

BE SURE TO use the Internet Explorer Web browser to navigate to your Microsoft Dynamics CRM Web site, if necessary, before beginning this exercise.

1. In the **Marketing** area, click **Campaigns**.

2. Open the **New Product Advertising** campaign.

3. In the left navigation area, click **Campaign Activities**.

4. Select the **New Product Introduction Follow-Up Phone Call** activity without opening the record.

Reports

5. In the grid toolbar, click the **Reports** button, and then click **Campaign Activity Status**.

The Select Records dialog box opens. This dialog box lets you specify whether you want to run the report for all campaign activities or only for those highlighted when the report button was clicked.

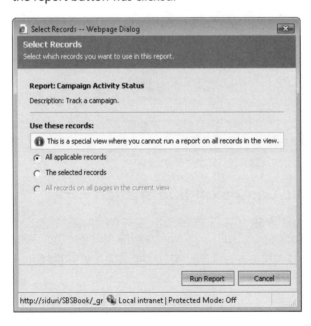

6. Click **The selected records**, and then click **Run Report**.

The Campaign Activity Status report appears. Here you can see information about the campaign activity, including the status of the distributed campaign activities, and assignment by activity owner.

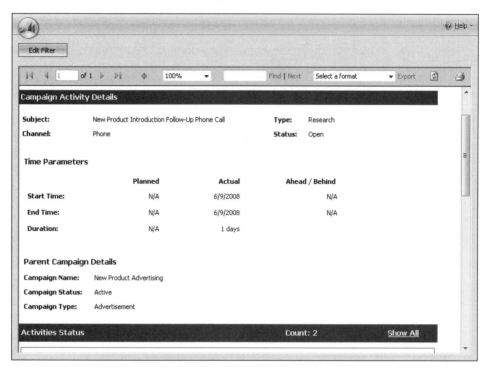

If you want to see the records that make up the charts in the report, you can click Show All or click on the chart directly to see a list of the specific records.

 CLOSE the Campaign Activity Status report.

See Also Chapter 15, "Using Advanced Find," discusses in detail the additional reporting capabilities available in Microsoft Dynamics CRM with Advanced Find and system views. Chapter 16, "Using the Report Wizard," provides more information about the additional reporting capabilities of the Report Wizard.

Key Points

- Campaign activities allow you to track the campaign-specific communications related to a marketing campaign.

- You can assign specific marketing lists to a campaign activity. Not all campaign marketing lists need to be used in a campaign activity.

- When you distribute campaign activities, the activities are created and assigned to customer record owners to be completed.

- You can choose to send e-mail campaign activities immediately when they are distributed.

- You can record a campaign response in several ways. In addition to manually creating a campaign response, you can record a response by converting a campaign activity, allow e-mail responses to automatically create campaign activities, or import campaign responses by using the import wizard.

- Campaign responses can be converted to other Microsoft Dynamics CRM record types, such as leads, accounts, contacts, opportunities, quotes, or orders.

- Microsoft Dynamics CRM includes several reports that let you view the results of marketing campaigns and campaign activities. Two examples are the Campaign Performance report and the Campaign Activity Status report.

Part IV

Service

Chapter at a Glance

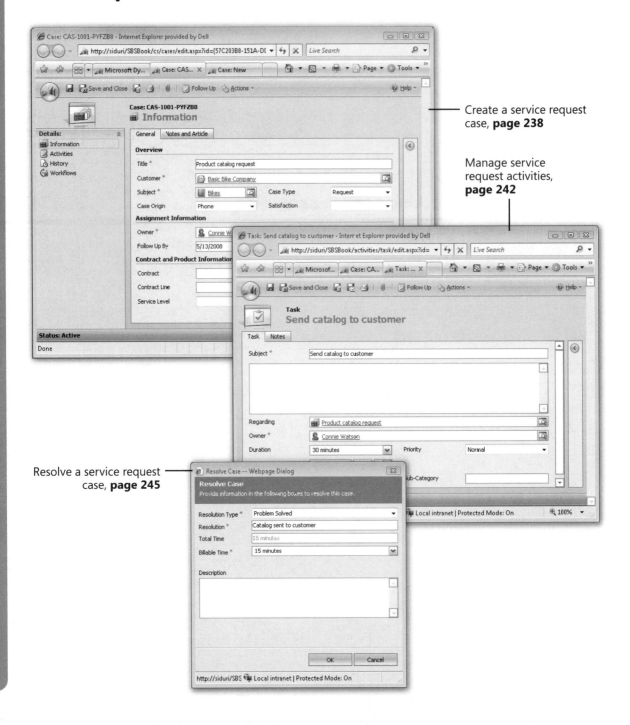

Create a service request case, **page 238**

Manage service request activities, **page 242**

Resolve a service request case, **page 245**

11 Tracking Service Requests

In this chapter, you will learn to

✔ Create and assign a service request case.

✔ Manage service request activities.

✔ Resolve a service request case.

✔ Cancel and reopen a service request case.

Many CRM system implementations are initiated by sales and marketing teams to build a shared, central repository of customer sales and order data. In the previous chapters of this book, you've learned how Microsoft Dynamics CRM can be used to manage marketing activities, prospective customers (leads), sales opportunities, and orders. Of course, after a sale is completed, your company's relationship with the customer does not end! To ensure that the customer is satisfied with the sale, customer service teams can use the information gathered during the marketing and sales processes to manage the post-sale relationship with the customer.

Consider the following scenario: You've just purchased a flight to your favorite vacation locale from a travel Web site. The day before you're scheduled to leave, you receive an e-mail indicating that your flight has been canceled and you'll need to contact the travel Web site's customer service team for more information. You call the customer service number listed in the e-mail, only to be routed through three customer service representatives, explaining your situation to each before someone finally books you on another flight.

Regardless of the purchase, this scenario is not uncommon when customer support issues are involved, which is why a system that allows customer service teams to share sales and support information is such a powerful concept. All communications regarding the support request can be captured in one location and viewed by everyone on the team to ensure a speedy resolution. As the archive of service requests accumulates, customer service managers can identify common issues and trends that can then be used to drive enhancements to the sales process, to service, or to product development.

In Microsoft Dynamics CRM, service requests are called *cases*. A case represents any request or support incident for a customer. Typically, a case includes a description of the service issue or problem reported by the customer and the related notes and follow-up activities that service representatives use to resolve the issue.

Providing an avenue for customers to submit requests or issues during and after the sales process is critical to ensuring that customers are satisfied and willing to do business with your company in the future. In this chapter, you'll learn how customer service teams can create, update, and resolve cases in Microsoft Dynamics CRM.

Important There are no practice files for this chapter.

Troubleshooting Graphics and operating system–related instructions in this book reflect the Windows Vista user interface. If your computer is running Windows XP and you experience trouble following the instructions as written, refer to the "Information for Readers Running Windows XP" section at the beginning of this book.

Important The images used in this book reflect the default form and field names in Microsoft Dynamics CRM. Because the software offers extensive customization capabilities, it's possible that some of the record types or fields have been relabeled in your Microsoft Dynamics CRM environment. If you cannot find the forms, fields, or security roles referenced in this book, contact your system administrator for assistance.

Important You must know the location of your Microsoft Dynamics CRM Web site to work the exercises in this book. Check with your system administrator to verify the Web address if you don't know it.

Creating and Assigning a Service Request Case

Each case in Microsoft Dynamics CRM contains the details of a customer request or issue, as well as follow-up dates, resolution steps, and other details. Multiple cases can be tracked for each customer, and each case has its own follow-up dates and status value. Because of the flexibility of the case record and the ability to customize forms and fields in Microsoft Dynamics CRM, cases are often used to track more than just support requests. Examples of how we've seen cases used include:

- Resolving call center support requests for customers of a financial services firm.
- Managing concierge requests for top-tier clients of a hospitality provider.

- Tracking safety requests to fix potholes and replace broken streetlights for a municipal government.
- Capturing end-user requests for the CRM system itself.
- Tracking warranty requests for residential home sales.

In this exercise, you'll create a new case for a customer who is requesting a product catalog. After creating the case with the appropriate details from the customer, you'll assign it to a customer service representative.

See Also Cases can be assigned to queues as well as to individual representatives. For more information about queues, see Chapter 13, "Working with Contracts and Queues."

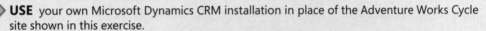

USE your own Microsoft Dynamics CRM installation in place of the Adventure Works Cycle site shown in this exercise.

BE SURE TO use the Windows Internet Explorer Web browser to navigate to your Microsoft Dynamics CRM Web site before beginning this exercise.

1. In the **Service** area, click **Cases** to view the case manager.

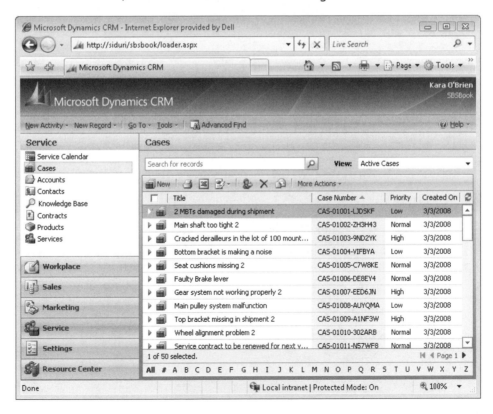

New Case

2. In the grid toolbar, click the **New** button to launch the **New Case** form.

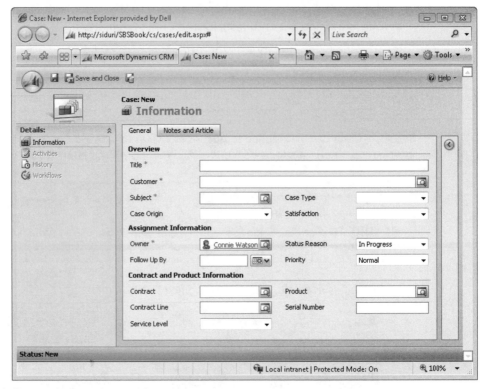

3. In the **Title** field, enter **Product catalog request**.

Look Up

4. Click the **Look Up** button next to the **Customer** field, and select an account.

> **Tip** Each case must be related to a customer account or contact. In addition to
> customers, cases can also be related to service contracts and products.

5. Select a **Subject** category for the case.

See Also For more information on subjects and the subject tree, see the "Configuring
the Subject Tree" sidebar at the end of this chapter.

6. Set the **Case Origin** field to **Phone** to indicate that the customer called with this
request.

7. Set the **Case Type** field to **Request**.

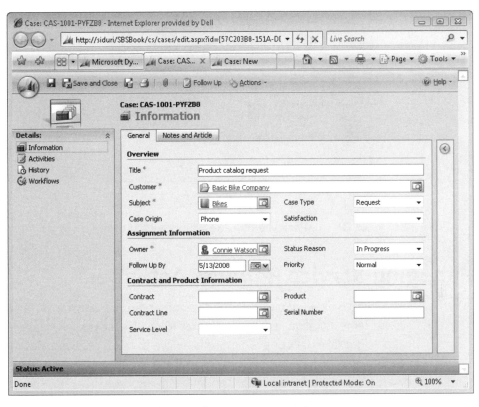

Save

8. In the form toolbar, click the **Save** button to create the case.

> **Tip** Microsoft Dynamics CRM automatically assigns a number to each case when it is first saved. Case auto-numbering can be configured by system administrators in the Administration section of the Settings pane. By default, each case is created with a three-character prefix (*CAS*), a four-digit code, and a six-character identifier—for example, *CAS-1001-PYFZB8*.

Actions

9. In the form toolbar, click the **Actions** button, and then select **Assign** to assign the case to a customer service representative.

10. In the **Assign to Queue or User** dialog box, select **Assign to another user or queue**, and click the Look Up button to select another user record.

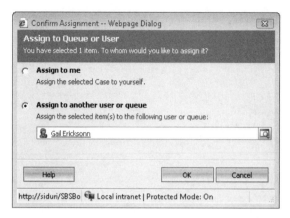

11. Click **OK** to assign the record to the selected user.

Managing Service Request Activities

Depending on the complexity of the customer request or issue, it might take a customer service representative just a few minutes to resolve a case, whereas more complicated cases might take days or even months before they are resolved. Because the workload of a customer service team is subject to the requests and support issues created each day, it's important for teams to continuously resolve issues and track progress on new issues as they are logged.

For example, the catalog request example in the previous section has a straightforward resolution: The customer service representative will create a task for the fulfillment clerk to send a catalog to the customer, and after this has been completed, no additional follow-up is required with the customer.

Many requests require more research, either internally or with the customer. After submitting an initial warranty claim for a malfunctioning stereo system, a customer might be asked to speak to a service representative on the phone several times and schedule an appointment at a service center before the stereo is fixed. And if it can't be fixed, the customer might be asked to ship the broken stereo to the manufacturer for replacement.

For customer service managers, tracking the steps taken during a case provides a way of identifying the best solution to frequently logged issues and managing the amount of time each representative spends on a case.

In this exercise, you'll log a follow-up activity for the case created in the previous section, creating a task activity to track time spent on the service request.

See Also For more information about activities, see Chapter 4, "Working with Activities and Notes."

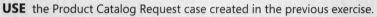

USE the Product Catalog Request case created in the previous exercise.
BE SURE TO use the Internet Explorer Web browser to navigate to your Microsoft Dynamics CRM Web site, if necessary, before beginning this exercise.

Follow Up

1. On the form toolbar of the **Case** form, click the **Follow Up** button to create a follow-up activity.

2. In the **Form Assistant** pane on the right side of the form, ensure that **Task** is selected in the **Activity Type** field.

> **Tip** Activities can also be created from the Activities view accessed in the left navigation area of the Case form. For more information, see Chapter 4.

3. Enter the following in the **Subject** field: **Send catalog to customer**.

4. In the **Due** field, select a date three business days from today's date.

5. Click the **Save and Open** button to create the follow-up task and view the new record.

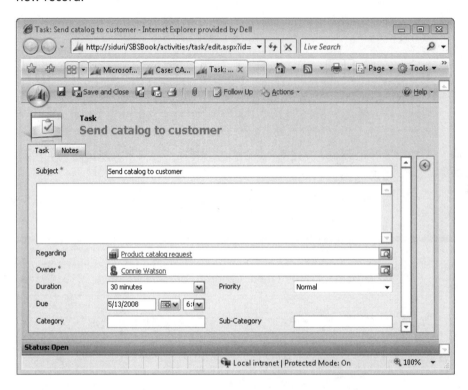

> **Tip** If you do not want to view the new activity after creating it from the Form Assistant, click the Save button instead of Save And Open. After the activity has been created, a notification appears below the save buttons, indicating that the activity was created.

6. Set the **Duration** field on the **Task** form to **15 minutes**. (The duration is the anticipated time the task will take to complete.)

7. Click the **Save as Completed** button to mark the task as completed.

Save as
Completed

After the status of the task is updated to Completed, the Task form automatically closes.

Resolving a Service Request Case

As customer service teams work toward resolving service request questions and incidents, it's important to maintain an accurate status value for each case to ensure that new cases are addressed in a timely manner and worked on until a resolution is identified. When a case is resolved to the customer's satisfaction, customer service representatives can update the status of the case to Resolved, which will maintain the case record in the Microsoft Dynamics CRM database but remove it from the active cases view.

Before a case can be marked as resolved, all open, related activities must be completed or canceled. The duration value of each completed activity regarding the case will be totaled when the case is resolved, so customer service managers can track the amount of time spent working on the case.

In this exercise, you'll mark the case created in a previous exercise as resolved.

> **USE** the Product Catalog Request case you created earlier in this chapter.
>
> **BE SURE TO** use the Internet Explorer Web browser to navigate to your Microsoft Dynamics CRM Web site, if necessary, before beginning this exercise.

1. On the **Case** form toolbar, click the **Actions** menu, and select **Resolve Case** to mark the case as resolved.

> **Important** A case cannot be resolved until all open activities regarding the case have been closed. Before resolving the case, ensure that all activities for the case have been marked as completed or canceled.

2. In the **Resolve Case** dialog box, in the **Resolution** field, enter **Catalog sent to customer**. Leave **15 minutes** selected in the **Billable Time** field.

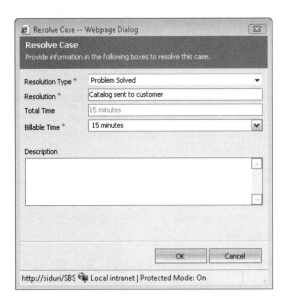

> **Tip** By default, Microsoft Dynamics CRM includes only one status option for the Resolved case status: Problem Solved. This value automatically appears in the Resolution Type field in the Resolve Case dialog box. The status reason values for cases can be modified to match your business needs with the customization tools in Microsoft Dynamics CRM. Contact your system administrator for assistance.

3. Click **OK** to update the case status to Resolved.

All fields are saved and made read-only on the form. Microsoft Dynamics CRM automatically creates a Case Resolution activity that stores the details of the resolution in the case's history.

4. In the left navigation area of the case, click **History** to view the completed activities for the case.

5. Open the case resolution activity. Note that the resolution and total time for the case are stored in the history for reporting and analysis.

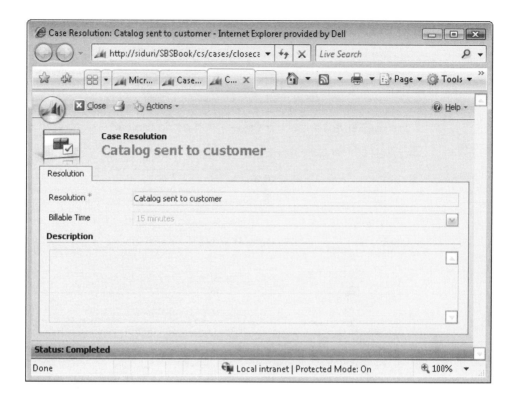

Canceling and Reopening a Service Request Case

There will be times when a case drops off the customer's priority list or the customer resolves an issue internally. Imagine a situation in which a customer submits a warranty claim for a refrigerator he recently purchased. The day after the case was logged with the appliance company's customer service team, the company issues a recall of the customer's refrigerator model, having seen several similar cases logged against it in previous months. The customer service team sets up a new case tracking category to manage recall requests and logs a new case under it for the customer. To prevent the initial case from remaining in the customer service team's active cases list, the case is canceled. Canceled cases are deactivated so that all fields on the form are read-only, but these cases can still be searched and referenced as necessary.

Sometimes the reverse happens—a case that was previously resolved or canceled is reopened if the issue recurs for the customer. Resolved and canceled cases can be reactivated in Microsoft Dynamics CRM so that customer service teams can continue working with them. Software development companies often have cases that require ongoing customer input; these cases might be canceled if no response is received from the customer for a long period of time. Such a case could be reopened in Microsoft Dynamics CRM if the customer contacts the support team at a later date.

In this exercise, you'll mark a case as Canceled and then reopen it.

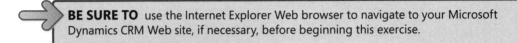

> **BE SURE TO** use the Internet Explorer Web browser to navigate to your Microsoft Dynamics CRM Web site, if necessary, before beginning this exercise.

1. In the **Service** area, click **Cases**. On the grid toolbar, click **New** to create a new case.

2. On the **New Case** form, type or select values in the required fields, as follows:

Field	Value
Title	**Unable to register new software licenses**
Customer	**Sonoma Partners**, or any account in your system
Subject	**Default Subject**, or any subject in your system

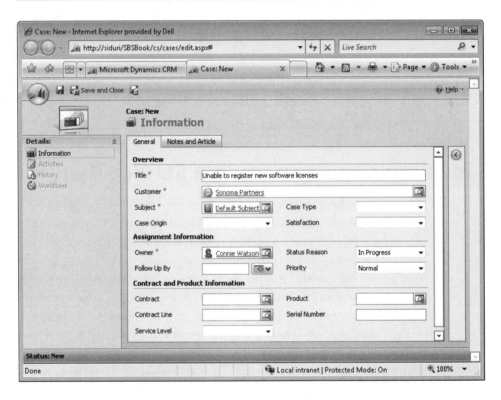

3. Click **Save** to create the case.

4. On the form toolbar, click **Actions**, and select **Cancel Case**.

   The Case Cancel Confirmation dialog box opens.

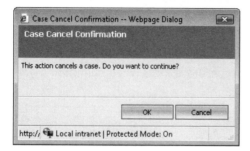

5. In the dialog box, click **OK** to confirm that you want to cancel the case.

   After you click OK, the case updates to Canceled status and all fields on the form are read-only.

6. In the form toolbar, click **Actions**, and select **Reactivate**.

   The Reactivate The Selected Case dialog box opens.

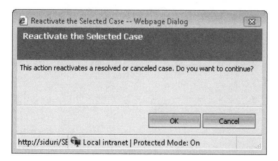

7. In the dialog box, click **OK** to reactivate the case.

   This updates the case to Active status, and all the fields in the form are editable again.

Configuring the Subject Tree

Subjects are categories used to organize products, sales literature, cases, and knowledge base articles in Microsoft Dynamics CRM. Consider the subject tree as an index of topics related to your business. A hierarchical subject tree can be used in Microsoft Dynamics CRM to categorize your business information. Because subject categories are applied across sales and service records, it's important to consider the best categories for your business when configuring your Microsoft Dynamics CRM system.

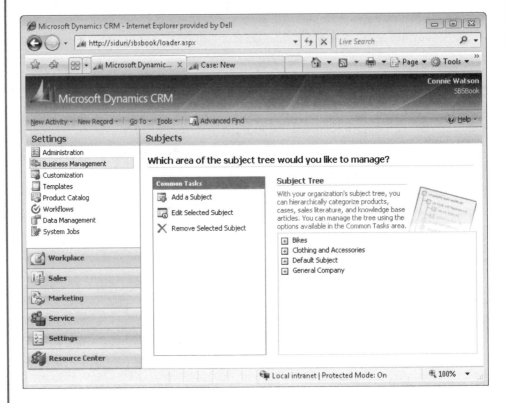

Your subject tree might be aligned to your products or business divisions, or perhaps you want to track customer invoicing questions without relating them to a specific product or service. The following table includes sample subject trees for different industries.

Business type	Sample subject tree

Financial services firm	- Brokerage services
	  - Product A
	    + Client relations
	    + Confirmations
	    + Settlements
	  + Product B
	  + Financial planning
	  + Foreign exchange

Software consulting company	+ Billing
	- Product support
	  + Product A
	  + Product B
	+ Sales and marketing
	+ Service agreements
	- Services
	  + Application development
	  + Consulting

Residential real estate developer	+ Buyers
	- Conversion management
	  + Tenants
	+ Marketing materials
	- Projects
	  - Property A
	    + Units
	    + Other inventory
	    + Warranties
	  + Property B

The subject tree is accessed and updated from the Business Management section of the Settings area in Microsoft Dynamics CRM. Because the right to create, edit, and remove subjects for your organization is considered an administrator function, it is outside the scope of this book. For assistance with creating the subject tree in your Microsoft Dynamics CRM environment, contact your system administrator.

> **Tip** By default, the Subject field is required on the New Case form in Microsoft Dynamics CRM. If you want to create cases before your subject tree is configured, you can make the field optional on the form by using the customization tools. This modification can be made by users with system administrator or system customizer security privileges.

Key Points

- A case represents any service request or support incident for a customer in Microsoft Dynamics CRM. Customer service teams can use cases to manage customer requests and problems.

- Customer service managers can analyze case data to identify frequently occurring customer issues, improve product or service offerings, and streamline the time it takes service representatives to resolve issues.

- By default, Microsoft Dynamics CRM requires that a case be assigned a Subject value. The subject tree allows you to categorize sales and support records in Microsoft Dynamics CRM and should be configured by a system administrator.

- Follow-up activities ensure that steps are taken to resolve a case. A follow-up activity might be a simple task to send a catalog or update a customer's address, or it could be more involved, such as a series of phone calls with the customer, service appointments, or research tasks.

- By tracking activities to a case, customer service managers can add the duration of each completed activity to the total time spent on the case. This total is automatically calculated in the Resolve Case dialog box.

- Maintaining the status value of each case accurately is important to ensure that new issues are addressed in a timely manner and resolved as quickly as possible.

- Cases can be marked as Resolved or Canceled to remove them from the active case list. Updating a case to Resolved or Canceled status makes the case read-only in Microsoft Dynamics CRM; however, cases in these statuses can be reactivated if the customer reports the problem again or additional edits to the case are necessary.

Chapter at a Glance

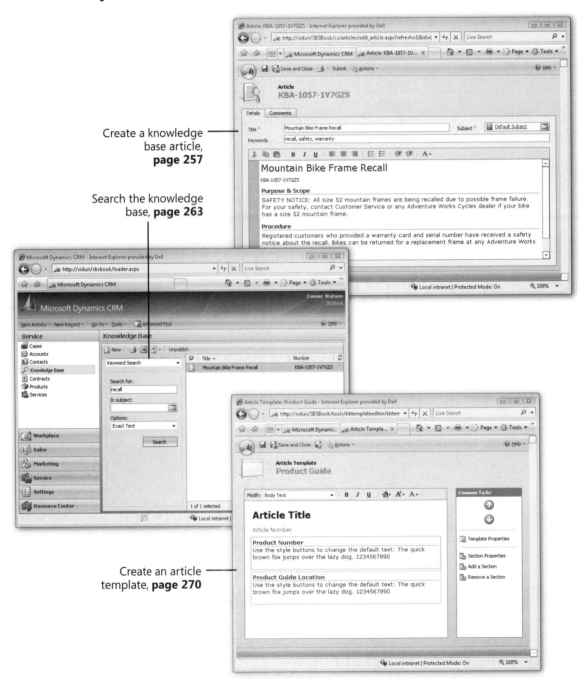

Create a knowledge base article, **page 257**

Search the knowledge base, **page 263**

Create an article template, **page 270**

12 Using the Knowledge Base

In this chapter, you will learn to

✔ Create and submit a knowledge base article.

✔ Publish a knowledge base article.

✔ Search for a knowledge base article.

✔ Remove an article from the knowledge base.

✔ Create and modify a knowledge base article template.

In the previous chapter, you learned how to manage service requests in Microsoft Dynamics CRM. Whether your organization tracks the questions, comments, and problems submitted by your customers as cases in Microsoft Dynamics CRM or elsewhere, over time there will probably be common themes or patterns in the service requests. This should make recurring cases easier to resolve, but often the organizational knowledge collected in service requests is lost in the sheer volume of cases managed by each representative. Another challenge in retaining experience and organizational knowledge on customer service teams is the high turnover common on many teams.

Beyond quantitative analysis of case-related metrics—such as the number of cases per customer or the average time it takes to resolve a case—customer service teams can benefit from a qualitative repository of case summaries, whittled down to include the information that will help the team respond to future service requests quickly and accurately. Combined, the qualitative and quantitative stores of data can become a powerful source for improving service to customers and driving sales, marketing, and product development processes to better meet customers' needs.

In this chapter, you'll learn how to build a *knowledge base*—a collection of *articles* in Microsoft Dynamics CRM that can be referenced by customer service representatives when answering questions about an organization's products or services. Articles are text based and can include product user guides, summaries of recurring problems and their solutions, and frequently asked questions (FAQs) assembled by the customer service team. Any information that can be used to quickly answer questions from customers, prospects, and other parties can be stored in your organization's knowledge base.

Like service request cases, knowledge base articles are assigned a subject, tying knowledge base articles to the same business categories used to group other sales and service records in Microsoft Dynamics CRM. For articles, subjects also provide the user with a quick way to search for information on a particular topic even if the specific article title is not known. Because a subject value is required for each article, you should make sure your subject tree is configured before you create an article. For assistance with creating the subject tree in your Microsoft Dynamics CRM environment, contact your system administrator.

See Also For more information about subject trees, see the "Configuring the Subject Tree" sidebar in Chapter 11, "Tracking Service Requests."

> **Tip** Although many fields can be marked as optional instead of required in Microsoft Dynamics CRM forms, the Article form *cannot* be modified. However, during the installation process, a *Default Subject* value is created in the subject tree. You can select the *Default Subject* value for articles prior to configuring your subject tree, if necessary.

A well-organized knowledge base can reduce the amount of time customer service representatives spend searching for answers and reference documents on behalf of customers. In this chapter, you will learn how to build a knowledge base by creating, publishing, searching for, and modifying articles in Microsoft Dynamics CRM.

> **Important** There are no practice files for this chapter.

> **Troubleshooting** Graphics and operating system–related instructions in this book reflect the Windows Vista user interface. If your computer is running Windows XP and you experience trouble following the instructions as written, refer to the "Information for Readers Running Windows XP" section at the beginning of this book.

> **Important** The images used in this book reflect the default form and field names in Microsoft Dynamics CRM. Because the software offers extensive customization capabilities, it's possible that some of the record types or fields have been relabeled in your Microsoft Dynamics CRM environment. If you cannot find the forms, fields, or security roles referenced in this book, contact your system administrator for assistance.

> **Important** You must know the location of your Microsoft Dynamics CRM Web site to work the exercises in this book. Check with your system administrator to verify the Web address if you don't know it.

Creating and Submitting a Knowledge Base Article

In addition to a subject value, each article contains a title, a list of search keywords, and the content, which varies by article template. You'll learn more about configuring article templates later in this chapter. For this first exercise, you'll use one of the templates included with Microsoft Dynamics CRM.

Knowledge base articles are not assigned to customers; instead, the information contained in each article is typically applicable to a subset of customers—or even all customers. In this exercise, you will create a new article detailing a product recall and then submit it to the customer service manager for review.

USE a user account that has the Customer Service Representative security role or another role with privileges to create, read, and write knowledge base articles.

BE SURE TO use the Windows Internet Explorer Web browser to navigate to your Microsoft Dynamics CRM Web site before beginning this exercise.

1. In the **Service** area, click **Knowledge Base** to view the article queue.

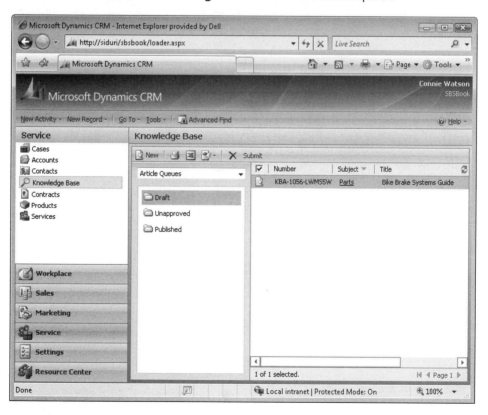

New Article

2. In the grid toolbar, click the **New** button.

The Select A Template dialog box opens.

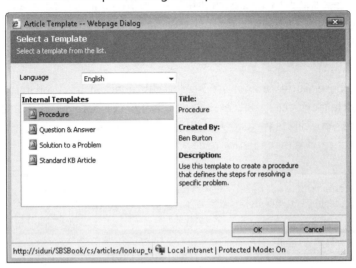

3. In the dialog box, select the **Procedure** template, and then click **OK**.

4. In the **New Article** form, in the **Title** field, enter **Mountain Bike Frame Recall**.

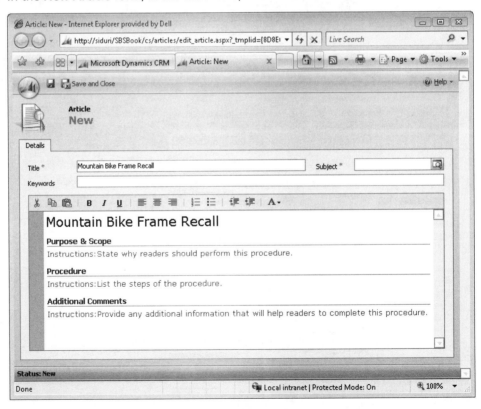

> **Tip** As you update the Title field, your title automatically updates in the article's text editor.

5. In the **Subject** field, select **Default Subject** or any other subject in your system.

6. In the **Keywords** field, enter the following: **recall, safety, warranty**.

> **Tip** Keywords allow users to quickly find articles. Even though Microsoft Dynamics CRM does not require you to provide keywords, consider entering common words or phrases relevant to your article.

7. In the article text editor, click the red text under the **Purpose & Scope** section heading and enter the following: **SAFETY NOTICE: All size 52 mountain frames are being recalled due to possible frame failure. For your safety, contact Customer Service or any Adventure Works Cycles dealer if your bike has a size 52 mountain frame.** Note that the instruction text is automatically hidden when you begin typing in each section.

8. In the **Procedure** section, enter the following: **Registered customers who provided a warranty card and serial number have received a safety notice about the recall. Bikes can be returned for a replacement frame at any Adventure Works Cycles dealer.**

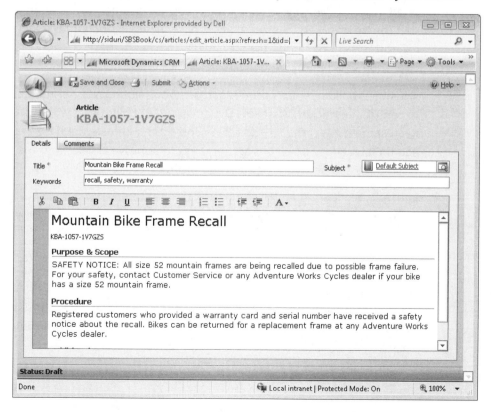

Save

9. Click the **Save** button to create the article.

> **Tip** When an article is saved for the first time, it is automatically assigned an article number. Article auto-numbering is configured by system administrators in the Administration section of the Settings area. By default, each article is created with a three-character prefix (*KBA*), a four-digit code, and a six-character identifier—for example, *KBA-1057-1V7GZS*. If you have security rights to modify auto-numbering settings in your Microsoft Dynamics CRM system, you can modify the article prefix applied to each new article.

 10. Click the **Submit** button in the form toolbar to move the article into the **Unapproved** queue so that it can be reviewed by a customer service manager.

 CLOSE the new article record created in the exercise.

Publishing a Knowledge Base Article

After you have created a knowledge base article in Microsoft Dynamics CRM, the article is saved as a draft. When you submit the article, it is moved to an Unapproved article queue so it can be reviewed by a customer service manager and either rejected for further revisions or approved into the searchable knowledge base. A knowledge base article cannot be searched by other users before it is published.

When first building your knowledge base, you might ask other members of your team to contribute articles. Microsoft Dynamics CRM allows users with the Customer Service Representative security role to create and submit knowledge base articles; however, additional security privileges are required to approve articles into the Published queue, where they can be searched and referenced by other users.

> **Tip** The Publish Articles security privilege can be modified on the Service tab of any security role. To grant article publishing rights to a user, contact your system administrator.

The submit-and-publish process for articles allows many members of a team to contribute articles, but as a best practice, only a few team members should be able to review the articles and publish them into the knowledge base. Those with publishing rights should be tasked with making the articles as comprehensive and accurate as possible.

In this exercise, you'll publish the article submitted in the previous section into the knowledge base.

USE a user account that has the CSR Manager security role or another role with privileges to publish knowledge base articles, and use the bike frame recall article you created in the previous exercise.

BE SURE TO use the Internet Explorer Web browser to navigate to your Microsoft Dynamics CRM Web site, if necessary, before beginning this exercise.

1. In the **Service** area, click **Knowledge Base**, select the **Unapproved** article queue, and then select the mountain bike frame recall article without opening it.

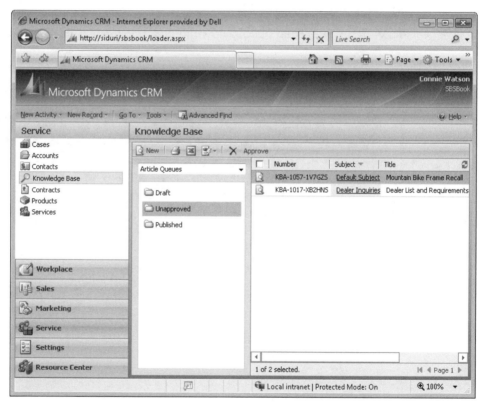

2. In the grid toolbar, click the **Approve** button to mark the article as approved.

Approve

> **Tip** You can approve multiple articles by selecting all of the articles you want to publish and then clicking the Approve button. Alternatively, you can also publish individual articles from the Article form.

The Article Submittal Confirmation dialog box opens.

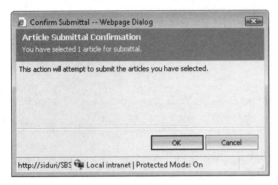

3. In the dialog box, click **OK**.

4. View the **Published** queue and verify that the article is displayed there.

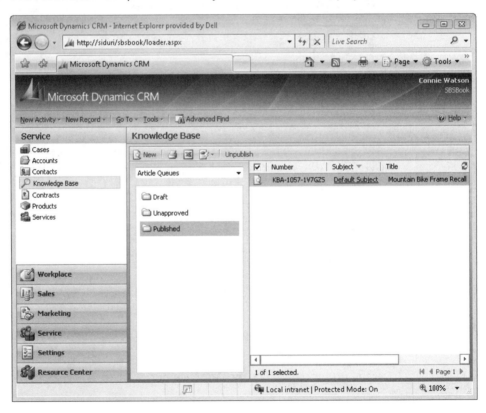

Searching for a Knowledge Base Article

Published articles can be searched by article text, title, number, or keywords. Additionally, you can browse the subject tree to find all articles for a specific subject. The knowledge base search page can be accessed in two places in Microsoft Dynamics CRM:

- In the Service area, by clicking Knowledge Base in the left navigation pane, and then selecting the search type.

- In the Workplace area, by clicking Articles in the left navigation pane.

From both locations, Microsoft Dynamics CRM provides the following options to browse or search the knowledge base articles in your system.

Search option	Description
Article Queues	Lists articles by status in one of three queues: Draft, Unapproved, or Published.
Full Text Search	Searches article content based on the text you enter.
Keyword Search	Searches articles by the keyword field that the article's author completed. This approach is useful for quickly finding relevant articles but requires the author to properly complete the keywords field.
Title Search	Searches article titles based on the text you enter.
Article Number Search	Searches articles based on the article number you enter.
Subject Browse	Lists articles by the assigned subject values.

In this exercise, you'll submit a keyword search to retrieve the mountain bike frame recall article published in the previous exercise.

USE a user account that has the Customer Service Representative security role or another role with privileges to read subjects and articles, and use the mountain bike frame recall article you published in the previous exercise.

BE SURE TO use the Internet Explorer Web browser to navigate to your Microsoft Dynamics CRM Web site, if necessary, before beginning this exercise.

1. In the **Service** area, click **Knowledge Base** to view the article queue.

2. Click the arrow next to **Article Queues**, and select **Keyword Search** from the list.

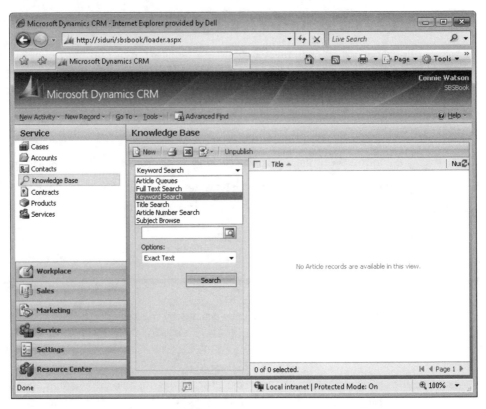

3. In the **Search for** field, enter **recall** as the keyword. Leave **Exact Text** selected in the Options field, and then click the **Search** button.

> **Tip** The Exact Text option limits your search to those articles that match your keyword exactly. For example, if you enter *recalls* in your search, Microsoft Dynamics CRM will *not* return an article that has *recall* listed in the keyword field. You can expand your search to include articles with keywords that match a portion of a word or a similar word by selecting Use Like Words.

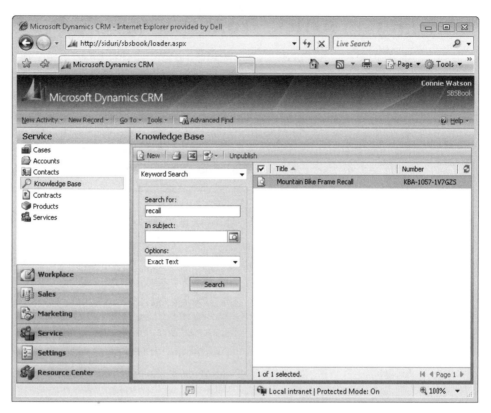

4. Double-click the mountain bike frame recall article in the results pane to view the article. Note that the article is read-only and cannot be edited.

 CLOSE the knowledge base article.

Removing an Article from the Knowledge Base

After an article has been published to the knowledge base, it cannot be edited by any users, regardless of their security roles. So what happens when the product guide included in an article is updated or the recall period for a product ends? Articles can be unpublished from the knowledge base for updates or revisions, or they can be removed by being deleted from the database. Each knowledge base article must be in one of the three article queues in Microsoft Dynamics CRM—Draft, Unapproved, or Published. Articles can move from one queue to another as shown in the following table.

Article queue	Action	Description
Draft	Submit	Moves the article into the Unapproved queue for management review.
Draft	Delete	Deletes the article record from Microsoft Dynamics CRM.
Unapproved	Reject	Moves the article back to the Drafts queue for further revisions.
Unapproved	Approve	Moves the article to the Published queue so it can be searched and referenced by other users.
Unapproved	Delete	Deletes the article record from Microsoft Dynamics CRM.
Published	Unpublish	Removes the article from the active knowledge base and returns it to the Unapproved queue.

Important The availability of these actions varies based on the security privileges for each user. If you do not see one or more of the above options in the toolbar on the Article form, you might not have the necessary security privileges to perform that action.

Tip As articles move through each queue, users have the ability to add comments to indicate updates that need to be made or other notes about the article. The comments are accessed on a tab on the Article form, so users can quickly reference the notes for each article. However, the comments are not searchable.

In this exercise, you'll unpublish the article approved earlier in this chapter and assign it back to the Draft queue so it can be updated with additional information about the product recall.

USE the mountain bike frame recall article created and approved earlier in this chapter.

BE SURE TO use the Internet Explorer Web browser to navigate to your Microsoft Dynamics CRM Web site, if necessary, before beginning this exercise.

OPEN the Published article queue in Microsoft Dynamics CRM.

1. In the **Published** article queue, locate the mountain bike frame recall article.

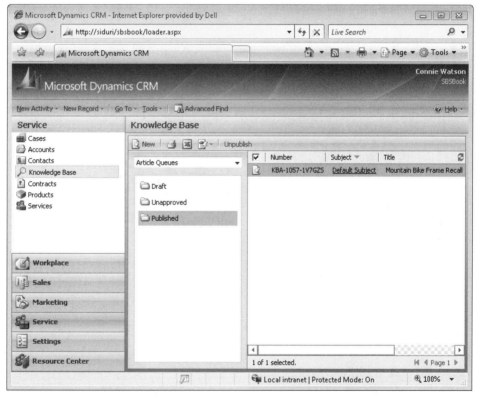

2. Select the article and, in the grid toolbar, click the **Unpublish** button.

The Article Unpublish Confirmation dialog box opens.

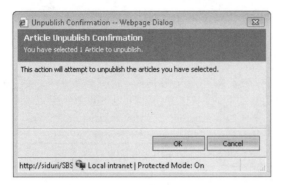

3. In the dialog box, click **OK** to verify that you want to unpublish the article.

4. Go to the **Unapproved** article queue and open the mountain bike frame recall article.

5. In the form toolbar, click the **Reject** button to move the article to the **Draft** queue so that a customer service representative can update it with additional recall information.

6. In the **Provide a Reason** dialog box, enter the following reason for rejecting the article: **Update with serial numbers for recall information.**

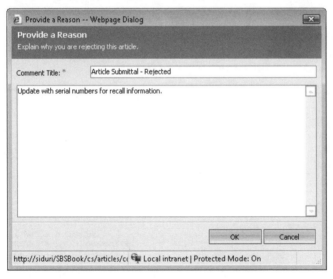

7. Click **OK** to move the article to the **Draft** queue.

8. On the **Article** form, click the **Comments** tab to verify that the rejection note appears, so that the customer service representative knows what updates are needed for the article.

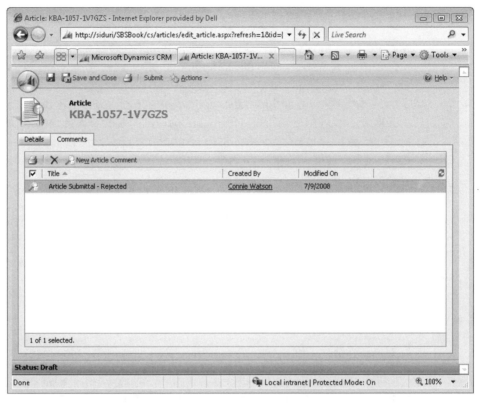

By double-clicking the comment, you can view the additional details about why the article was rejected.

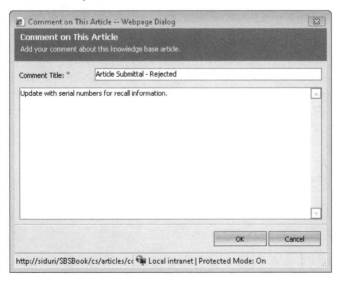

CLOSE the article.

Creating and Modifying Article Templates

Microsoft Dynamics CRM includes several templates for formatting knowledge base articles. The templates typically contain one or two sections, such as a Question section and an Answer section, which provide the people tasked with creating knowledge base articles with content and formatting guidelines for each article type. You might want to add a section to an existing template or even create a custom template to capture knowledge base information specific to your organization. Customer service managers can change section heading names and add instructional text to article templates, as well as modifying the font face, size, and color.

For example, assume that the customer service manager at the bike company wants to make sure that part numbers are included for all product articles. To ensure that this information is included in the knowledge base articles created by the customer service team, each template will be updated with a new section called Product Number.

In this exercise, you'll create a new product guide template for the bike company that includes a section specifically for the product number.

> **Important** The CSR Manager security role in Microsoft Dynamics CRM has privileges to create and modify article templates. If the role has been altered in your environment or if you do not have rights to modify the templates, contact your system administrator. Rights to modify article templates are configured on the Service tab of each security role.

> **Tip** If you do not want your customer service team to use one of the templates included with Microsoft Dynamics CRM, you can remove the template from the Select A Template dialog box that displays when a new article is created. You do this by deactivating the template. To deactivate a template, click Templates in the Settings page, and then click Article Templates. Select the template you want to remove, and select Deactivate from the More Actions menu in the grid toolbar.

> **USE** a user account that has the CSR Manager security role or another role with privileges to create and update article templates.
>
> **BE SURE TO** use the Internet Explorer Web browser to navigate to your Microsoft Dynamics CRM Web site, if necessary, before beginning this exercise.

1. In the **Settings** area, click **Templates**, and then click **Article Templates**.

New Article
Template

2. Click the **New** button to create a new article template.

3. In the **Article Template Properties** dialog box, enter the following values:

Field	Value
Title	Product Guide
Description	Details and location of product guide
Language	English

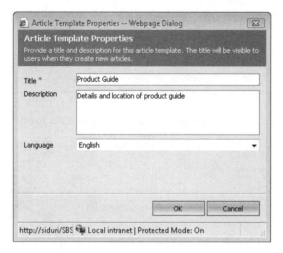

4. Click **OK**.

The New Article Template form opens.

5. In the **Common Tasks** pane on the right side of the form, click **Add a Section**.

6. In the **Add a New Section** dialog box, enter the following values:

Field	Value
Title	Product Number
Instructions	Specify the product number.

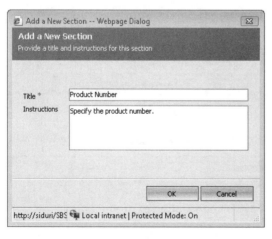

7. Click **OK**.

8. Click the **Add a Section** button again to add a second section to the template.

9. In the **Add a Section** dialog box, enter the following values:

Field	Value
Title	Product Guide Location
Instructions	Enter the URL for the product guide.

10. Click **OK**.

11. Click the **Save** button to create the new article template.

> **Tip** The instructions entered in the template will display when new articles are created from the template, so use the Instructions field to provide as much detail as possible for the people creating your articles when adding sections to templates. In addition to listing the desired content in the Instructions field, you might also consider providing sample formatting or other examples.

 CLOSE the article template.

Key Points

- The knowledge base in Microsoft Dynamics CRM is a store of useful product and service information and other resources relevant to your organization.

- One objective of the knowledge base is to capture the collective "know-how" of the customer service team so that it can be easily searched and referenced by other team members when answering common customer requests.

- Knowledge base articles can include any information that helps customer service representatives provide more timely and accurate customer service. Examples of article content include user guides, data sheets or schematics for products or services, frequently asked questions (FAQs), or summaries of recurring problems and their solutions.

- Articles are automatically moved through a workflow as they are published in Microsoft Dynamics CRM. As they are reviewed, articles are moved between three queues: Draft, Unapproved, and Published.

- Only customer service managers have the right to publish articles into the knowledge base so that they can be searched by other users, but customer service representatives can contribute to the knowledge base by creating and submitting articles for management approval.

- Only published articles are available to other members of the organization. Articles with Draft or Unapproved status cannot be searched or accessed by other users.

- Knowledge base articles can be searched by title, keywords, text, subject, and article number. The knowledge base search screen can be accessed from the Workplace or Service pages in Microsoft Dynamics CRM.

- Microsoft Dynamics CRM includes several templates to provide a framework for the layout and content of knowledge base articles. Customer service managers can create or modify article templates in the Settings section if additional information is needed on templates.

Chapter at a Glance

Create a contract
template, **page 279**

Create a service
contract, **page 279**

Assign a case to a
service queue, **page 294**

Accept a case from a
service queue, **page 294**

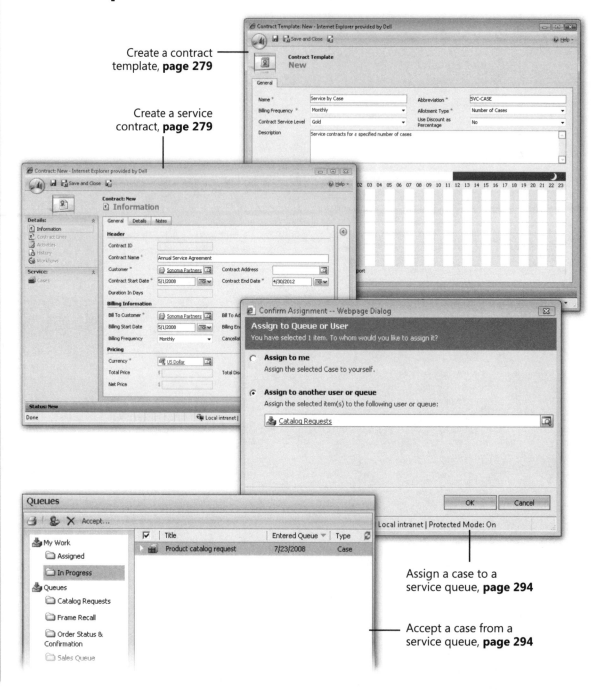

13 Working with Contracts and Queues

In this chapter, you will learn to

✔ Create a contract template.

✔ Create a service contract with a contract line.

✔ Activate and renew a contract.

✔ Create a queue and assign a case to it.

✔ Accept a case from a queue.

In the previous chapters, you learned about cases and knowledge base articles, which capture the customer requests and product information used by customer service teams to address support issues. Most of the service requests your company receives are not likely to be resolved by referencing a single knowledge base article. Instead, each request is probably routed through an involved process that includes verifying a customer's information and service agreement terms, obtaining details about the problem, and escalating to the correct customer service representative to resolve the case. Large customer service teams typically have several tiers of support resources, so that senior-level representatives can focus on complex or advanced issues while level-one representatives take calls from customers and verify basic information.

To manage the routing process of service requests, Microsoft Dynamics CRM allows customer service teams to manage multiple service agreement types and submit cases to service *queues*. Service contracts are agreements that define the support terms offered to a customer, either during a specified time period or for a specified number of cases or hours. Each *contract* contains one or more contract lines, which are the line-item details such as service term, pricing, and other conditions for the services specified in the contract. Contracts are valuable if your organization offers support services to its customers, because they allow customer service representatives to quickly identify each customer's eligibility for support.

After verifying that a customer is eligible for customer service, the level-one representative creates a case detailing the issue and submits it to the team's work queue so that another representative can research the solution. A queue is a holding bin of open cases and activities that need to be completed. Queues can be accessed by multiple members of a team so that individuals can accept new work items as they complete old ones.

Contracts and queues are used to manage customer service processes to ensure that customer requests are handled efficiently. In this chapter, you'll learn how to create, activate, and renew service contracts for your customers and use queues to distribute cases to your customer service team.

Important The exercises in this chapter require only records created in earlier chapters; none are supplied on the companion CD. For more information about practice files, see "Using the Companion CD" at the beginning of this book.

Troubleshooting Graphics and operating system–related instructions in this book reflect the Windows Vista user interface. If your computer is running Windows XP and you experience trouble following the instructions as written, refer to the "Information for Readers Running Windows XP" section at the beginning of this book.

Important The images used in this book reflect the default form and field names in Microsoft Dynamics CRM. Because the software offers extensive customization capabilities, it's possible that some of the record types or fields have been relabeled in your Microsoft Dynamics CRM environment. If you cannot find the forms, fields, or security roles referenced in this book, contact your system administrator for assistance.

Important You must know the location of your Microsoft Dynamics CRM Web site to work the exercises in this book. Check with your system administrator to verify the Web address if you don't know it.

Creating a Service Contract

Even if you don't work at a call center, your company probably provides some type of post-sale support to customers. To offset support costs within an organization, many companies sell service agreements to customers to ensure that the customer's questions or problems are addressed within predefined terms, such as response time, guarantee of resolution, and availability. The terms of a service agreement vary for different organizations and industries. For example, a large manufacturing company might offer warranties on parts and repair calls, and a professional services firm might offer support for a set number of incidents or a specified period of time.

Microsoft Dynamics CRM provides the flexibility to set up several different types of *contract templates*, which provide the framework for service contracts. Each contract template has an *allotment type* that indicates the units of service, such as number of cases, coverage dates, or time. You can create as many templates as needed in your organization. The following table details the components of a contract template.

Field	Description
Name	The name of the contract template.
Abbreviation	An abbreviation of the template name. This is displayed with the name when you create a new contract.
Billing Frequency	The invoice frequency for the contract, such as monthly, bi-monthly, quarterly, or annually.
Allotment Type	The service units of the contract, which could be number of cases, coverage dates, or time.
Contract Service Level	The rating of the customer service level. The default values are Gold, Silver, and Bronze.
Use Discount As Percentage	A configuration field in which you can set discount amounts as a percentage or as a fixed dollar value.
Description	Additional comments or a description of the contract template.
Calendar	The hours of availability by day for the contract. This is typically set to include regular business hours but can be configured for 24-hour, 7-days-a-week support.

> **Tip** Because you can't create a contract without a contract template, Microsoft Dynamics CRM includes a default contract template named Service. You can access this template in the Templates section of the Settings area.

In Microsoft Dynamics CRM, each contract must be created from a contract template. The values from the contract template drive the content of each contract record, although some values—such as the service level and the discount type—can be overridden at the contract level. After creating a contract, customer service managers add line items (*contract lines*) to specify the details of the agreement. The following list describes some typical examples of contracts and contract lines:

- A local park district provides contracts to refreshment vendors to manage cleanup and facility maintenance requests. In this example, contract lines are allotted a number of minutes to be used toward maintenance.

- A plumber offers two types of service contracts, one to provide a one-year warranty on services and another to track incident-based requests. In this example, contract lines are allotted coverage dates for the first type of contract and a number of cases for the second type.

- A financial services firm offers incident-based support to large brokerage clients to ensure that preferred customers receive high-priority, 24/7 support. In this example, contract lines are allotted a number of cases.

- A medical supply provider manages setup and maintenance of home health care supplies for patients on behalf of hospitals and insurance companies. In this example, contract lines are allotted a fixed number of service calls for particular products.

In this exercise, you will create a contract template for a case-based service agreement and then use it to create a contract that provides 20 service cases.

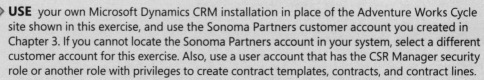

USE your own Microsoft Dynamics CRM installation in place of the Adventure Works Cycle site shown in this exercise, and use the Sonoma Partners customer account you created in Chapter 3. If you cannot locate the Sonoma Partners account in your system, select a different customer account for this exercise. Also, use a user account that has the CSR Manager security role or another role with privileges to create contract templates, contracts, and contract lines.

BE SURE TO use the Windows Internet Explorer Web browser to navigate to your Microsoft Dynamics CRM Web site before beginning this exercise.

1. In the **Settings** area, click **Templates**, and then click **Contract Templates** to view the available templates.

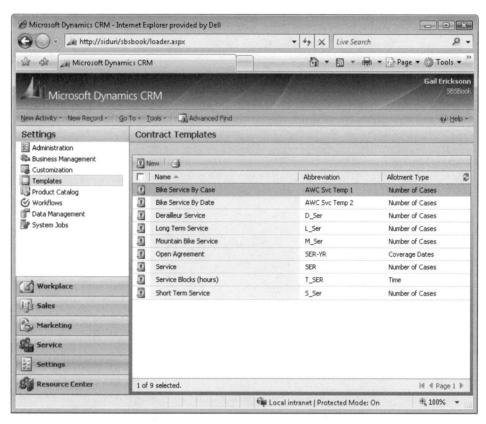

New Contract
Template

2. Click the **New** button to launch the **New Contract Template** form.

3. Complete the **New Contract Template** form with the following values:

Name	Service by Case
Abbreviation	SVC-CASE
Billing Frequency	Monthly
Allotment Type	Number of Cases
Contract Service Level	Gold
Use Discount as Percentage	No
Description	Service contracts for a specified number of cases

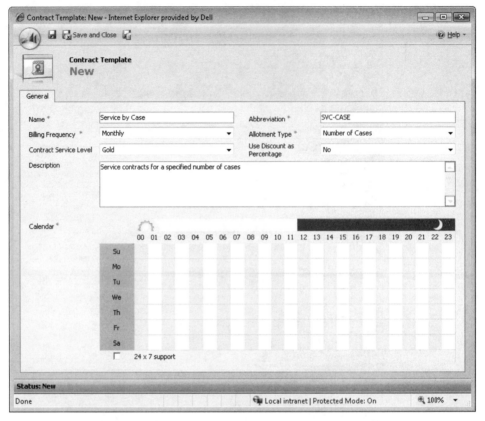

4. In the **Calendar** area, click the days and hours to designate the availability of service resources for the agreement from 09:00 until 17:00, Monday through Friday.

> **Tip** The Calendar hours are based on a 24-hour day, so 5:00 P.M. displays as 17:00. When configuring the availability dates for your contract templates, you can click the day (row) or hour (column) headings in the Calendar area to toggle the settings for all cells of that value. For example, if you click the 08 column heading, all of the days will be set to available for 08:00. If you click the column heading again, you will toggle all of the days to unavailable at 08:00.

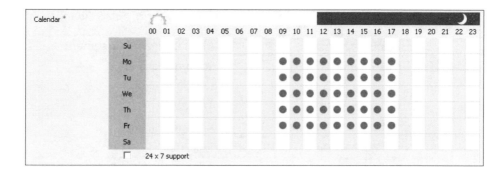

> **Important** At least one time slot must be marked for availability in the Calendar area before you can save a contract template. Green dots indicate the times that support is offered. If your organization does not limit when customer service is offered, select the 24 x 7 Support check box below the calendar to mark all days as available. Calendar settings are not enforced when service requests are created.

Save and Close

5. In the form toolbar, click the **Save and Close** button to finish creating the contract template.

6. Navigate to the **Service** area, and click **Contracts**.

New Contract

7. Click the **New** button to launch the **New Contract** form.

The Template Explorer dialog box opens.

8. In the **Template Explorer** dialog box, select the **SVC-CASE - Service by Case** template, and then click **OK**.

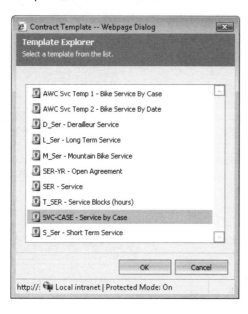

9. On the **General** tab of the **New Contract** form, enter the following values:

Contract Name	Annual Service Agreement
Customer	Sonoma Partners
Contract Start Date	5/1/2008
Contract End Date	4/30/2012
Bill To Customer	Sonoma Partners
Billing Start Date	5/1/2008
Billing End Date	4/30/2012
Billing Frequency	Monthly

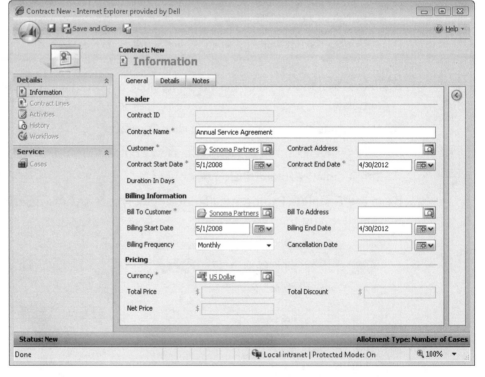

10. On the **Details** tab of the **New Contract** form, verify that the **Discount** type is set to **Amount** and the **Service Level** field is set to **Gold**, based on the template settings.

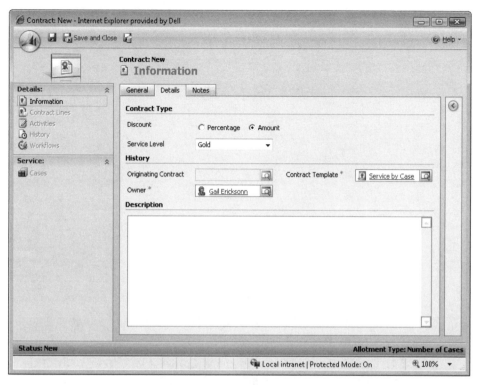

11. Click the **Save** button to create the contract.

Save

> **Tip** Microsoft Dynamics CRM automatically assigns a unique identifying number to each contract when it is first saved. Similar to auto-numbering for cases and knowledge base articles, contract numbering can be configured by system administrators in the Administration section of the Settings pane. By default, each case is created with a three-character prefix (*CNR*), a four-digit code, and a six-character identifier—for example, *CNR-1006-V7PQMB*.

12. In the left navigation area of the new contract, click **Contract Lines**.

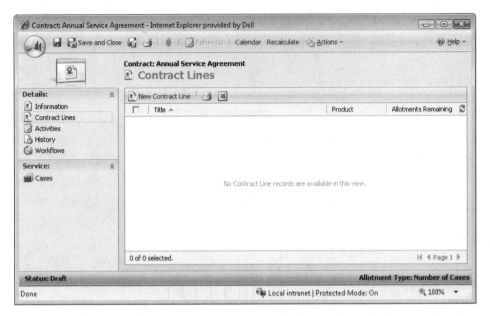

New Contract
Line

13. Click the **New Contract Line** button in the grid toolbar to launch the **New Contract Line** form.

14. On the **General** tab of the **New Contract Line** form, in the **Title** field, enter **FY2008-2009 Agreement**.

15. Verify that the **Start Date** and **End Date** fields default to **7/1/2008** and **6/30/2009**, respectively.

> **Important** Microsoft Dynamics CRM validates the start and end dates entered in the contract line to ensure that the end date does not occur in the past and that both the start and end dates are within the Contract Start Date and Contract End Date fields specified on the Contract form. If the end date of 6/30/2009 occurs in the past, you will need to change it to a future date to complete this exercise.

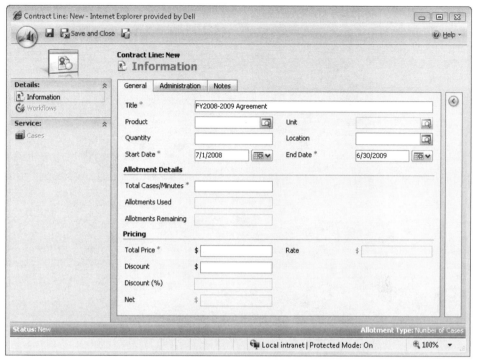

16. In the **Total Cases/Minutes** field, enter 20.

> **Tip** For this example, the Total Cases/Minutes field will be required on the form, because the associated contract template allots a number of cases to the contract. When a contract template with an allotment type of Coverage Dates is used, the Total Cases/Minutes field will be read-only on the form, because the contract covers a time period rather than a set number of cases or minutes.

17. In the **Total Price** field, enter **10,000**. In the **Discount** field, enter **2,500**.

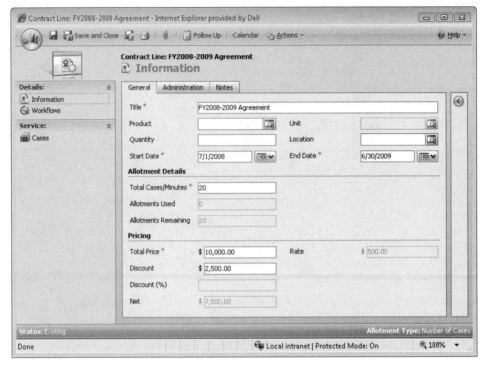

18. Click **Save** to create the contract line.

> **Important** Each time the Contract Line form is saved, several fields are updated automatically based on system calculations. In the Allotment Details section, the total allotted cases or minutes logged against the contract line is subtracted from the Total Cases/Minutes value to display the Allotments Remaining. In the Pricing section, the net charge is recalculated based on the Total Price and Discount values, and a rate per case is calculated based on the Total Price and Total Cases/Minutes values.

19. Click **Save and Close** to save and close the contract line.

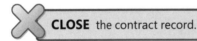 **CLOSE** the contract record.

Activating and Renewing a Contract

When a contract is created in Microsoft Dynamics CRM, the system assigns a default status of Draft to the contract. Only contracts in Draft status can be edited; once a contract has been processed to Invoiced or Active status, the fields in the contract are locked. At this point, service cases can be logged against the contract and a running tally of used cases or time is tracked against the total allotment specified in the contract line.

Given the need for a business to lock down the terms of a contract while still allowing for flexibility as the company's needs change, the life cycle of a contract can become complicated. Consider the following scenarios for why a service contract might change:

- A company's internal team takes over support for a software application, so it cancels its support agreement with a consulting firm.

- A customer service manager receives notification from her company's accounting department that a customer has several past due invoices for support services, so the manager places the customer's service contract on hold to prevent any new cases from being created until the balance is paid.

- Upon the expiration of a year-long service agreement, a customer decides to renew the contract for another year of service.

Not every contract will follow a fixed life cycle from start to finish, so it's important to understand how contract statuses are managed in Microsoft Dynamics CRM and what actions are allowed for each status. The following table provides an overview of contract statuses and actions.

Status	Description	Actions
Draft	Default status when a contract is created.	Can be edited or deleted. No cases can be assigned. Cannot be placed on hold, canceled, or renewed.
Invoiced	Indicates that the contract has been accepted by the customer and has a pending start date. A contract cannot be moved to this status until it has at least one contract line.	Cannot be edited or deleted. No cases can be assigned. Can be placed on hold or canceled. Cannot be renewed.
Active	Indicates that the contract is within the specified start and end dates and eligible for support cases. Each contract is automatically moved to this status on the specified start date.	Cannot be edited or deleted. Cases can be assigned. Can be placed on hold or canceled. Can be renewed.

(continued on the next page)

Status	Description	Actions
On Hold	Indicates that the contract is on hold from Active status, typically for further review or negotiation with the customer.	No actions can be taken against the contract until the hold is released. No cases can be assigned.
Canceled	Indicates that the contract was canceled prior to the end date by the organization or the customer.	Cannot be edited or deleted. No cases can be assigned. Can be renewed.
Expired	Indicates that the contract has passed the specified end date without being renewed.	Cannot be edited or deleted. No cases can be assigned. Can be canceled. Can be renewed.

In this exercise, you will move the contract created in the previous section to Invoiced status, log a case against it, and then renew it.

USE your own Microsoft Dynamics CRM installation in place of the Adventure Works Cycle site shown in this exercise, and use the contract created in the previous exercise. Also, use a user account that has the CSR Manager security role or another role with privileges to create and edit contracts, contract lines, and cases.

BE SURE TO use the Internet Explorer Web browser to navigate to your Microsoft Dynamics CRM Web site, if necessary, before beginning this exercise.

1. In the **Service** area, click **Contracts**, and then double-click the contract created in the previous exercise.

Actions

2. On the form toolbar, click the **Actions** button, and then select **Invoice Contract**.

Important After you select Invoice Contract, the contract's status is updated to Invoiced if the start date is in the future, or Active if the start date is the current date or a past date. When a contract is in Invoiced or Active status, all fields on the contract are read-only.

3. In the left navigation area of the contract, click **Cases** to view the case manager for the contract.

New Case

4. On the grid toolbar, click the **New Case** button to open a new case against the contract.

5. In the **New Case** form, enter the following values:

Title	Replace water line for company coffee machine
Customer	Sonoma Partners
Subject	Default
Case Type	Problem
Case Origin	Phone
Contract	**Annual Service Agreement** (created in the previous exercise)
Contract Line	**FY2008-2009 Agreement** (created in the previous exercise)

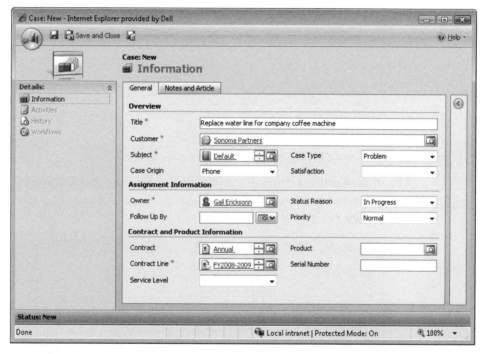

6. Click **Save** to create the case.

7. On the form toolbar, click **Actions**, and then click **Resolve Case** to mark the case as resolved.

> **Tip** Only resolved cases are counted against the total allotment specified on the contract line. For each resolved case, the remaining allotment is recalculated. For example, if a contract line has five cases specified in the Total Cases/Minutes field, it's possible to log six or more cases against it, as long as no more than five of those cases are in Resolved status.

8. In the **Resolve Case** dialog box, in the **Resolution** field, enter **Water line replaced**.

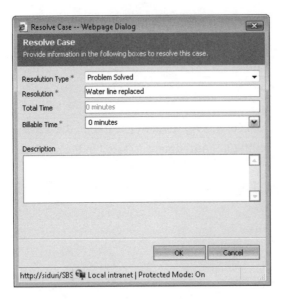

9. Click **OK** to mark the case as resolved.

Close

10. Click the **Close** button to close the case window.

Refresh

11. In the **Contract** form, in the left navigation area, click **Contract Lines**. Then click the **Refresh** button, if needed, to verify that the **Allotments Remaining** value is updated to 19.

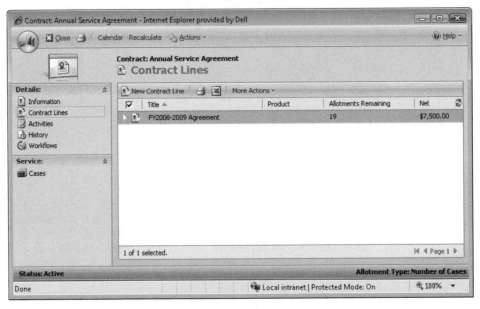

12. On the form toolbar, click **Actions**, and then click **Renew Contract** to renew the contract for another term.

> **Tip** Use the Actions menu on the form toolbar to update the status of a contract. From this menu, you can also cancel or place a contract on hold. The actions that are available vary, depending on the current status of the contract.

13. In the **Renew Contract** dialog box, leave the **Include canceled contract lines** check box selected, and then click **OK**.

> **Important** When a contract is renewed, Microsoft Dynamics CRM automatically creates a copy of the contract with updated start and end dates. The new contract defaults to Draft status and has the same contract number as the original.

14. Close the active contract.

In the Service area, in the Contracts view, note that a new contract in Draft status has been created with the same number as the active contract.

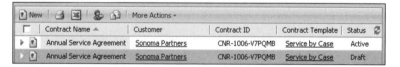

15. Double-click the renewed contract in **Draft** status, and verify that the start and end dates are automatically calculated as an extension of the original contract.

> **Tip** Microsoft Dynamics CRM creates a link between the original contract and the renewed contract. You can find this information in the Originating Contract field on the Details tab of the Contract form.

 CLOSE the contract record.

Working with Service Queues

In addition to managing the number of cases or service hours billed to customers with contracts, customer service teams can use service queues to improve the routing of cases and ensure that each request is handled efficiently. In Microsoft Dynamics CRM, a queue is a public listing of open cases and activities. Queues are typically set up based on team assignments or subject matter expertise on a product or service.

When a case is assigned to a service queue, it is shared by the group of users that have access to the queue until it is accepted by or assigned to a customer service representative. Microsoft Dynamics CRM displays your queue information within the Workplace area. In the *My Work* folder, you will notice the following two folders:

- **Assigned.** Open activities and cases assigned to the user, but not yet accepted by the user.

- **In Progress.** Open activities and cases owned by the user (including activities and cases not related to a queue).

Customer service managers can create queues in the Business Management section in the Settings area. A user can accept items from queues or assign items from his or her *Assigned* or *In Progress* folder to a group queue or to another user. After a case is accepted by a user, it is moved to the user's *In Progress* folder and cannot be accepted by other team members.

In Microsoft Dynamics CRM, most records—such as accounts and contacts—can be assigned only to users. Therefore, queues cannot own an activity or case, but Microsoft Dynamics CRM allows you to assign a record to a user *or* a queue. When you assign an activity or case to a queue, the owner of the activity or case is always a system user, but the record also appears in the specified queue. When the record has been assigned to a queue, other queue users can accept the record out of the queue, at which point Microsoft Dynamics CRM changes the record ownership to the accepting user.

See Also With the workflow manager in Microsoft Dynamics CRM, you can set up routing rules to automatically assign cases to the appropriate queue. Although the workflow feature is beyond the scope of this book, you can learn more about it in *Working with Microsoft Dynamics CRM 4.0*, by Mike Snyder and Jim Steger (Microsoft Press, 2008).

If you enter an e-mail address when you create a queue, you can have service requests received by that e-mail address delivered directly to the queue. All inbound e-mail messages to that address are then created as e-mail activity records in Microsoft Dynamics CRM and are displayed in the queue so that customer service representatives can accept each e-mail message and follow up accordingly. You can select from the following options when configuring e-mail messages to automatically display in a queue:

- All e-mail messages sent to the specified address.

- All e-mail messages sent to the specified address in response to messages sent from Microsoft Dynamics CRM.

- All e-mail messages sent to the specified address from a lead, contact, or account in your Microsoft Dynamics CRM database.

You do not need to supply an e-mail address when setting up a queue, but this feature is helpful for customer service teams that receive a lot of service requests via e-mail.

Tip You can remove e-mail messages from a queue by selecting the records to remove and then clicking Delete. This will remove the messages from the queue without deleting them from Microsoft Dynamics CRM. Only e-mail messages can be removed from queues this way. Deleting any other activity or case from a queue deletes it completely from Microsoft Dynamics CRM!

In this exercise, you will create a service queue and assign a case to it. You will then accept the case into your In Progress queue.

USE your own Microsoft Dynamics CRM installation in place of the Adventure Works Cycle site shown in this exercise, and use the Product Catalog Request case you created in Chapter 11. If you cannot locate the Product Catalog Request case, select a different active case for this exercise. Also, use a user account that has the CSR Manager security role or another role with privileges to create queues and cases.

BE SURE TO use the Internet Explorer Web browser to navigate to your Microsoft Dynamics CRM Web site, if necessary, before beginning this exercise.

1. In the **Settings** area, click **Business Management**, and then click **Queues** to view the available queues.

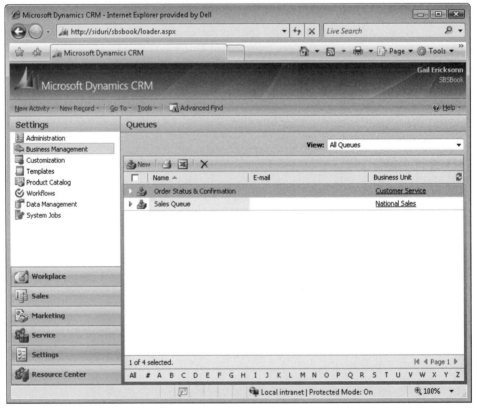

2. Click the **New** button to launch the **New Queue** form.

New Queue

3. In the **New Queue** form, enter the following information:

Queue Name	Catalog Requests
Business Unit	This will vary among individual systems. Select any business unit.
E-mail	someone@example.com
Owner	This will vary among individual systems, so select your user account.
Description	**Catalog fulfillment requests**
Convert to e-mail activities	**All e-mail messages**
E-mail access type - Incoming	None
E-mail access type - Outgoing	None

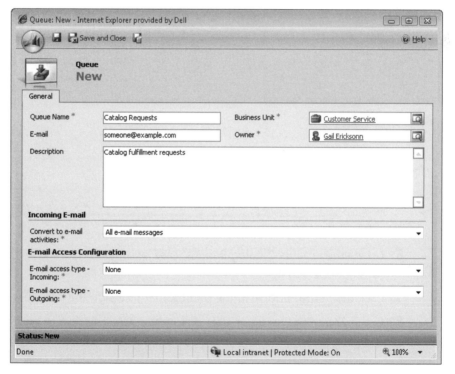

4. Click **Save and Close** to create the queue.

5. In the **Service** area, click **Cases** to view the case manager.

6. Locate the Product Catalog Request case, and then select the record in the grid (without opening it).

Assign

7. Click the **Assign** button in the grid toolbar to assign the case to a queue.

8. In the **Assign to Queue or User** dialog box, select **Assign to another user or queue**, and select the **Catalog Requests** queue. Then click **OK**.

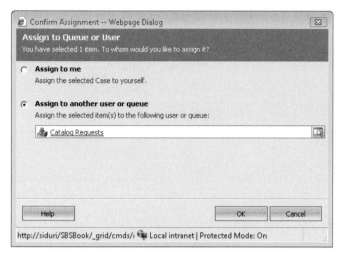

9. In the **Workplace** area, click **Queues**, and then click the **Catalog Requests** queue to verify that the case you assigned appears.

10. Ensure that the case is selected. Then, in the queue toolbar, click the **Accept** button to accept the case into your personal queue.

The Move Items To In Progress dialog box opens.

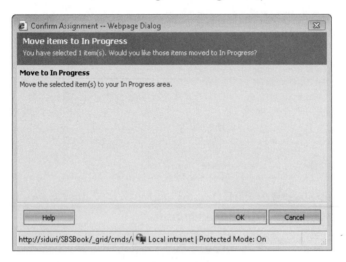

11. Click **OK** to verify that you are accepting the case.

12. In the queue manager, click the **In Progress** queue and verify that the case now appears.

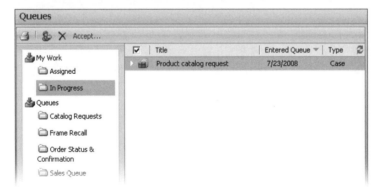

Key Points

● Service contracts can be used to manage support requests from customers. Each contract includes the duration of the agreement, the number of incidents or hours of service, pricing, and customer billing information. Multiple contract lines can be assigned to a contract to store the particular terms of each agreement.

● Customer service managers can create contract templates to establish the framework for service contracts. Each contract must be created from a contract template.

● Contracts can be edited only while in Draft status, so it's important that customer service representatives complete the contract terms as thoroughly and accurately as possible before moving the contract to Invoiced status.

● Each contract in Invoiced status is automatically moved to Active status on the specified start date and moved from Active to Expired status on the end date if the contract has not been renewed.

● Cases can be logged against only those contracts that are in Active status.

● A contract can be renewed while in Active, Canceled, or Expired status. When renewing a contract, Microsoft Dynamics CRM creates a copy of the original contract and stores a link to the originating contract on the new record.

● Contracts can be placed on hold or canceled to prevent new cases from being logged against them.

● Customer service teams can share cases and other work activities in queues to ensure that all service requests are routed to the correct people and resolved quickly.

● By default, each user has two queues in the Workplace area: an Assigned queue to manage cases and activities assigned to the user, and an In Progress queue of items accepted by the user.

● Cases remain in a queue until they are accepted by a customer service representative, who assumes responsibility for handling them or escalating them to another representative.

● Service requests submitted via e-mail can be assigned to a queue automatically, if an e-mail address was assigned to the queue during setup.

Part V

Data Management

Chapter at a Glance

Create duplicate
detection rules,
page 306

Use the Duplicate
Detection Wizard,
page 311

View duplicate
detection jobs,
page 315

Resolve potential
duplicate records,
page 315

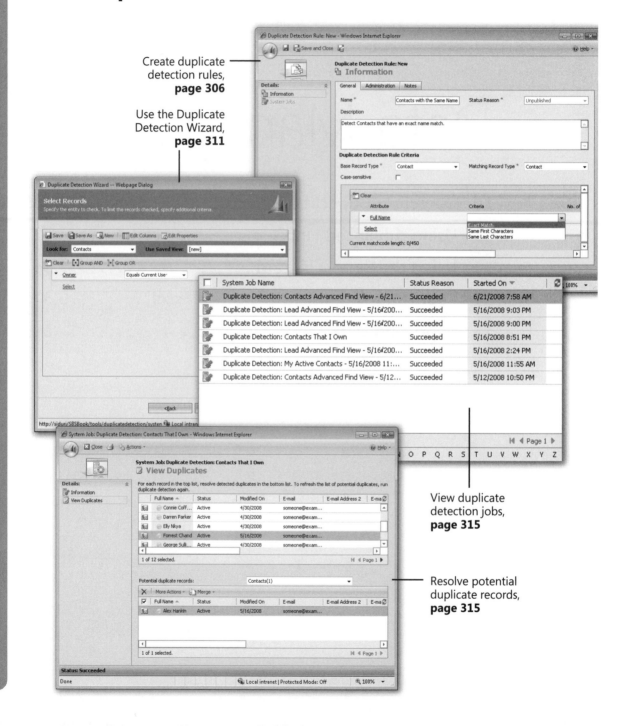

14 Detecting Duplicate Records

In this chapter, you will learn to

✔ Create duplicate detection rules.

✔ Use the Duplicate Detection Wizard.

✔ View the results of a duplicate detection job.

✔ Resolve duplicate records.

✔ Create advanced duplicate detection rules.

Data quality is a key factor in the success of your Microsoft Dynamics CRM application. A pristine database leads to accurate reporting and higher user adoption. A large threat to data consistency is duplicate records. Although it is easy to enter a duplicate record in CRM applications, Microsoft Dynamics CRM provides you with a great tool that lets you detect duplicates before and after they are entered. Common examples of duplicate records are:

● A company entered under both its legal name and an acronym (for example, *Affordable Sports Equipment* and *ASE*).

● A contact entered under the individual's full name and a nickname (for example, *Michael Alexander and Mike Alexander*).

In this chapter, you will learn how to create duplicate detection rules to keep your Microsoft Dynamics CRM database free of duplicates. You will also learn how to detect duplicate records and react appropriately by using delete, deactivate, or merge functionality.

> **Important** There are no practice files for this chapter.

> **Troubleshooting** Graphics and operating system–related instructions in this book reflect the Windows Vista user interface. If your computer is running Windows XP and you experience trouble following the instructions as written, refer to the "Information for Readers Running Windows XP" section at the beginning of this book.

> **Important** The images used in this book reflect the default form and field names in Microsoft Dynamics CRM. Because the software offers extensive customization capabilities, it's possible that some of the record types or fields have been relabeled in your Microsoft Dynamics CRM environment. If you cannot find the forms, fields, or security roles referenced in this chapter, contact your system administrator for assistance.

> **Important** You must know the location of your Microsoft Dynamics CRM Web site to work the exercises in this book. Check with your system administrator to verify the Web address if you don't know it.

Creating Duplicate Detection Rules

Many organizations define duplicate records uniquely. Some have simple rules that include a single field match (for example, e-mail address), and others determine duplicates based on multiple field matching criteria using both partial and complete text. Consider the following scenarios, along with their related pros and cons.

Duplicate detection rule	Pros	Cons
Detect contact records with the same e-mail address	If you are working with contacts at companies, each person typically has a unique e-mail address.	If you are working with contacts unrelated to a company, contacts might be using a shared email address (for example, *TheSmiths@example.com*).
Detect account records with the same street address, city, and state	Most street addresses will belong to just one company, especially if you are diligently capturing suite numbers.	If you are working with companies in metropolitan areas, it is common to have many companies at one street address. (For example, more than 100 companies work in the Sears Tower in Chicago.)

Microsoft Dynamics CRM empowers you to determine the logic that is right for your needs and allows you to implement that logic by using a simple wizard. System administrators can specify when duplicate detection rules run. For example, duplicate detection rules can be set to run at the following times:

- When a record is created or updated
- When Microsoft Dynamics CRM for Outlook goes from offline to online
- During data import

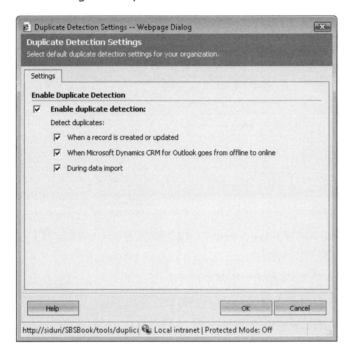

In this exercise, you will create duplicate detection rules.

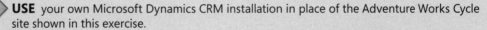

USE your own Microsoft Dynamics CRM installation in place of the Adventure Works Cycle site shown in this exercise.

BE SURE TO use the Windows Internet Explorer Web browser to navigate to your Microsoft Dynamics CRM Web site before beginning this exercise.

1. In the **Settings** area, click **Data Management**, and then select **Duplicate Detection Rules**.

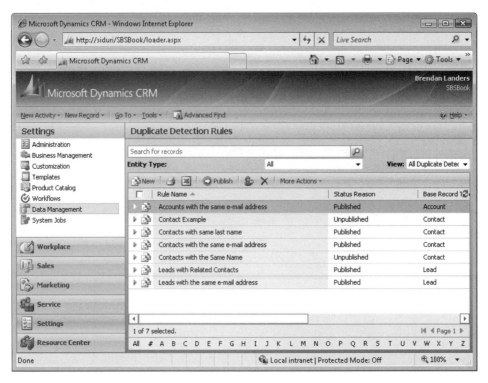

Some duplicate detection rules might be already listed. Microsoft Dynamics CRM includes three default rules:

- Accounts with the same e-mail address
- Contacts with the same e-mail address
- Leads with the same e-mail address

These rules are self-explanatory; any two account, contact, or lead records with the same e-mail address will be considered duplicates when these rules are run.

> **Tip** As you can see from the three default rules, each duplicate detection rule runs within a single record type (accounts, contacts, or leads). If you would like to run the same rule across more than one record type, you must create a rule for each record type.

New Duplicate
Detection Rule

2. In the grid toolbar, click the **New** button.

The New Duplicate Detection Rule form opens.

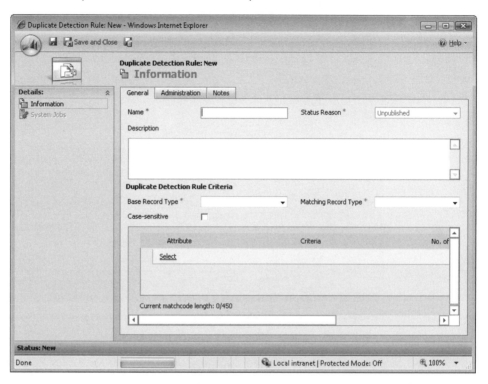

3. Complete the **New Duplicate Detection Rule** form by using the following values:

Name	Contacts with the same name
Description	Detect Contacts that have an exact name match.
Base Record Type	Contact
Attribute	Full Name
Criteria	Exact Match

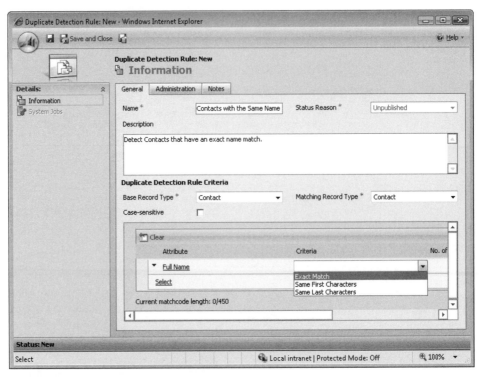

Save and Close

4. In the form toolbar, click the **Save and Close** button.

5. Select the newly created duplicate detection rule, and click **Publish**.

You have successfully created a duplicate detection rule. Now, when a duplicate detection job is run against contacts, this rule will run along with any other rules that exist.

Duplicate Detection Rule Field Criteria

The criteria available for creating a duplicate detection rule vary depending on the data type of the field selected in the Attribute list. The only type of field not available for use in duplicate detection rules is a yes/no (or bit) field, usually represented by a check box or radio button. The following table illustrates the criteria available for each related field type.

Field Type	Available Criteria
Text	Exact match Same first characters Same last characters
Integer	Exact match
Date	Same date Same date and time
Pick List	Exact match

Using the Duplicate Detection Wizard

In this section, you will learn how to leverage the Duplicate Detection Wizard to identify duplicate records. The Duplicate Detection Wizard allows you to check for duplicate account, contact, and lead records. You can detect duplicates for all records or specify a subset of records for which you would like to detect duplicates.

For example, imagine that you are a sales representative who is assigned several hundred customer records. You are sure that you have duplicate contact records in the system due to a lack of historical maintenance, and you want to check all contacts that you own for duplicates. You can limit the records checked to only those that are assigned to you with the Duplicate Detection Wizard. The Duplicate Detection Wizard is located within Microsoft Dynamics CRM and walks you through an intuitive process of detecting duplicates.

In this exercise, you will run the Duplicate Detection Wizard and detect duplicate records in your Microsoft Dynamics CRM environment.

USE your own Microsoft Dynamics CRM installation in place of the Adventure Works Cycle site shown in the exercise.

BE SURE TO use the Internet Explorer Web browser to navigate to your Microsoft Dynamics CRM Web site, if necessary, before beginning this exercise.

1. In the application menu toolbar, click **Tools**.

2. Click **Duplicate Detection**.

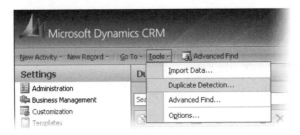

The Duplicate Detection Wizard opens.

3. Click **Next**.

The Select Records dialog box opens. This dialog box allows you to specify which records you would like to check for duplicates. You can specify filter criteria in this dialog box or choose a saved view to leverage its filter criteria. Additionally, you can select a saved view to populate default criteria and modify the default criteria to meet your needs.

4. In the **Look for** list, select **Contacts**.

5. Click **Select** and scroll through the possible filter fields to select **Owner**.

6. Select the **Equals Current User** operator.

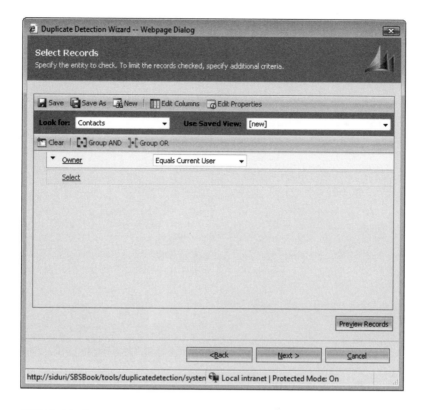

> **Tip** You can click Preview Records at any point to ensure that the expected records are returned. This is helpful to ensure that you have defined your filter criteria correctly.

7. Click **Next**.

In the Select Options dialog box that opens, you can name the duplicate detection job, specify the start time, select a desired recurrence, and identify who should be notified after the job has completed.

8. In the **Name** box, enter **Duplicate Detection: Contacts That I Own**. Leave the default start time, and click **Next**.

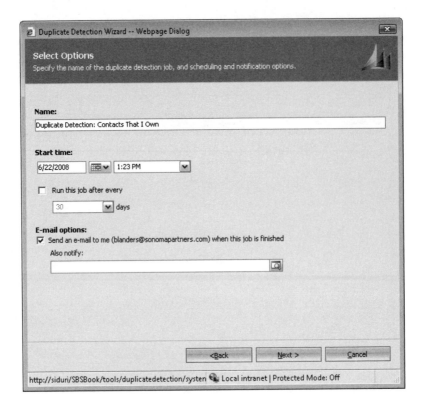

> **Tip** You are creating a system job when you complete the Duplicate Detection Wizard. Microsoft Dynamics CRM allows you to schedule the job at intervals of 7, 30, 90, 180, and 365 days. If you would like to run the job on a different frequency, you can schedule multiple jobs to accomplish. For example, if you would like to run a job every 15 days, you can create two jobs that run every 30 days with different start dates.

9. Click **Finish**.

The duplicate detection job is run when you click the Finish button. The job identifies duplicate records but does not automatically merge or delete records that are identified. The next step is to view the results of the job and take the appropriate actions.

Viewing the Results of a Duplicate Detection Job

Detecting potential duplicates is relatively simple. Detecting absolute duplicates and automatically taking action against those records is a very dangerous concept. You probably would not want a record to automatically be deactivated or deleted because it is potentially a duplicate. Therefore, Microsoft Dynamics CRM handles the detection of duplicate records and provides the mechanism for you to evaluate the potential duplicate and take the appropriate actions.

Consider the following example. Assume that you have a duplicate detection rule that has the following criteria:

- Match on first three letters of First Name
- Exact match on Last Name
- Exact match on Address 1: Street 1
- Exact match on Address 1: ZIP/Postal Code

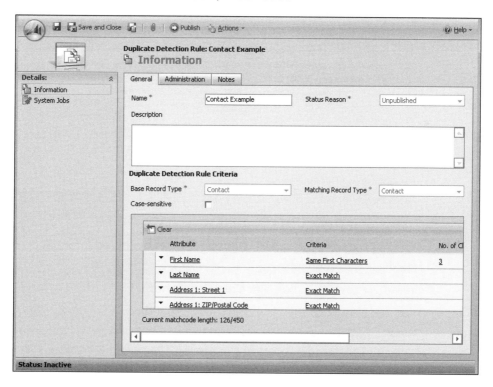

If there are two contacts—say, Michael Alexander and Michelle Alexander—associated to the same account in your system and you execute the above duplicate detection rules, Microsoft Dynamics CRM will find a potential duplicate. Although most of the potential duplicates identified would be actual duplicates, exceptions such as this will occur.

In this exercise, you will review potential duplicate records and take action against those records.

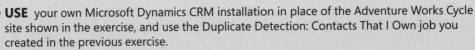

USE your own Microsoft Dynamics CRM installation in place of the Adventure Works Cycle site shown in the exercise, and use the Duplicate Detection: Contacts That I Own job you created in the previous exercise.

BE SURE TO use the Internet Explorer Web browser to navigate to your Microsoft Dynamics CRM Web site, if necessary, before beginning this exercise.

1. In the **Workplace** area, click **Duplicate Detection**.

The list of duplicate detection jobs appears.

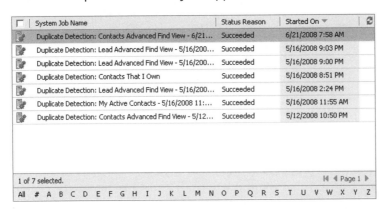

2. Open the **Contacts That I Own** job.

The information page opens. This page shows high-level information about the duplicate detection job.

3. In the left navigation bar, click **View Duplicates**.

Two lists appear on the View Duplicates page. The top list shows all records for which a potential duplicate was found. The bottom list shows the potential duplicates for the record selected in the top list. The potential duplicate list refreshes dynamically based on the record selected in the top list.

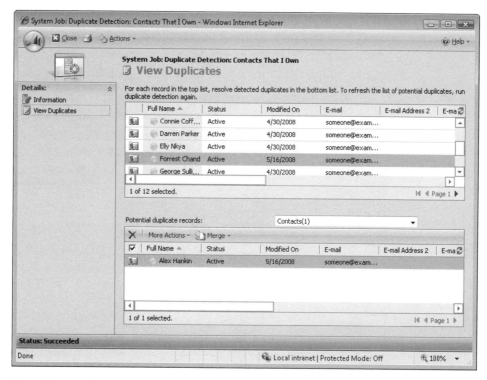

Now that you know the list of potential duplicates, you can take action on these records. You can take the following actions on the potential duplicate records by using the menu options on the toolbar:

Menu	Action	Outcome
Merge	Automatically	The potential duplicate record is merged with the selected record in the top list and deactivated.
Merge	Select Master	The native merge dialog box is presented, on which the user can select master fields.
More Actions	Edit	The potential duplicate record is opened for the user to modify.
More Actions	Deactivate	The potential duplicate record is deactivated.
More Actions	Activate	The potential duplicate record is activated.
Delete	Delete	The potential duplicate record is deleted.

4. Select the top record in the list that has an actual duplicate record in the bottom list.

5. Select the duplicate record in the bottom list.

Merge

6. On the toolbar at the top of the **Potential duplicate records** area, click the **Merge** button, and then click **Select Master**.

The Merge Records dialog box opens. This dialog box allows you to combine data fields from two records into a single record, which is considered the master. After you have completed the merge process, the master record inherits all of the child records of the subordinate record, and the subordinate record is deactivated.

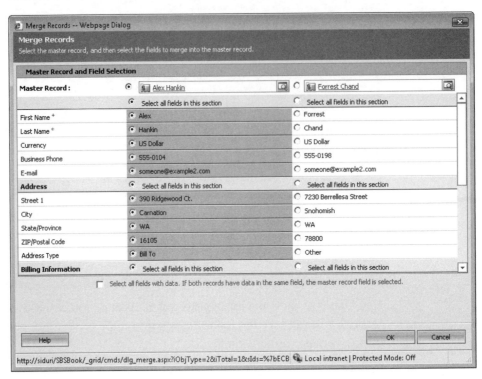

7. Choose the correct master record fields, and click **OK**.

8. Now that you have resolved the first duplicate record, select the next record in the list and determine the appropriate course of action. Continue until all potential duplicates have been resolved.

You have completed the duplicate detection process. As you can see, you have flexibility over the rules, over when duplicate detection runs, and over the available actions to take and their related outcomes.

The process just described *reactively* addresses duplicate records. Microsoft Dynamics CRM also allows you to address duplicate records *proactively.* When you save or update a record, if a potential duplicate record is found, you are presented with the potential duplicate record. You can then decide which action to take, such as:

● Canceling the save of the record

● Saving the record

● Editing the potential duplicate records

● Deactivating the potential duplicate records

● Activating the potential duplicate records

Creating Advanced Duplicate Detection Rules

So far in this chapter, you have identified and executed simple duplicate detection rules. Simple rules might not solve all of your duplicate detection needs, however. In this section, you will learn how to implement more complex duplicate detection rules.

In this exercise, you will create a single duplicate detection rule that will include the following scenarios:

● The rule will include partial match criteria. For example, you could match on the first three letters of the first name plus the last name.

● The rule will identify a duplicate record based on a different record type. For example, you could identify active leads that have a corresponding active contact.

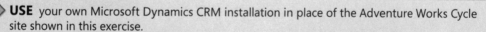

USE your own Microsoft Dynamics CRM installation in place of the Adventure Works Cycle site shown in this exercise.

BE SURE TO use the Internet Explorer Web browser to navigate to your Microsoft Dynamics CRM Web site, if necessary, before beginning this exercise.

1. In the **Settings** area, click **Data Management**.

2. Click **Duplicate Detection Rules,** and then click the **New** button.

3. Complete the **New Duplicate Detection Rule** form with the following values:

Name	**Leads with related contacts**
Base Record Type	**Lead**
Matching Record Type	**Contact**
Base Record Attribute	**First Name**
Matching Record Attribute	**First Name**
Criteria	**Same First Characters**
No. of Characters	**3**
Base Record Attribute (second row)	**Last Name**
Matching Record Attribute (second row)	**Last Name**
Criteria (second row)	**Exact Match**

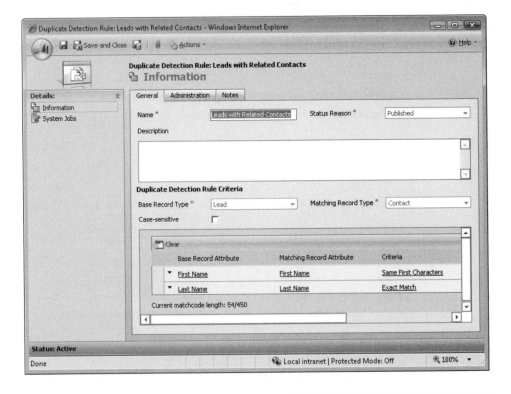

> **Tip** You can compare a base record attribute with any matching record attribute. For example, you might want a duplicate detection rule that compares the base record's First Name field to the matching record's Nickname field.

4. In the form toolbar, click **Save and Close**.

You have now created a duplicate detection rule that uses a partial match and compares one type of record (leads) against another (contacts). The process of resolving the duplicates is largely the same as checking a single entity, but be aware of the following:

- You cannot merge records of two different types (for example, a lead and a contact). However, you can delete or deactivate the potential duplicate record.

- In the potential duplicate records list, you might have to toggle between record types to see all potential duplicates.

Key Points

- The user can configure duplicate detection rules. Your organization can have many different duplicate detection rules that run in parallel to search for potential duplicates.

- The Duplicate Detection Wizard allows you to create a duplicate detection job that can be run at a predefined time or on a recurring basis.

- Microsoft Dynamics CRM allows you to decide how to take action against a potential duplicate record. You can merge the records, delete a record, or update a record's status by activating or deactivating it.

- Advanced duplicate detection rules can be set up to include partial match searching and detection across multiple record types.

Chapter at a Glance

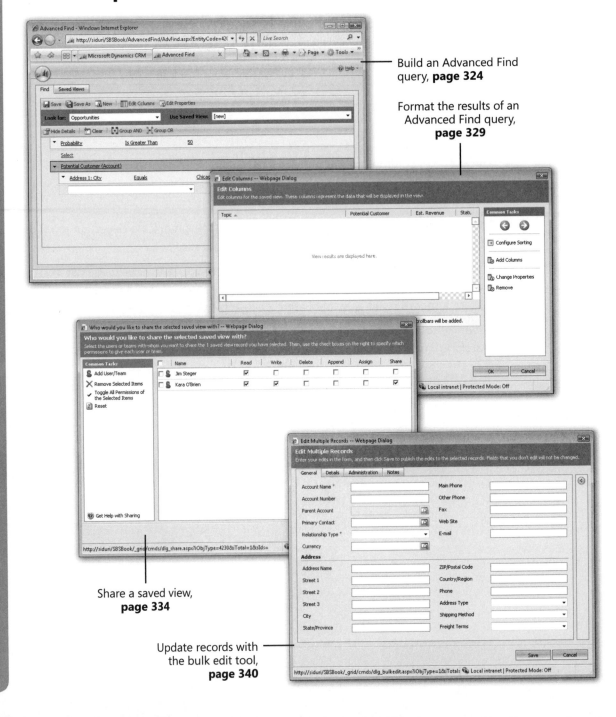

Build an Advanced Find query, **page 324**

Format the results of an Advanced Find query, **page 329**

Share a saved view, **page 334**

Update records with the bulk edit tool, **page 340**

15 Using Advanced Find

In this chapter, you will learn to

✔ Perform ad hoc queries by using Advanced Find.

✔ Organize and format Advanced Find results.

✔ Create a saved view.

✔ Use saved views to share your queries with other users.

✔ Build a complex query to search data.

✔ Use bulk edit and bulk assign to take action on query results.

An important benefit of CRM systems is the central repository of customer data that builds as sales, marketing, and customer service teams track their interactions with customers. As this store of data grows, managers face the need to report on and analyze the data to understand trends and identify areas for improvement. Microsoft Dynamics CRM provides a variety of tools for extracting data and presenting it in a simple and easy-to-use format. This chapter focuses on the best tool for this task: Advanced Find. The Advanced Find tool lets you create your own queries through a simple interface. When end users are empowered to create reports and filter the results to return a specific data set, they rely less on IT resources to do their job. In addition, this flexibility will increase an organization's IT resources to focus on more complex business requirements.

In this chapter, you will learn to harness the power of the Advanced Find tool by creating a query, saving it as a system view that can be shared with others, and updating multiple records in the results set.

> **Tip** Advanced Find respects the security settings of the end user. As a rule of thumb, you can assume that if a user can see the record elsewhere in the application, that user will be able to gain access to it within Advanced Find.

> **Important** There are no practice files for this chapter.

> **Troubleshooting** Graphics and operating system–related instructions in this book reflect the Windows Vista user interface. If your computer is running Windows XP and you experience trouble following the instructions as written, refer to the "Information for Readers Running Windows XP" section at the beginning of this book.

> **Important** The images used in this book reflect the default form and field names in Microsoft Dynamics CRM. Because the software offers extensive customization capabilities, it's possible that some of the record types or fields have been relabeled in your Microsoft Dynamics CRM environment. If you cannot find the forms, fields, or security roles referenced in this chapter, contact your system administrator for assistance.

> **Important** You must know the location of your Microsoft Dynamics CRM Web site to work the exercises in this book. Check with your system administrator to verify the Web address if you don't know it.

Performing Advanced Find Queries

Business needs can change frequently over the course of a project and, as a result, reporting needs also change. Therefore, ad hoc reporting has become a standard feature within most business applications, because expecting end users to define all of their reporting needs before a system is implemented is unrealistic. The Advanced Find tool within Microsoft Dynamics CRM provides a flexible interface to query, view, analyze, and update data on an ongoing basis, so that predefined queries can be saved as the system is implemented and new queries can be created as the reporting needs of your business change. Examples of how Advanced Find is commonly leveraged by end users include:

- Configuring a customized to-do list to follow up on open opportunities.
- Determining leads that fall into a specific geographical region for distribution and assignment.
- Finding all activities due on the current date for a specific customer service representative who has called in sick, so that the activities can be reassigned to a different representative.
- Obtaining a list of contacts that have not been modified in more than two years, so that they can be considered for deactivation.

Advanced Find queries rely on an intuitive set of operators that you select when building a query. The data fields you select in your query determine the operators that will be available for filtering. The following table highlights the operators available for the different data fields.

Data type	Operators	
User (Owner)	Equals Current User	Contains
	Does Not Equal Current User	Does Not Contain
	Equals	Begins With
	Does Not Equal	Does Not Begin With
	Contains Data	Ends With
	Does Not Contain Data	Does Not End With
Text	Equals	Does Not Contain
	Does Not Equal	Begins With
	Contains Data	Does Not Begin With
	Does Not Contain Data	Ends With
	Contains	Does Not End With
Numeric	Equals	Is Less Than
	Does Not Equal	Is Less Than Or Equal To
	Is Greater Than	Contains Data
	Is Greater Than Or Equal To	Does Not Contain Data
Date	On	This Year
	On Or After	Last X Hours
	On Or Before	Next X Hours
	Yesterday	Last X Days
	Today	Next X Days
	Tomorrow	Last X Weeks
	Next 7 Days	Next X Weeks
	Last 7 Days	Last X Months
	Next Week	Next X Months
	Last Week	Last X Years
	This Week	Next X Years
	Next Month	Any Time
	Last Month	Older Than X Months
	This Month	Contains Data
	Next Year	Does Not Contain Data
	Last Year	

For each query, you can specify as many search criteria as you need. You must designate the primary record type you want returned in the results, but you can also include data fields from related records in your query. For example, you might search for top sales opportunities that are assigned to sales representatives in a certain geographical region. Your search could include the data fields the sales team uses to rate opportunities as well as the sales region field for the user records to which opportunities are assigned.

In this exercise, you will create an Advanced Find query to view the opportunities that have a probability value greater than 50 for accounts in the city of Chicago.

USE your own Microsoft Dynamics CRM installation in place of the Adventure Works Cycle site shown in this exercise.

BE SURE TO use the Windows Internet Explorer Web browser to navigate to your Microsoft Dynamics CRM Web site before beginning this exercise.

Advanced Find

1. On the application menu toolbar, click the **Advanced Find** button.

The Advanced Find screen opens.

2. In the **Look for** list, select **Opportunities**.

This specifies the primary entity for which you will be executing the query.

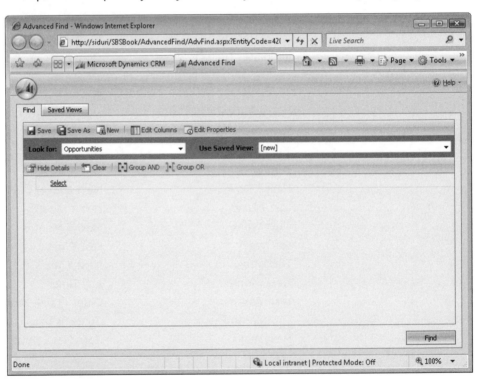

3. In the **Select** field, choose **Probability** to set the search criteria for the opportunity's **Probability** field.

A second list of operators is displayed to the right of the Select field.

> **Tip** The Select field shows all searchable fields for the specified entity. System administrators can modify the selection of fields that are searchable in the database.

4. In the **Operator** field, select **Is Greater Than**. Then, in the **Enter Value** field, enter **50**.

> **Tip** The Select field turns into a list when you click on it, and a new row automatically appears below each row you add to your query, so you can add as many rows as needed in your search criteria.

5. In the second row of the Advanced Find query, in the **Select** field, scroll to the bottom of the list to the **Related** section and select **Potential Customer (Account)** to add a data field from the account record type to your search.

This allows you to filter on attributes of the account related to the opportunities.

6. In the **Select** field, choose **Address 1: City**.

7. In the **Operator** field, leave **Equals** selected, and in the **Enter Value** field, enter **Chicago**.

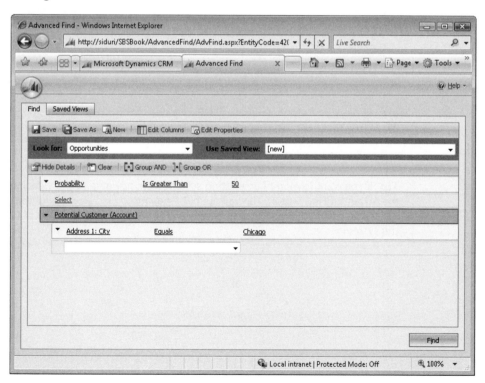

8. Click the **Find** button in the lower right corner of the screen.

The results of your search are displayed.

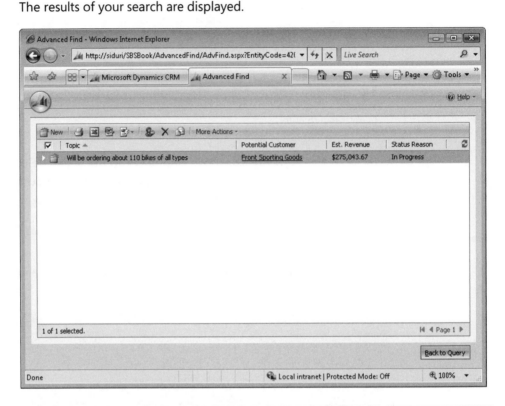

 BE SURE TO leave the query open so that you can use it in the next exercise.

Tip If you want to modify an existing system view, navigate to the view before clicking the Advanced Find button. This will open the Advanced Find screen with the criteria from the system view already set. This also allows you to easily understand the criteria used in the system views.

Organizing and Formatting Advanced Find Results

As you can see, Microsoft Dynamics CRM gives you the power to create a report that contains a set of records based on specific, user-defined criteria that is simple to put together. In addition to building your own search query, you can also format Advanced Find results to include additional data columns and sort, order, and size the results columns to meet your reporting needs. You can do the following:

- Add any column you want to the results.
- Adjust the order of the columns.
- Modify the size of each column.
- Define the sort order of the output.

For example, you might want to create a list of contacts that includes the contact name and primary address fields in a specific order. This can be accomplished with ease in Microsoft Dynamics CRM.

In this exercise, you will use the search query you created in the previous exercise, modifying the columns that appear in the output to include the Probability field for each opportunity as well as the Industry field for the customer account. In addition, you will sort and format your results.

USE your own Microsoft Dynamics CRM installation in place of the Adventure Works Cycle site shown in this exercise.

Edit Columns

1. In the **Advanced Find** criteria screen, click the **Edit Columns** button.

The Edit Columns dialog box opens. Here you can modify the column order, set the column width, add or remove columns, and configure sorting.

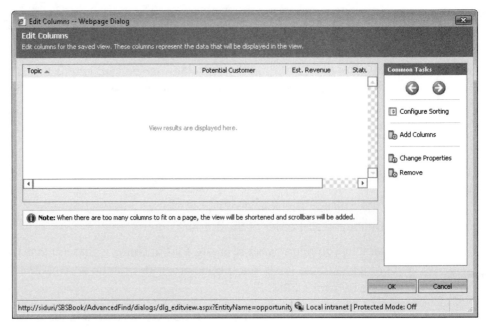

2. In the **Common Tasks** area, click **Add Columns**.

   The Add Columns dialog box opens.

3. Locate the **Probability** field, and select the check box next to it to add the field to your results.

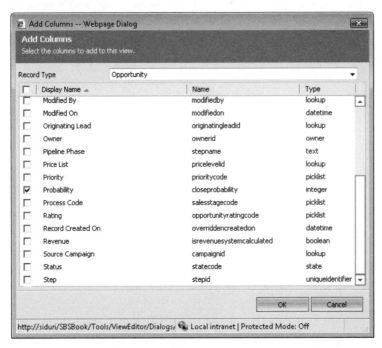

4. In the **Record Type** list at the top of the form, change the record type to **Potential Customer (Account)**.

Notice that you can add columns from related record types in addition to those from the primary record type.

5. Select the **Industry** check box, and then click **OK**.

The newly added columns appear to the right of the original columns.

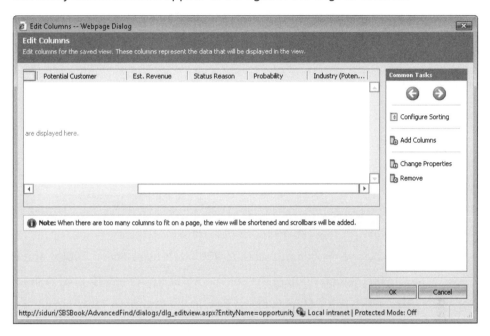

> **Important** For each record type in Microsoft Dynamics CRM, system administrators can configure the default columns that appear in each Advanced Find results set. The images in this chapter show the default view for opportunities in Microsoft Dynamics CRM. It's possible that your results will include different columns. If there is a column you find yourself adding frequently to your searches, ask your system administrator about adding it to the default Advanced Find view.

6. In the **Edit Columns** dialog box, click (don't double-click) the **Industry** column heading.

The border color changes to green.

7. In the **Common Tasks** area, click the left arrow until the **Industry** column is the first column in the results grid.

8. Double-click the **Industry** column.

The Change Column Properties dialog box opens.

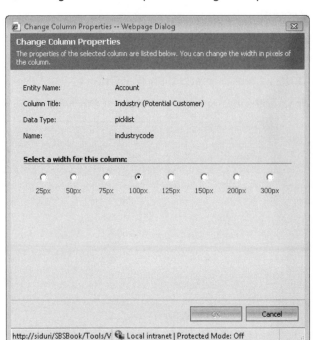

9. Change the column width to 200 pixels by selecting **200px**, and then click **OK**.

   This setting doubles the column width from the 100-pixel default.

10. In the **Edit Columns** dialog box, in the **Common Tasks** pane, click **Configure Sorting**.

    The Configure Sort Order dialog box opens.

11. In the **Column** list, select **Probability**, and in the **Order** field, select **Descending Order**, and then click **OK**.

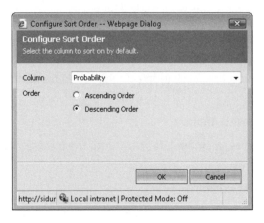

This sorts the results so that the opportunities with the highest closing probability appear at the top of the report.

> **Tip** Although the sort option includes only one sort level, you can sort by multiple columns on any grid within Microsoft Dynamics CRM if you hold the Shift key and click the column header.

12. In the **Edit Columns** dialog box, click **OK** to close the dialog box.

13. On the **Advanced Find** query form, click **Find**. The search results appear with the new columns you added.

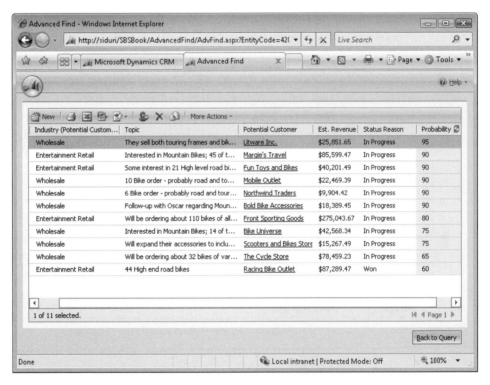

 BE SURE TO leave the query open so that you can use it in the next exercise.

Creating and Sharing a Saved View

What if, sometime in the future, you want to run the same Advanced Find query for which you have already defined the criteria, specified the output format, and defined the sort order to address your needs? You would find it frustrating if you had to go through all of these steps each time you wanted to produce the report. Fortunately, Microsoft Dynamics CRM allows you to create saved views to save your Advanced Find queries for future use. Saved views can be run or modified at a later date, sparing you from recreating reports that you run on a regular schedule.

> **Tip** Although saved views store the specified criteria and formatting settings, results are dynamic and reflect the records that match your search criteria at the time the saved view is accessed. Saved views are not point-in-time data snapshots.

In addition to saving a view for yourself, it's likely that your reports will also be useful to your colleagues. Rather than trying to articulate the steps it took for you to create a view, you can *share* the view with other users in Microsoft Dynamics CRM. Typically, a sales manager or other "power user" creates a saved view that will be valuable to other team members. These saved views solve business-critical reporting needs without requiring advanced programming skills.

Saved views can be shared with other users or teams, which are groups of users that can share access privileges for certain records. By default, each user or team is granted Read access when you share a saved view. This allows the user or team to access the saved view but not modify it. You can assign additional permissions when you share a saved view. The following table outlines the security privileges available when sharing a view.

Privilege	Description
Read	Shared users can access the view but not modify it.
Write	Shared users can modify the view to include additional criteria, results fields, or other formatting.
Delete	Shared users can delete the view from the Microsoft Dynamics CRM database.
Append	Shared users can associate other records to the view.
Assign	Shared users can assign the view to an additional system user.
Share	Shared users can share the view with additional users or teams while maintaining their own access to the view.

In this exercise, you will save the view you created in the previous section so that you can access it in the future.

> **USE** your own Microsoft Dynamics CRM installation in place of the Adventure Works Cycle site shown in this exercise.

Save As

1. On the **Advanced Find** screen that includes the query you created in the previous section, click the **Save As** button.

2. In the **Name** field of the **Provide Information For This View** dialog box, enter **Hot Opportunities in Chicago Market**.

3. In the **Description** field, enter **Opportunities in Chicago with a probability greater than 50**.

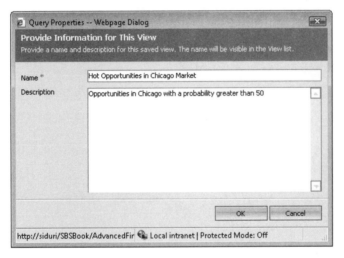

4. In the **Advanced Find** query form, click the **Saved Views** tab to see the newly created saved view.

   In addition to being accessible from the Saved Views tab, the saved view will appear in the View list on the Opportunities grid.

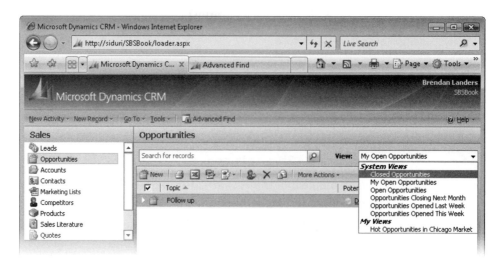

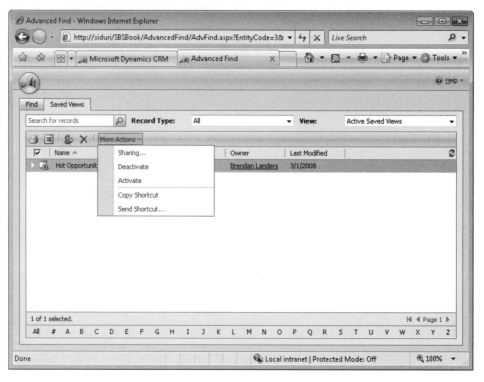

5. In the **Saved Views** tab, click the **More Actions** button, and then click **Sharing**.

The Who Would You Like To Share The Selected Saved View With? dialog box opens.

6. In the **Common Tasks** pane, click **Add User/Team**.

The Look Up Records dialog box opens.

7. Enter the name of another system user in the **Look for** field, and then click **Find**.

8. Select a user record, and click the right arrow to move the record from the **Available Records** box to the **Selected Records** box. Then click **OK**.

The selected user has been returned to the shared user screen. By default, the user receives Read rights to your view. Besides Read rights, you can empower the user to Write, Delete, Append, Assign, and Share your view with others.

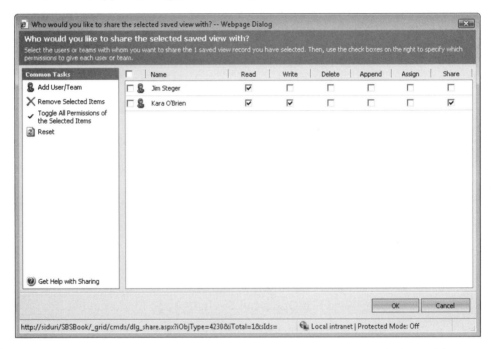

9. Click **OK** in the **Who would you like to share the selected saved view with?** dialog box.

With just a few clicks, your colleagues can now benefit from the reports you created.

Using Advanced Filter Criteria

By default, Microsoft Dynamics CRM applies AND logic to queries that include two or more search criteria. This means that results are limited to those records that meet all search criteria in the query. However, you also might be required to produce a report with records that match any of the search criteria. In this instance, you could use OR logic in Advanced Find to search multiple fields to find records that have matching data in any of the fields.

In this exercise, you will use the Group AND and Group OR functionality of the Advanced Find tool. As you saw earlier, the original criteria we applied to the Hot Opportunities In Chicago Market saved view included all opportunities that met the following criteria:

● The opportunity probability is greater than 50.

● The accounts are in the city of Chicago.

Now you will expand the criteria to include opportunities in Des Moines in addition to those in Chicago.

USE your own Microsoft Dynamics CRM installation in place of the Adventure Works Cycle site shown in this exercise.

BE SURE TO use the Internet Explorer Web browser to navigate to your Microsoft Dynamics CRM Web site, if necessary, before beginning this exercise.

1. Launch **Advanced Find** if it is not open already.

2. In the **Advanced Find** query screen, in the **Look for** field, select **Opportunities**, and then select **Hot Opportunities in Chicago Market** in the **Use Saved View** list.

The criteria for the saved query is displayed.

Show Details

3. Click the **Show Details** button.

> **Tip** By default, the Advanced Find mode is set to Simple, which means that the details of the query are not shown until you click the Show Details button. You can change this setting on the General tab in the Personal Options area, which is accessible from the Tools menu on the application menu toolbar.

4. In the **Potential Customer (Account)** section, click the **Select** field underneath the row that specifies the city as **Chicago**.

5. In the **Select** field, choose **Address 1: City**.

6. In the **Enter Value** field, enter **Des Moines**.

Because Microsoft Dynamics CRM uses AND logic by default, if you click Find at this point, your search will not return any results, because no single account record can have a primary address in both Chicago and Des Moines.

7. Click the arrow to the left of the first **Address 1: City** field, and click **Select Row**.

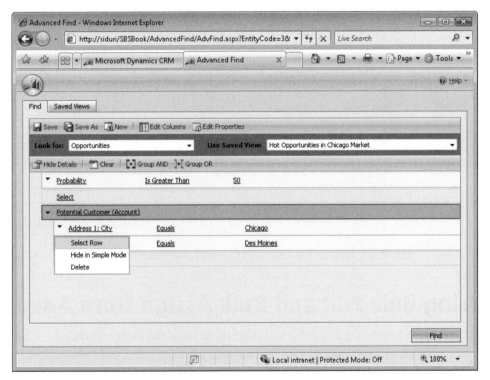

8. Click the arrow to the left of the second **Address 1: City** field, and click **Select Row**.

Group OR

9. On the toolbar, click the **Group OR** button.

This selection will update the logic so that records that have a primary address in the city of Chicago or Des Moines will be returned in the results.

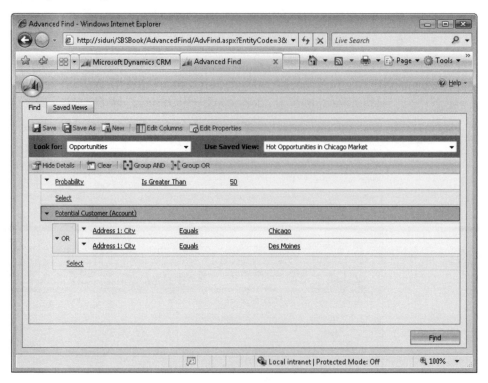

10. Click **Find** to see the results matching your new query.

Using Bulk Edit and Bulk Assign from Advanced Find

It is certainly powerful and exciting to have the ability to create a list of records that match your specific criteria. The ability to take action on those records to strengthen your Microsoft Dynamics CRM database and adapt it to your business as it evolves is equally important. With Microsoft Dynamics CRM, you can take many actions on the results of an Advanced Find query. For example, you can perform the following actions:

- Export the data to Microsoft Office Excel.
- Bulk edit the records.
- Bulk assign the records.
- Deactivate the records.

In this section, we focus on the bulk edit and bulk assign functionalities. With the Microsoft Dynamics CRM bulk edit functionality, you can make a change to many records at one time from any grid. For example, you might use bulk edit or bulk assign if:

- You realize that data has been entered incorrectly for several records.

- You add a new attribute that you would like to populate for all records.

- An employee decides to leave your company, and you need to distribute the records that the employee owns to other team members.

> **Important** Bulk edit rights might not be available for every user. Your ability to use bulk edit is configured by the system administrator in your security role.

In this exercise, you will edit the Address 1: City field of multiple records by using the bulk edit tool. In addition, you will use the bulk assign functionality to assign ownership of multiple records to another user.

USE your own Microsoft Dynamics CRM installation in place of the Adventure Works Cycle site shown in the exercise.

BE SURE TO use the Internet Explorer Web browser to navigate to your Microsoft Dynamics CRM Web site, if necessary, before beginning this exercise.

1. In the **Workplace** area, click **Accounts**.

The default view appears in the grid.

> **Important** You will see My Active Accounts as the default view. This view includes the Account Name, Main Phone, Address 1: City, Primary Contact, and E-mail (Primary Contact) fields for the accounts you own. The default view can be modified and therefore might be different in your environment.

2. On the application menu toolbar, click **Advanced Find**.

The criteria from the current view populates the Show Details section.

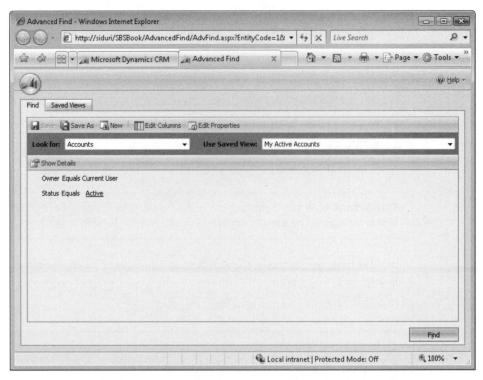

3. Click the **Show Details** button to view the details of the query, and then add a new search field by choosing **Address 1: City** in the **Select** field.

4. Leave the operator as **Equals**, and enter **NY** in the **Enter Value** field.

5. Click **Find**.

All active accounts that you own with a city value of *NY* are displayed. Next you will update the city to *New York* by using the bulk edit tool.

> **Important** If your search did not return at least two results, modify the query before continuing with this exercise.

6. Select several records by holding the Ctrl key while clicking the records you want to update.

7. On the grid toolbar, select **More Actions**, and then choose **Edit**.

The Edit Multiple Records dialog box opens. It resembles a blank Account form.

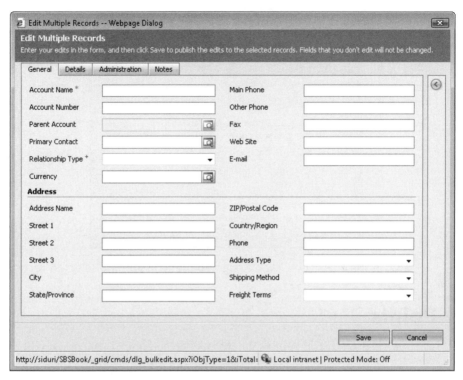

8. Enter **New York** in the **City** field, and then click **Save**.

> **Important** This action cannot be undone.

After you have clicked Save, the underlying records are updated. If you refresh the grid, you will no longer see these records.

> **Tip** If your query results return multiple pages, you will need to edit records one page at a time. The number of records returned on a page can be modified in the Personal Options area to a maximum of 250.

9. In the results grid, select at least two additional records by pressing the ⌷Ctrl⌷ key while clicking them.

Assign

10. In the grid toolbar, click the **Assign** button.

The Assign Accounts dialog box opens.

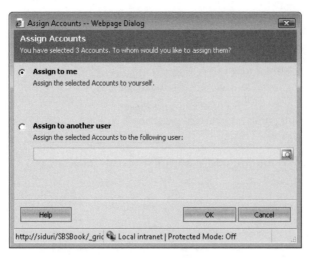

11. In the dialog box, click **Assign to me** to assign the selected records to yourself.

Key Points

- The Advanced Find tool in Microsoft Dynamics CRM allows you to search data in your system. You can filter results and display columns from the primary record type you are searching as well as from related record types.

- You can format and sort the output of your query to meet your specific needs.

- You can save your Advanced Find views for later use.

- With sharing, you can distribute your saved views to other users.

- You can create complex queries by using Group AND and Group OR logic.

- You can take action on the results of an Advanced Find query by using the bulk edit and bulk assign functionalities to update multiple records at a time.

- Similar to other views, Advanced Find results can be exported to Excel.

Chapter at a Glance

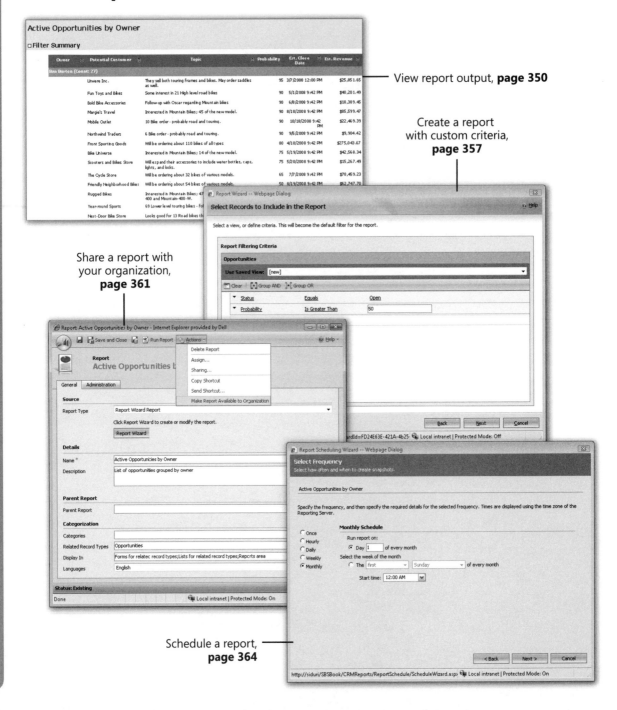

View report output, **page 350**

Create a report
with custom criteria,
page 357

Share a report with
your organization,
page 361

Schedule a report,
page 364

16 Using the Report Wizard

In this chapter, you will learn to

✔ Create a report with the Report Wizard.

✔ Modify a report.

✔ Share a report.

✔ Schedule a report.

✔ Categorize a report.

In Chapter 15, "Using Advanced Find," you learned how to use the Advanced Find tool to create and format data into reports. Although those options are powerful and will meet many of your reporting needs, Microsoft Dynamics CRM also uses Microsoft SQL Server Reporting Services for advanced reporting capabilities. Programmers can create advanced reports by working directly within Microsoft SQL Server Reporting Services, but Microsoft Dynamics CRM also includes a Report Wizard that provides users of all skill levels with a tool to create Microsoft SQL Server Reporting Services reports. The following table compares the features of Advanced Find with those of the SQL Server Reporting Services Report Wizard.

	Advanced Find	SQL Server Reporting Services Report Wizard
Report output	Microsoft Dynamics CRM grids that can be exported to Microsoft Office Excel format	Web-based reports that can be exported to additional formats, such as Excel, PDF, and CSV
Skill level required to create or modify reports	Beginner	Beginner
Ability to schedule reports for e-mail delivery	No	Yes
Support for charts and graphs	No	Yes

(continued on the next page)

347

	Advanced Find	SQL Server Reporting Services Report Wizard
Ability to include data from multiple record types in results	Yes	Yes
Ability to include data from multiple record types in the report query	Yes	Yes
Ability to prompt users to enter parameters before running reports	No	Yes
Ability to restrict access for some users	Yes	Yes
Respect for Microsoft Dynamics CRM record-level security settings by default	Yes	Yes

Microsoft Dynamics CRM includes 24 standard SQL Server Reporting Services reports in the base product. You can find these reports by navigating to the Workplace area and clicking the Reports link.

You will find that these reports solve some of your reporting needs and will probably serve as a solid starting point for your organization. The reports also give you a high-level understanding of the possibilities that exist with Microsoft SQL Server Reporting Services. The following table summarizes the reports and their applicability within the Marketing, Sales, Service, and Administrative areas of Microsoft Dynamics CRM.

Report Name	Marketing	Sales	Service	Administrative
Account Distribution	X	X	X	
Account Overview	X	X	X	
Account Summary	X	X	X	
Activities				X
Campaign Activity Status	X			
Campaign Comparison	X			
Campaign Performance	X			
Case Summary Table			X	
Competitor Win Loss		X		
Invoice		X		
Invoice Status		X		
Lead Source Effectiveness	X	X		
Neglected Accounts		X		
Neglected Cases			X	
Neglected Leads		X		
Order		X		
Products By Account		X		
Products By Contact		X		
Quote		X		
Sales History		X		
Sales Pipeline		X		
Service Activity Volume			X	
Top Knowledge Base Articles			X	
User Summary				X

In this chapter, you will learn how to create, modify, and format reports by using the Microsoft Dynamics CRM Report Wizard. You will also learn how to share a report with other users, schedule delivery of a report, and categorize a report. Finally, you will learn to use the advanced features of the Report Wizard to create complex reports.

> **Important** There are no practice files for this chapter.

> **Troubleshooting** Graphics and operating system–related instructions in this book reflect the Windows Vista user interface. If your computer is running Windows XP and you experience trouble following the instructions as written, please refer to the "Information for Readers Running Windows XP" section at the beginning of this book.

> **Important** The images used in this book reflect the default form and field names in Microsoft Dynamics CRM. Because the software offers extensive customization capabilities, it's possible that some of the record types or fields have been relabeled in your Microsoft Dynamics CRM environment. If you cannot find the forms, fields, or security roles referenced in this book, contact your system administrator for assistance.

> **Important** You must know the location of your Microsoft Dynamics CRM Web site to work the exercises in this book. Check with your system administrator to verify the Web address if you don't know it.

Creating a Report with the Report Wizard

The Report Wizard allows you to create sophisticated reports within the Microsoft Dynamics CRM interface by guiding you through a step-by-step process that is easy to understand. It allows you to produce grouped, summary-level data in addition to record-level data. Consider the following scenarios:

- You need to create an Opportunity Pipeline report that shows all opportunities by owner and includes the sum of all estimated revenue across those opportunities.

- You need to compare the number of accounts assigned to each user to determine account distribution levels.

With the Report Wizard, you can get the aggregated summary numbers for these types of reports.

In this exercise, you will use the Report Wizard to create a report that shows active opportunities by owner.

> **USE** your own Microsoft Dynamics CRM installation in place of the Adventure Works Cycle site shown in this exercise, and log in as a user that has privileges to create reports.
>
> **BE SURE TO** use the Windows Internet Explorer Web browser to navigate to your Microsoft Dynamics CRM Web site before beginning this exercise.

New Report

1. In the **Workplace** area, click **Reports**.

2. In the grid toolbar, click the **New** button to launch the **New Report** form.

3. In the **Source** section of the form, click the **Report Wizard** button.

   The Report Wizard Get Started page opens.

4. In the Report Wizard, leave **Start a new report** selected, and then click **Next** to move on to the **Report Properties** page.

5. In the **Report name** field, enter **Active Opportunities by Owner**, and in the **Report description** field, enter **List of opportunities grouped by owner**.

6. In the **Primary record type** field, select **Opportunities**.

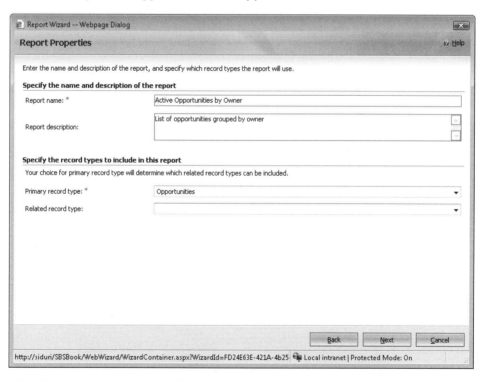

7. Click **Next** to move on to the **Select Records to Include in the Report** page.

8. In the **Report Filtering Criteria** section, replace the default **Modified On** search parameter by choosing **Status** instead of **Modified On** in the **Select** list.

9. Leave **Equals** in the operator field, and in the **Enter Value** field, select **Open**.

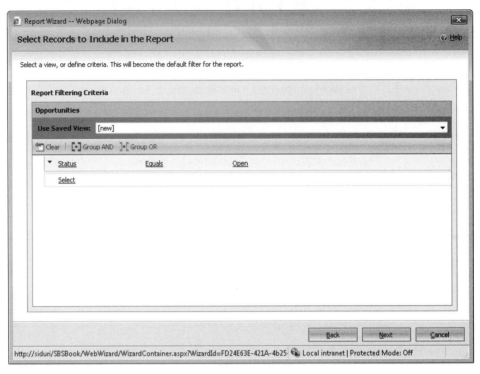

10. Click **Next** to move on to the **Lay Out Fields** page.

11. Click in the **Click here to add a grouping** field.

The Add Grouping dialog box opens.

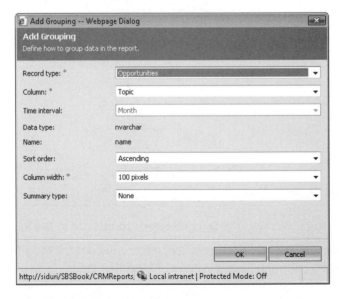

12. In the **Column** list, select **Owner**.

13. In the **Summary Type** field, select **Count**, and then click **OK** to add this grouping to your report.

This summary type allows you to see how many active opportunities exist for each owner.

14. Click **Click here to add a column**.

The Add Columns dialog box opens.

15. In the **Column** field, select **Potential Customer**. Set the **Column Width** to **150 pixels**, and click **OK** to add the column to your report.

16. To the right of **Potential Customer**, click in the **Click here to add a column** field to add another column to your report. Continue this process to add the following fields and related information:

Column	Column width	Summary type
Topic	300 pixels	None
Probability	75 pixels	None
Est. Close Date	100 pixels	None
Est. Revenue	100 pixels	Sum

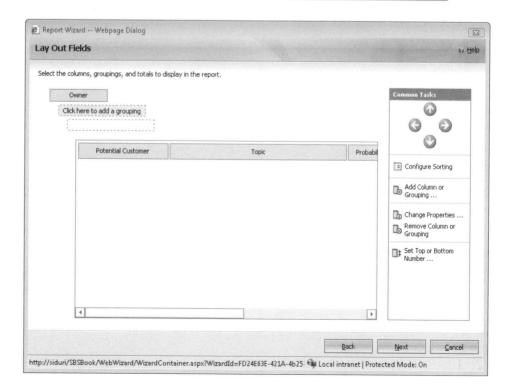

17. In the **Common Tasks** pane, click **Configure Sorting**.

The Configure Sort Order dialog box opens.

18. In the **Column** field, select **Probability**, and then click **Descending Order**.

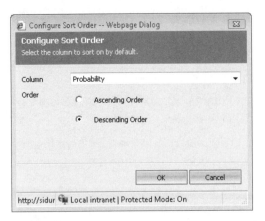

19. Click **OK**, and then click **Next** to move on to the **Format Report** page.

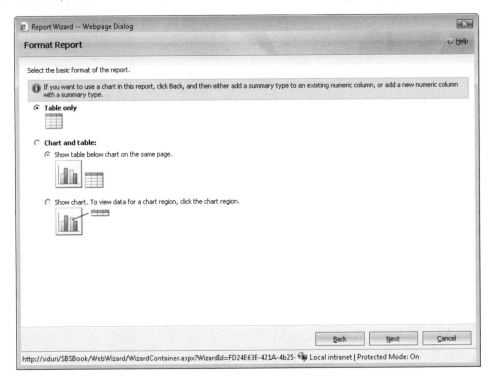

20. Leave **Table only** selected for your report format, and then click **Next**.

The Report Summary screen displays your report selections.

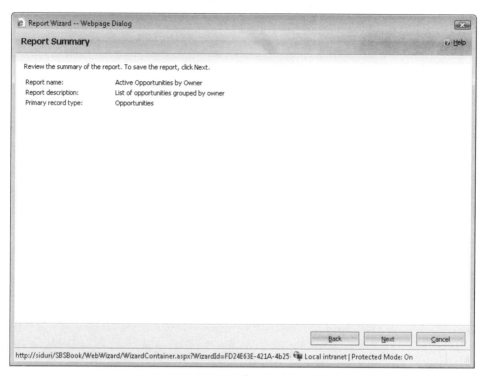

21. Review the report details, and then click **Next**.

The Report Successfully Created confirmation page opens, indicating that you have successfully created a report.

22. On the confirmation page, click **Finish** to exit the Report Wizard and return to the New Report form, which automatically updates to reflect the details of your report. To see the results, you need to run the report.

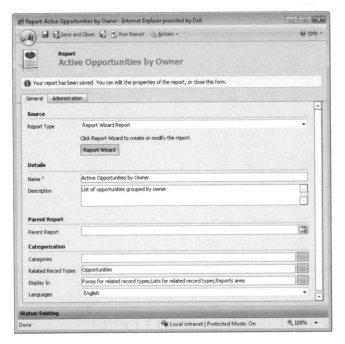

Run Report

23. On the form toolbar, click the **Run Report** button.

Your report displays within SQL Server Reporting Services. The resulting report provides insight into how many open opportunities exist for each owner.

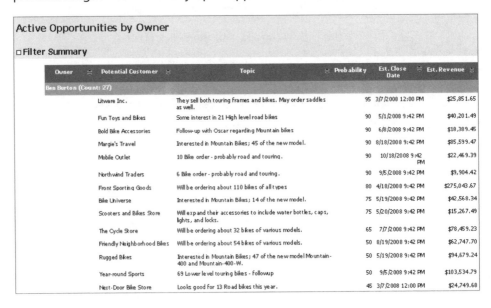

Owner	Potential Customer	Topic	Probability	Est. Close Date	Est. Revenue
Ben Burton (Count: 27)					
	Litware Inc.	They sell both touring frames and bikes. May order saddles as well.	95	3/7/2008 12:00 PM	$25,851.65
	Fun Toys and Bikes	Some interest in 21 High level road bikes	90	5/1/2008 9:42 PM	$40,201.49
	Bold Bike Accessories	Follow-up with Oscar regarding Mountain bikes	90	6/8/2008 9:42 PM	$18,389.45
	Margie's Travel	Interested in Mountain Bikes; 45 of the new model.	90	8/18/2008 9:42 PM	$85,599.47
	Mobile Outlet	10 Bike order - probably road and touring.	90	10/18/2008 9:42 PM	$22,469.39
	Northwind Traders	6 Bike order - probably road and touring.	90	9/5/2008 9:42 PM	$9,904.42
	Front Sporting Goods	Will be ordering about 110 bikes of all types	80	4/18/2008 9:42 PM	$275,043.67
	Bike Universe	Interested in Mountain Bikes; 14 of the new model.	75	5/19/2008 9:42 PM	$42,568.34
	Scooters and Bikes Store	Will expand their accessories to include water bottles, caps, lights, and locks.	75	5/20/2008 9:42 PM	$15,267.49
	The Cycle Store	Will be ordering about 32 bikes of various models.	65	7/7/2008 9:42 PM	$78,459.23
	Friendly Neighborhood Bikes	Will be ordering about 54 bikes of various models.	50	8/19/2008 9:42 PM	$62,747.70
	Rugged Bikes	Interested in Mountain Bikes; 47 of the new model Mountain-400 and Mountain-400-W.	50	5/19/2008 9:42 PM	$94,679.24
	Year-round Sports	69 Lower level touring bikes - followup	50	9/5/2008 9:42 PM	$103,534.79
	Next-Door Bike Store	Looks good for 13 Road bikes this year.	45	3/7/2008 12:00 PM	$24,749.68

> **Tip** After running the report, you can modify the filter to refine your report output, export to other formats (usually PDF or Excel), or view an opportunity record by clicking the topic in the output.

 CLOSE the report and the Report form.

Modifying a Report

Now that you have seen the power of the Report Wizard, you can use it to create reports that are relevant to your business needs. Business needs change over time, and your reports will need to change accordingly. Additionally, you will often want to make small tweaks to the reports you have already built. For example, you might want to add a column or a grouping level, or you might want to modify the sort order. You can use the same interface in the Report Wizard to modify existing reports without having to start over.

In this exercise, you will modify the Active Opportunities By Owner report that you created in the previous exercise. Specifically, you will modify the filter to include only those opportunities with a closing probability greater than 50 and group results by manager in addition to record owner.

 USE your own Microsoft Dynamics CRM installation in place of the Adventure Works Cycle site shown in this exercise, and use a user account that has privileges to create and update reports.

BE SURE TO use the Internet Explorer Web browser to navigate to your Microsoft Dynamics CRM Web site, if necessary, before beginning this exercise.

1. In the **Workplace** area, click **Reports**.

Edit Report

2. Select **Active Opportunities by Owner** without opening it, and click the **Edit Report** button in the grid toolbar.

The Report form opens.

3. In the **Report** form, click **Report Wizard** to launch the Report Wizard.

4. On the **Get Started** page of the Report Wizard, leave the default selections to work from your existing report, so that your changes overwrite the original settings. Click **Next** to proceed to the next step of the Report Wizard.

5. On the **Report Properties** page, leave the current settings intact, and click **Next** to proceed to the next step of the Report Wizard.

   The Select Records To Include In The Report screen opens, displaying the Status report parameter configured in the previous exercise.

6. Add a new row by clicking **Select** and then choosing **Probability**.

7. Select **Is Greater Than** as the operator.

8. In the **Enter Value** field, enter **50**.

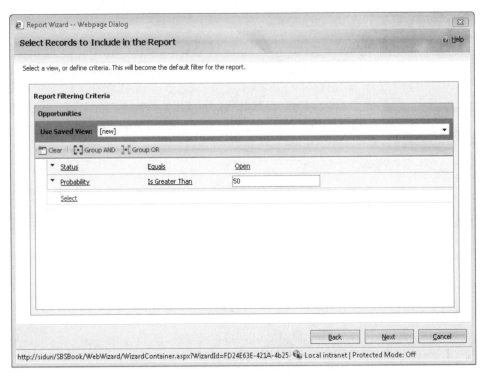

9. Click **Next** to proceed to the next step of the Report Wizard.

   This selection refines your results to include only records with a probability value greater than 50.

10. On the **Lay Out Fields** page, revise the report format by clicking in the **Click here to add a grouping** field.

    The Add Grouping dialog box opens.

11. In the **Record type** field, select **Owner**.

12. In the **Column** field, choose **Manager**.

13. In the **Summary type** field, select **Count**.

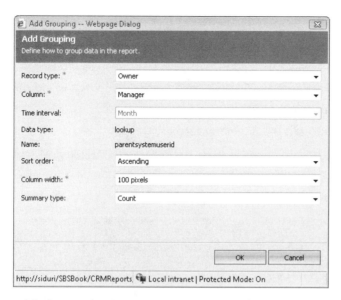

With these selections, you are adding the owner's manager to the report as an additional grouping level.

14. Click **OK** to close the **Add Grouping** dialog box.

The new grouping level is added below the existing Owner grouping level in the report.

15. In the **Common Tasks** pane, click the Up arrow.

This moves the manager grouping level above the owner so that the opportunities for each sales owner are grouped by the sales managers.

> **Troubleshooting** You might see a warning message showing that the table exceeds the width of one printed page. This is due to the total pixel count of all columns in the report. To keep the report under one page wide for printing purposes, ensure that the sum of your column pixels is less than 960.

16. Click **Next** to proceed to the next step of the Report Wizard.

The Format Report screen opens.

17. In this screen and in the Report Summary screen that follows, click **Next** to maintain the current selections.

The Report Successfully Created confirmation page opens, indicating that you have successfully updated the report.

18. Click **Finish** to exit the Report Wizard.

The Report Wizard closes and you are returned to the Report form. The changes to your report are automatically saved.

19. In the form toolbar, click Run Report to view the report with your changes.

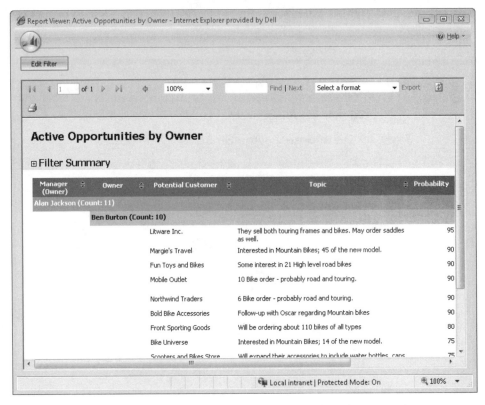

The report now includes an additional grouping level that shows total open opportunities at the manager level as well as at the owner level, and includes only those opportunities with a closing probability greater than 50. You can continue to refine your reports at any time with the Report Wizard.

 CLOSE the report and the Report form.

Sharing a Report

The report you created in the previous exercise will reside in the Reports view of the Workplace area but will display only for you; most other users will *not* be able to see the report, unless they have system administrator or other security rights. By default, Microsoft Dynamics CRM prevents other users from being able to use your report at this point, although it does allow you to share the report with other users as you see fit. This is desirable because:

- Many reports might be created by several different users with the Report Wizard. If all reports are immediately available to everyone, the number of reports in the list will grow quickly and may lead to confusion.

- You might need a report for a very specific reason that other users will not need, and therefore there is no reason to share it.

Although the reports are not shared immediately, you can share them with other users in just a few steps.

In this exercise, you will share the report created in the previous section with a specific user and then make it available to all users in your Microsoft Dynamics CRM environment.

> **USE** your own Microsoft Dynamics CRM installation in place of the Adventure Works Cycle site shown in this exercise, and use a user account that has a security role with privileges to publish reports.
>
> **BE SURE TO** use the Internet Explorer Web browser to navigate to your Microsoft Dynamics CRM Web site, if necessary, before beginning this exercise.

1. In the **Workplace** area, click **Reports**.

2. Select **Active Opportunities by Owner** without opening the report.

 3. In the grid toolbar, click the **More Actions** button, and then select **Sharing**.

   The Who Would You Like To Share The Selected Report With? sharing dialog box opens.

4. In the **Common Tasks** pane, click **Add User/Team**.

   The Look Up Records dialog box opens.

5. Search for system users and select any user. Then add the user to the **Selected Records** area, and click **OK**.

   The selected user displays in the sharing dialog box, with Read rights assigned by default. You can modify the sharing rights to suit your specific needs.

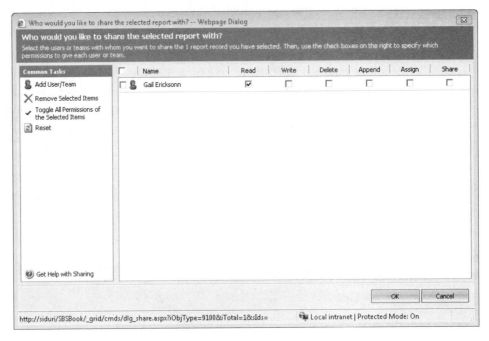

6. Click **OK** to save your sharing settings for the report.

   The specified user can now see the report in the Reports view of the Workplace area.

   Occasionally you might want to make the report available for every user rather than for specific users. Although you could select all users in the sharing dialog box, users that join your organization at a later time will not automatically have access to the report. In the next steps, you will make a report available to the entire organization so that even users who are added later are still able to access your report.

7. In the **Reports** view, select the **Active Opportunities by Owner** report without opening it, and in the grid toolbar, click **Edit Report**.

   The Report form displays.

Actions

8. In the form toolbar, click the **Actions** button, and then select **Make Report Available to Organization**.

> **Troubleshooting** If the Make Report Available To Organization option does not appear in the Actions menu, you do not have rights to publish reports. Contact your system administrator about adding the Publish Reports privilege to your security role.

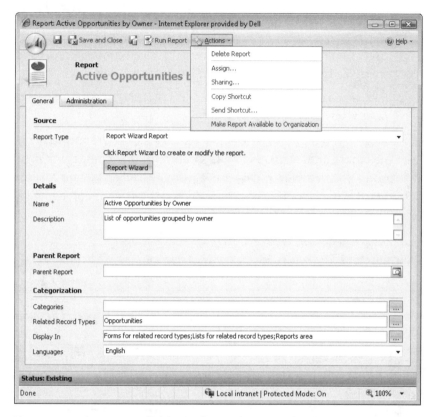

Your report is now available to the entire organization. You can also make the report a personal report again by following steps 7 and 8 and selecting Revert to Personal Report.

 CLOSE the Report form.

Scheduling a Report

When you run a report by using Microsoft SQL Server Reporting Services in Microsoft Dynamics CRM, the report runs in real time and reflects the current data in the system. This works very well for most of your reporting needs, but it can also pose challenges. For instance:

- Users who run the report at different times can communicate conflicting information, which leads to confusion and data integrity concerns.

- Real-time reports provide no historical perspective for comparison or trending purposes.

For example, you might want to run a monthly pipeline report to understand how the pipeline looks at the beginning of each month and to compare to previous months. Microsoft Dynamics CRM provides a Report Scheduling Wizard to address this need. The wizard allows you to generate report snapshots either on demand or at a regularly scheduled time.

> **Important** The Report Scheduling Wizard is not available in Microsoft Dynamics CRM Online.

In this exercise, you will schedule a report to run once a month at midnight.

> **USE** your own Microsoft Dynamics CRM installation in place of the Adventure Works Cycle site shown in this exercise, and use a user account that has a security role with privileges to add reporting services reports.
>
> **BE SURE TO** use the Internet Explorer Web browser to navigate to your Microsoft Dynamics CRM Web site, if necessary, before beginning this exercise.

1. In the **Workplace** area, click **Reports**.

2. Select **Active Opportunities by Owner** without opening the report.

3. In the grid toolbar, click **More Actions,** and then click **Schedule Report**.

> **Troubleshooting** If the Schedule Report option does not appear in the More Actions menu, you do not have rights to schedule reports. Contact your system administrator about adding the Add Reporting Services Reports privilege to your security role.

The Report Scheduling Wizard opens. Here you can specify when you would like a snapshot to occur.

4. Select **On a Schedule**, and click **Next** to proceed to the next step of the Report Scheduling Wizard.

5. On the **Select Frequency** page, select **Monthly** and leave the default settings for the monthly schedule.

The default settings schedule the report for the first day of the month at midnight.

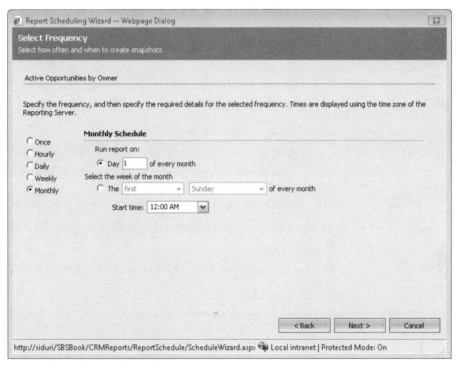

6. Click **Next** to proceed to the next step of the Report Scheduling Wizard.

7. On the **Select Start and End Dates** page, leave the current date as the default start date, and leave **No end date** selected.

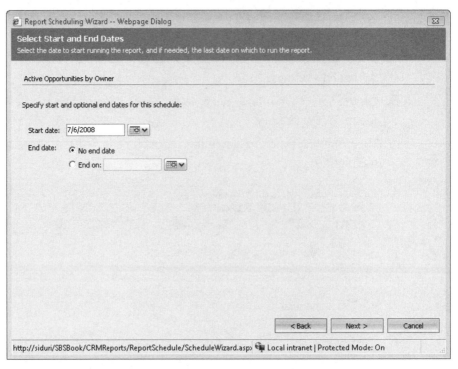

8. Click **Next** to proceed to the next step of the Report Scheduling Wizard.

   The Define Report Parameters page opens, indicating that there are no parameters for the selected report.

9. Click **Next** to proceed to the final step of the Report Scheduling Wizard.

   The Review Snapshot Definition page opens.

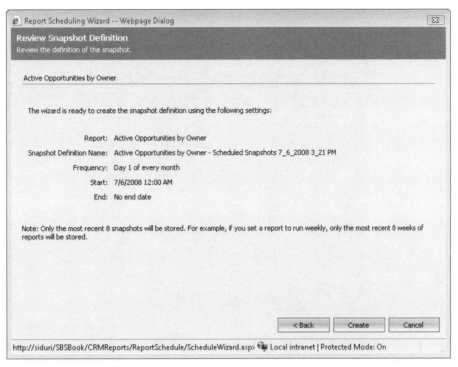

10. Verify that the settings are correct, and click **Create** to schedule your report.

A Completing The Report Scheduling Wizard confirmation page displays when the scheduling process is complete.

11. On the confirmation page, click **Finish** to exit the Report Scheduling Wizard.

You have successfully scheduled the report. On the first day of the next month, the report snapshot will be taken and will be available for all users who have access to the report. When the report is run, an additional report will appear in the list with a name similar to the original report that includes a timestamp of the report's run date.

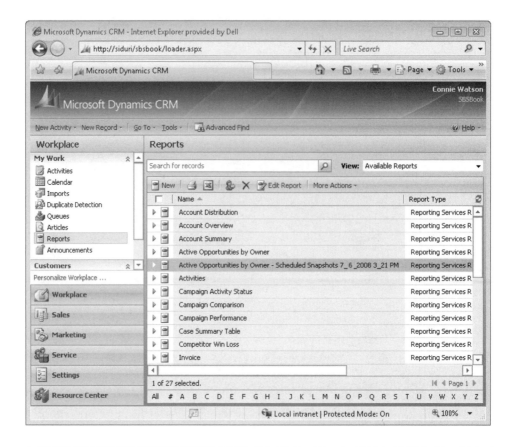

Tip The report will not display any results until the first snapshot is generated according to the schedule you specify in the Report Scheduling Wizard. Only the eight most recent report snapshots are stored. When the ninth report is created, the oldest report is deleted.

 CLOSE the Report form.

Categorizing a Report

You now know how to create, modify, share, and schedule reports. As you begin creating additional reports, you'll find proper categorization very helpful for organizing different types of reports into logical groupings. By default, the following categories are available for reports in Microsoft Dynamics CRM:

- Administrative Reports
- Marketing Reports
- Sales Reports
- Service Reports

> **Tip** Users with elevated security rights can modify and add report categories to match their business needs. This option is available on the Reporting tab of the System Settings dialog box, which is accessible in the Settings area. Contact your system administrator if you do not have access to this area.

In addition to providing local groupings for reports, the categorization feature provides other options, described in the following table.

Categorization field	Description
Related Record Types	This specifies the types of records relevant to the report. By default, this is set to the primary record type. In the Active Opportunities By Owner report, the Related Record Type is set to Opportunities.
Display In	This specifies where the report can be accessed within Microsoft Dynamics CRM. The available options are Forms For Related Record Types Lists For Related Record Types Reports Area
Languages	This shows the languages supported by the report.

Not only can reports be viewed in the Reports view in the Workplace area, they can also be viewed from the grid and form toolbars if they are configured to do so. The Display In option of each report allows you to designate where the report can be accessed. The Reports Area option is set by default and makes the report available under the Reports list in the Workplace area. The additional options are:

● **Forms for related record types.** This option allows a report to be run from within a record. For example, the Account Overview report can be run from within an account record.

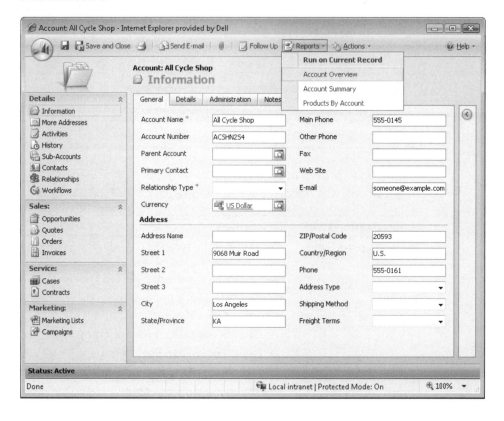

● **Lists for related record types.** This option allows a report to be run from the grid toolbar. Again, the native Account Overview report can be run from account grids. You can select multiple records to include in the report, or you can run it for a single record.

In this exercise, you will categorize the Active Opportunities By Owner report that you created earlier in this chapter.

USE your own Microsoft Dynamics CRM installation in place of the Adventure Works Cycle site shown in this exercise.

BE SURE TO use the Internet Explorer Web browser to navigate to your Microsoft Dynamics CRM Web site, if necessary, before beginning this exercise.

1. In the **Workplace** area, click **Reports**.

2. Select the **Active Opportunities by Owner** report without opening it, and in the grid toolbar, click the **Edit Report** button.

   The Report form displays.

Ellipsis

3. In the **Categorization** section, in the **Categories** field, click the ellipsis button.

   The Select Values dialog box appears.

4. In the **Available Values** section, click **Sales Reports**, and then click the right arrow button to select the value.

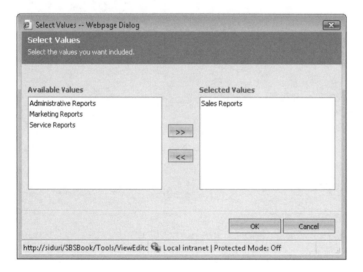

> **Tip** You can add multiple values to the Selected Values list to assign the report under multiple categories.

5. Click **OK** to close the dialog box.

![Save and Close] 6. On the Report form, click the **Save and Close** button to save the category selection.

Save and Close

7. In the **Reports** grid, in the **View** list, select **Sales Reports**.

   The Active Opportunities By Owner report now appears in the sales grouping.

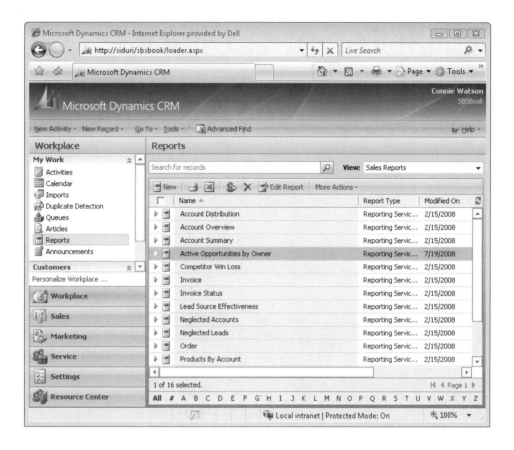

Key Points

- The Report Wizard allows you to create Microsoft SQL Server Reporting Services reports through an easy interface by using a step-by-step process.

- You can aggregate data by grouping fields with the Report Wizard. Additionally, you can specify which columns to include in the output of the report.

- Several report formatting options are available, including column width definition, column ordering, and sorting.

- You can modify Report Wizard reports by using the same wizard used to create reports.

- You can share your reports with individuals or with all users in your organization.

- Report scheduling allows you to record point-in-time snapshots of a report automatically by specifying a single or recurring run time. You can also record a report snapshot on demand at any time.

- Microsoft Dynamics CRM provides several report categorization options to enable you to specify how a report is grouped and where the report is available within the application.

Chapter at a Glance

Export data to Excel,
pages 377, 381, and 386

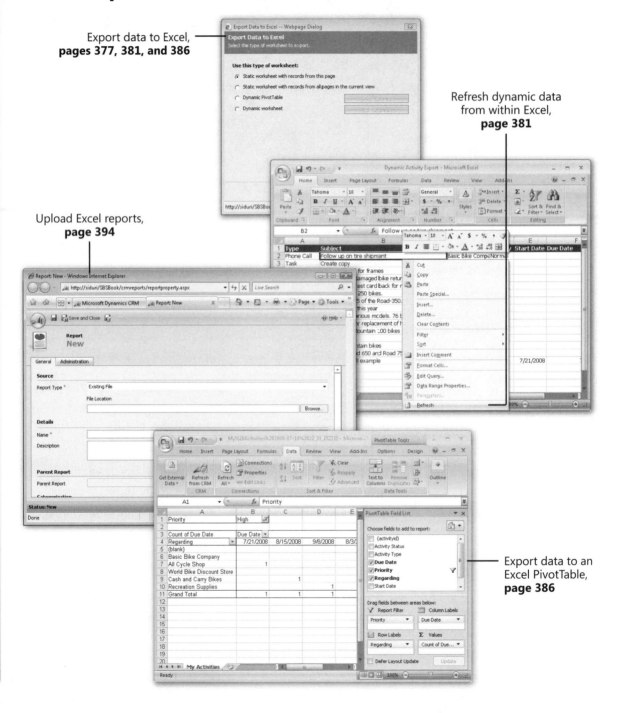

Refresh dynamic data
from within Excel,
page 381

Upload Excel reports,
page 394

Export data to an
Excel PivotTable,
page 386

17 Reporting with Microsoft Office Excel

In this chapter, you will learn to

✔ Export static data to Excel worksheets.

✔ Export dynamic data to Excel worksheets.

✔ Export dynamic data to Excel PivotTables.

✔ Upload Excel reports to the Reports list in Microsoft Dynamics CRM.

Microsoft Dynamics CRM provides several options for data reporting. The combination of Advanced Find views and the SQL Server Reporting Services Report Wizard make for a powerful suite of reporting tools. Microsoft Dynamics CRM provides an additional reporting option that many users like to use: you can export data to Microsoft Office Excel. The ability to export your Microsoft Dynamics CRM data to Excel within the Microsoft Dynamics CRM interface allows you to export data into a static worksheet, dynamic worksheet, or dynamic PivotTable for further analysis and reporting. By choosing a dynamic export option, you can ensure that the Excel file maintains a live connection to the Microsoft Dynamics CRM database, allowing you to refresh the data from within Excel. Consider how useful this functionality would be in the following scenarios:

● You have an Advanced Find view that you export weekly to print for a meeting. You can export to a dynamic file one time, format the report to your liking, and open it up from a saved location to get the most recent data.

● You have a PivotTable report that you use to view aggregated data. You can set up the PivotTable one time and reuse it as needed.

When you export data to Excel, Microsoft Dynamics CRM security settings apply: you can only export those records to which you have access in Microsoft Dynamics CRM.

In this chapter, you will learn how to create static and dynamic Excel reports. You will also learn how to create PivotTable reports that use data from Microsoft Dynamics CRM. Finally, you will learn how to upload an Excel report into the Reports area of Microsoft Dynamics CRM to share your Excel report with other users.

> **Important** There are no practice files for this chapter.

> **Troubleshooting** Graphics and operating system–related instructions in this book reflect the Windows Vista user interface. If your computer is running Windows XP and you experience trouble following the instructions as written, refer to the "Information for Readers Running Windows XP" section at the beginning of this book.

> **Important** The images used in this book reflect the default form and field names in Microsoft Dynamics CRM. Because the software offers extensive customization capabilities, it's possible that some of the record types or fields have been relabeled in your Microsoft Dynamics CRM environment. If you cannot find the forms, fields, or security roles referenced in this book, contact your system administrator for assistance.

> **Important** You must know the location of your Microsoft Dynamics CRM Web site to work the exercises in this book. Check with your system administrator to verify the Web address if you don't know it.

> **Important** The ability to export data to Excel is configurable at the user level. If you cannot see the export buttons and options referred to in this chapter, contact your system administrator for assistance.

Exporting Static Data to Excel Worksheets

Excel is a tool that most people in a traditional business environment are familiar with and use in some capacity. With Excel, you can organize, format, and analyze data. Many business applications give the end user the ability to export or download record-level data into Excel, and Microsoft Dynamics CRM is no exception.

It is very easy to export a list of records into Excel. If you have been using Microsoft Dynamics CRM for some time, you have probably already used this feature to export data to Excel.

For a simple, one-time report, you can export data from any grid in Microsoft Dynamics CRM in a *static* worksheet. The worksheet is described as static because the data will not be updated in Excel if it is changed in Microsoft Dynamics CRM after it is exported. A static data export reflects a point-in-time snapshot of a set of records in Microsoft Dynamics CRM.

When you export static data into Excel, the data is exported exactly as it appears in the Microsoft Dynamics CRM grid. The exported worksheet includes the fields that are displayed in the grid, using the same field order, sorting, and field widths. You can export most data grids into Excel, including the results of an Advanced Find.

Later in this chapter, you will learn to establish a live link with your Microsoft Dynamics CRM application by exporting *dynamic* data, which allows you to continually analyze your business data within Excel.

In this exercise, you will export a static Microsoft Dynamics CRM data view into Microsoft Office Excel.

> **USE** your own Microsoft Dynamics CRM installation in place of the Adventure Works Cycle site shown in this exercise.
>
> **BE SURE TO** use the Windows Internet Explorer Web browser to navigate to your Microsoft Dynamics CRM Web site before beginning this exercise.

1. In the **Workplace** area, click **Accounts**.

2. In the **View** field, select **Active Accounts**.

The data grid updates to display a list of active accounts.

3. On the grid toolbar, click the **Export to Excel** button.

Export to Excel

> **Tip** The Export To Excel button is available on most grids within Microsoft Dynamics CRM. You can export system-related information such as lists of reports or data imports, in addition to lists of core records such as accounts, contacts, and opportunities.

The Export Data To Excel dialog box opens.

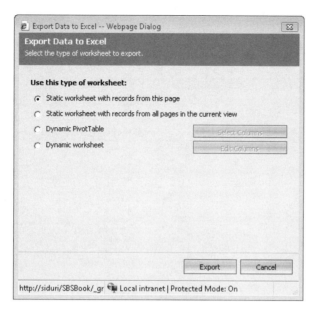

4. Leave **Static worksheet with records from this page** selected, and click the **Export** button.

The File Download dialog box opens.

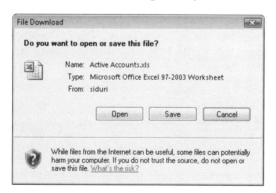

5. Click **Open** to launch Excel and open the export file. Alternatively, you can also click **Save** if you want to save the Excel file to your computer.

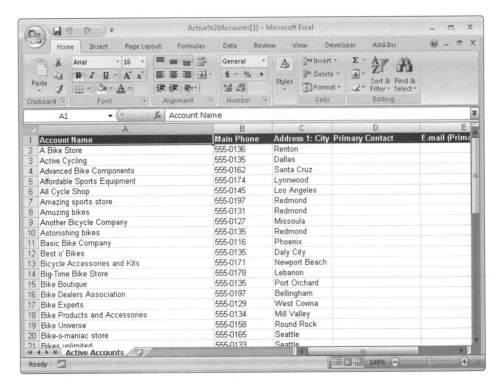

Important If you are using Excel 2007, you might get a warning indicating that the file you are trying to open is in a different format than specified by the file extension. Click Yes to proceed with the export.

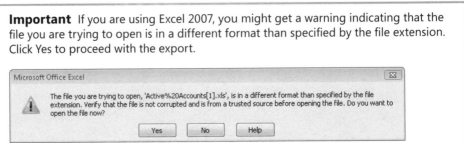

The first page of active account records has now been downloaded to Excel. You can format, modify, and analyze the data in Excel to meet your needs without affecting your Microsoft Dynamics CRM database.

> **Tip** If the records in the Active Accounts view span multiple pages, you will be presented with two options in step 4:
>
>   Static Worksheet With Records From This Page
>
>   Static Worksheet With Records From All Pages In The Current View
>
> These options allow you to choose whether to return all records from the view or just the records on the first page of the view results.

> **Important** If you do not have Excel installed on your computer, the file will not open. Contact your system administrator if you do not have Excel. Alternatively, Microsoft provides a tool called Excel Viewer, which allows you to open Excel files for viewing. Excel Viewer can be found at the Microsoft Download Center site: *http://www.microsoft.com/downloads*.

Exporting Dynamic Data to Excel Worksheets

If you are using Microsoft Dynamics CRM as it is intended, your data changes regularly. The number of records in your database on a given day will probably be different the next day, and the data captured within those records will be updated frequently. Consequently, the static data you exported to Excel in the past will probably be out of date after a day or two. You can easily export the static data again, but you will lose any formatting or additions you made to the Excel file. Fortunately, Microsoft Dynamics CRM lets you export dynamic data to Excel so that you can create your desired output once and refresh your data from within Excel. When you tap the power of dynamic worksheets, you can set up your file one time and simply open it when needed. You don't need to have Microsoft Dynamics CRM open to benefit from the data within the application.

Additionally, when you place the dynamic file on a "shared" network drive, other users can benefit from your report by seeing their data in the format you created. For example, in the exercise in this section you will create a dynamic file from the My Activities view, which shows only those activities assigned to you. When another user opens the file from his or her workstation, only that user's activities will appear.

In this exercise, you will export data to a dynamic Excel file. You will then update your Microsoft Dynamics CRM application and refresh your data from within Excel to see the power of the dynamic file in action.

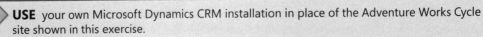

USE your own Microsoft Dynamics CRM installation in place of the Adventure Works Cycle site shown in this exercise.

BE SURE TO use the Internet Explorer Web browser to navigate to your Microsoft Dynamics CRM Web site, if necessary, before beginning this exercise.

1. In the **Workplace** area, click **Activities**.

The default activities view, My Activities, appears. If there are no activities in the default activities view, create a new activity for this exercise.

See Also For more information about creating activities, see Chapter 4, "Working with Activities and Notes."

2. Click the **Export to Excel** button.

The Export Data To Excel dialog box opens.

3. Select **Dynamic worksheet**.

The Edit Columns button becomes active. This button allows you to modify the columns in the output of your dynamic worksheet, in case you want to add columns or re-order the fields in the data grid.

4. Click the **Edit Columns** button to launch the **Edit Columns** dialog box.

See Also The Edit Columns screen functionality was reviewed earlier in this book. If you need a refresher on editing columns, see "Organizing and Formatting Advanced Find Results" in Chapter 15, "Using Advanced Find."

5. In the **Common Tasks** pane, click **Add Columns**.

The Add Columns dialog box opens.

6. Select the check box next to the **Last Updated** field to add the modified date to your export, and then click **OK**.

The Last Updated field is added to the grid preview in the Edit Columns dialog box.

7. Click **OK** to save your changes and return to the **Export Data to Excel** dialog box.

8. Click **Export** to export the dynamic data to Excel.

The File Download dialog box opens.

9. Click **Save**, and save the file to a familiar location after entering **Dynamic Activity Export** in the **File name** box.

The Download Complete dialog box opens after the file has been saved.

10. Click the **Open** button in the **Download Complete** dialog box to view the *Dynamic Activity Export* file.

The file includes the records from the My Activities view.

> **Important** You might get a security alert beneath the ribbon in Excel showing that data connections have been disabled. You can enable the content by clicking the Options button and selecting Enable This Content.

11. In the Excel file, rename the **Activity Type** column header to **Type**.

12. Press ⌃Ctrl + Ⓐ to select all rows in the Excel worksheet. In the **Font Type** field, select **Tahoma**.

13. Save the Excel file, and then close Excel.

14. Navigate back to the **My Activities** view within Microsoft Dynamics CRM.

New Activity ▾   **15.** Click the **New Activity** button to add a new activity.

The New Activity dialog box opens.

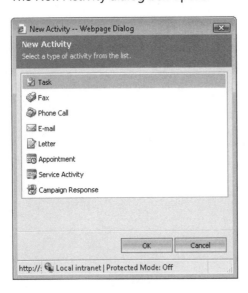

16. Select **Phone Call**, and then click **OK**.

The New Phone Call form opens.

17. Type in a subject, a **Regarding** value, and a due date.

Save and Close

18. Click the **Save and Close** button.

The new activity now appears in the My Activities view.

See Also Working with activities was discussed earlier in this book. If you need a refresher on this subject, see Chapter 4.

19. Open the *Dynamic Activity Export* file.

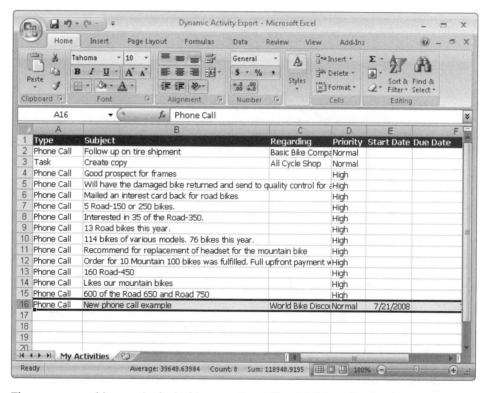

The new record is now included in your Excel file. Additionally, the formatting changes you made remain intact. Any time you open the file from now on, it will automatically refresh.

If you want to refresh the file without closing and reopening it, you can simply right-click within the resulting rows and select Refresh.

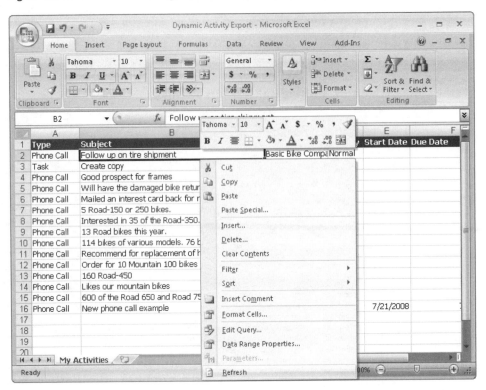

Exporting Dynamic Data to Excel PivotTables

In addition to letting you export data to dynamic Excel worksheets, Microsoft Dynamics CRM lets you export data to Excel PivotTables. Excel PivotTables give you the ability to cross-tabulate data to produce summarized reports.

Some people initially struggle with the concept of PivotTables. Consider the following example, in which you have this table of activities:

Activity Type	Owner	Due Date
Phone Call	Mike Snyder	8/15/2008
Task	Jim Steger	8/15/2008
Appointment	Jim Steger	8/12/2008
Phone Call	Kara O'Brien	8/19/2008
Phone Call	Jim Steger	9/1/2008
Task	Kara O'Brien	9/5/2008
E-mail	Mike Snyder	9/5/2008
Appointment	Kara O'Brien	9/7/2008
Task	Kara O'Brien	9/7/2008
Phone Call	Jim Steger	9/7/2008

This table consists of flat data in columns and rows. Flat data generally serves as the basis for a PivotTable. With a data set of this size, you can easily count the records to summarize the data in a variety of ways. For example:

- Four of the activities are phone calls.
- Mike Snyder is the owner of two activities.
- Three activities have a due date of 9/7/2008.

However, as your data set grows, summarizing the data at a glance becomes impossible. With a PivotTable, you can eliminate the manual calculation and *pivot* the data to get the answers. The following table is an example of a PivotTable on the flat data sample.

	Jim Steger	Kara O'Brien	Mike Snyder	Grand Total
Appointment	1	1		2
E-mail			1	1
Phone Call	2	1	1	4
Task	1	2		3
Grand Total	4	4	2	10

With the PivotTable, you can understand how many activities exist for each owner by type and in total. It also becomes clear how many total activities exist by type. You could have pivoted the data by due date rather than owner or activity type to see aggregates by due date.

> **Important** This chapter is not intended to teach you the full capabilities of PivotTables; it is meant to provide insight into basic PivotTable capability as it relates to your Microsoft Dynamics CRM data. For more information about PivotTables, see *Microsoft Office Excel 2007 Step by Step*, by Curtis D. Frye (Microsoft Press, 2007).

Although the concept of PivotTables might be intimidating at first, when you have obtained a comfort level with the process, you will be able to create powerful reports very efficiently. Similar to a dynamic worksheet, a dynamic PivotTable establishes a live link with your Microsoft Dynamics CRM database. Report setup is a one-time investment that you can benefit from continually. And learning how to use Excel PivotTables can help you solve reporting needs from other business-critical applications as well.

In this exercise, you will export data to a dynamic PivotTable to organize and summarize your Microsoft Dynamics CRM data.

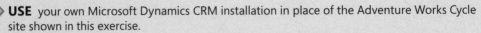

USE your own Microsoft Dynamics CRM installation in place of the Adventure Works Cycle site shown in this exercise.

BE SURE TO use the Internet Explorer Web browser to navigate to your Microsoft Dynamics CRM Web site, if necessary, before beginning this exercise.

1. In the **Workplace** area, click **Activities**.

   The default activities view, My Activities, appears.

2. Click the **Export to Excel** button.

   The Export Data To Excel dialog box opens.

3. Select **Dynamic PivotTable**.

   Notice that the Select Columns button is enabled.

4. Click the **Select Columns** button.

   The Select PivotTable Columns dialog box opens. The columns that appear in the My Activities grid are selected by default.

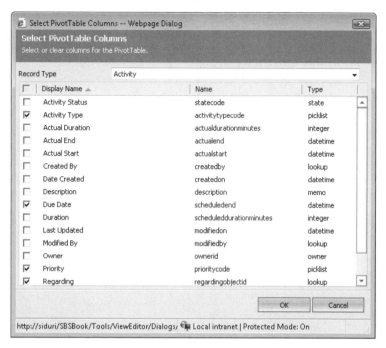

5. Select the check box for the **Activity Status** field, and then click **OK**.

This selection will make the Activity Status field available in the PivotTable.

6. Back in the **Export Data to Excel** dialog box, click **Export**.

The File Download dialog box opens.

7. Click **Open**.

This opens Excel with an empty PivotTable.

> **Important** You might get a security alert beneath the Microsoft Office Fluent Ribbon in Excel showing that data connections have been disabled. You can enable the content by clicking the Options button and selecting Enable This Content.

8. In the PivotTable field list on the right side of the screen, drag the **Due Date** field to the **Row Labels** section. Then drag the **Due Date** field to the **Values** section.

The PivotTable now shows a count of activities by due date.

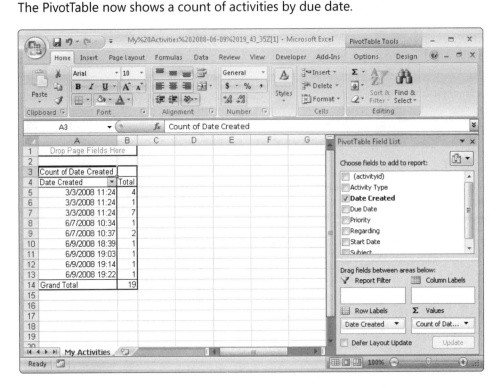

Tip While you are counting records, you can summarize numeric information in a variety of ways by changing the calculation type. To change the calculation type, click the arrow next to the field in the Values section, and click Value Field Settings. For example, you can modify the settings to summarize the data by Sum or Average.

9. Drag **Due Date** from the **Row Labels** section to the **Column Labels** section.

The same data is now pivoted in the opposite direction.

10. Drag the **Regarding** field into the **Row Labels** section.

The count of activities by due date for each Regarding option is now displayed.

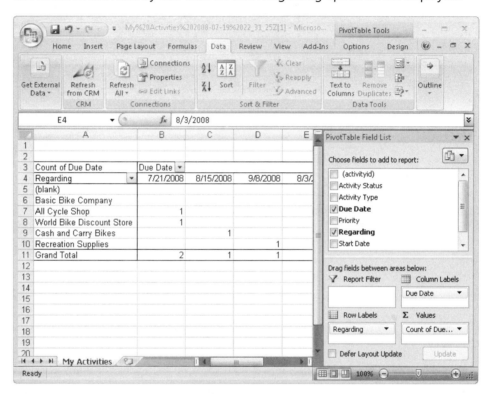

11. Drag the **Priority** field into the **Report Filter** section.

Priority now appears at the top of the PivotTable as a parameter. When you make a selection in the Priority field, the PivotTable results will refresh for records with the selected priority.

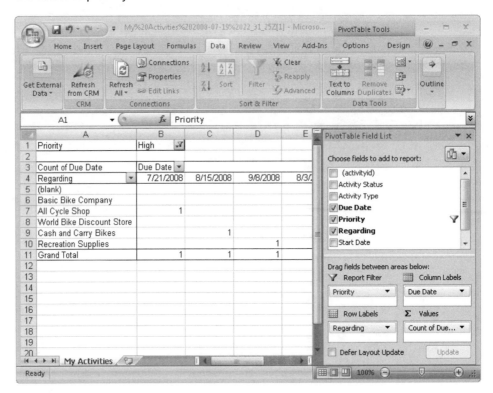

You can continue to add fields into the PivotTable report to refine your analysis.

Advanced PivotTables

With dynamic PivotTables, you can create countless summary-level reports with just a few clicks. To further illustrate the capabilities, here are two examples of dynamic PivotTables created from Microsoft Dynamics CRM data.

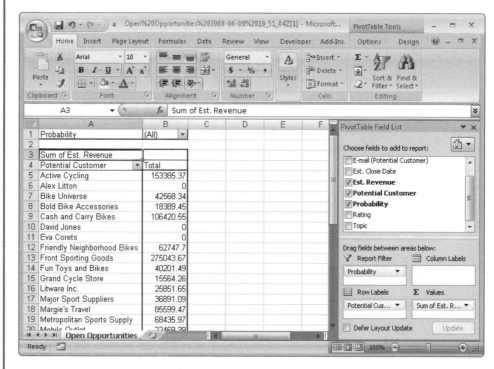

Example 1: Revenue by customer, filtered on closing probability

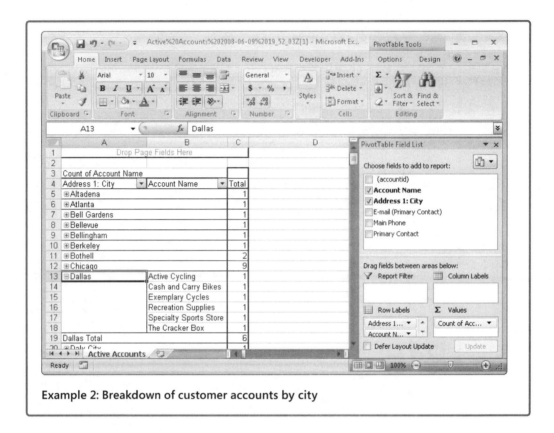

Example 2: Breakdown of customer accounts by city

Uploading Excel Reports to the Reports List in Microsoft Dynamics CRM

You are now able to create reports that have value to others in your organization. Although you learned that you can store dynamic Excel reports in a "shared" network location, this might be cumbersome and difficult to find. Microsoft Dynamics CRM allows you to also upload reports to the Reports area and share the reports to provide users with access to all of their reports within the application.

In this exercise, you will upload a report to the Reports area of Microsoft Dynamics CRM.

USE your own Microsoft Dynamics CRM installation in place of the Adventure Works Cycle site shown in this exercise.

BE SURE TO use the Internet Explorer Web browser to navigate to your Microsoft Dynamics CRM Web site, if necessary, before beginning this exercise.

1. In the **Workplace** area, click **Reports**.

The default Report view, Available Reports, appears.

2. Click the **New** button.

The New Report page opens.

New Report

3. In the **Report Type** field, select **Existing File**.

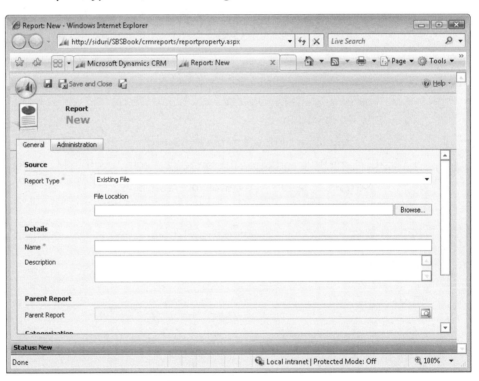

4. In the **Source** section of the page, click the **Browse** button.

The Choose File dialog box opens.

5. Navigate to the *Dynamic Activity Export* file created earlier in the chapter, and click the **Open** button.

The file path is returned to the Report screen.

6. Click the **Save and Close** button to save your report in Microsoft Dynamics CRM.

The report appears in the available reports list.

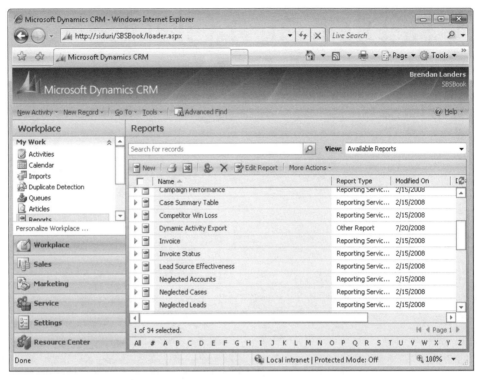

7. Double-click the **Dynamic Activity Export** report to launch your report.

You have successfully uploaded your report to Microsoft Dynamics CRM.

See Also The Reports area, Report Categorization, and Report Sharing were discussed earlier in this book. If you need a refresher on these subjects, see Chapter 16, "Using the Report Wizard."

Key Points

- You can export data to Excel from most record grids within Microsoft Dynamics CRM by clicking the Export To Excel button.
- When exporting data to Excel, you can choose to export static or dynamic data.
- Static data exports provide a snapshot of data as it exists at the time of export.
- Dynamic data exports establish a live link with the Microsoft Dynamics CRM database and can be refreshed at any time. Any formatting done on a dynamic Excel file is preserved after refreshing.
- A dynamic export to a PivotTable provides you with a mechanism to summarize data in a cross-tabbed, or pivoted, table.
- Dynamic exports can be uploaded and shared so that other users can benefit from the reports you create.

Chapter at a Glance

Create data maps, **page 400**

Resolve import errors, **page 414**

Import records by using the Import Data Wizard, **page 408**

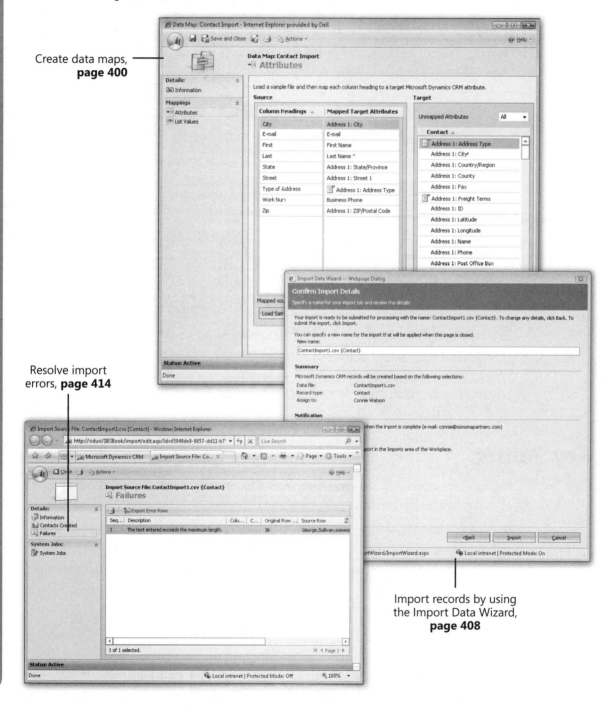

18 Importing Data

In this chapter, you will learn to

- ✔ Create data maps.
- ✔ Import records by using the Import Data Wizard.
- ✔ Map data automatically in the Import Data Wizard.
- ✔ View the results of an import.
- ✔ Resolve import errors.

Sales and marketing professionals often need to load bulk data into their Microsoft Dynamics CRM systems. Manually entering these records can be a time-consuming and expensive task. Examples of bulk data imports include:

- A list of leads, contacts, or accounts purchased from a third party.
- A list of contacts obtained from a recently attended conference.
- A file of business contacts brought by an employee who has recently joined the company.

Microsoft Dynamics CRM allows users to import data by using an easy-to-use Import Data Wizard. With this wizard, you can import hundreds or thousands of records in just a few clicks. In addition to core record types such as leads, contacts, and accounts, you can also use the Import Data Wizard to import other record types, including any custom record types created by your system administrator.

In this chapter, you will learn how to import data by using the Import Data Wizard. Additionally, you will learn how to enhance data imports by creating data maps, how to view the results of a data import, and how to troubleshoot import errors. Finally, you will learn how to save yourself time and frustration by taking advantage of automatic data mapping.

> **Important** Before you can use the practice files in this chapter, you need to install them from the book's companion CD to their default location. See "Using the Companion CD" at the beginning of this book for more information.

> **Troubleshooting** Graphics and operating system–related instructions in this book reflect the Windows Vista user interface. If your computer is running Windows XP and you experience trouble following the instructions as written, refer to the "Information for Readers Running Windows XP" section at the beginning of this book.

> **Important** The images used in this book reflect the default form and field names in Microsoft Dynamics CRM. Because the software offers extensive customization capabilities, it's possible that some of the record types or fields have been relabeled in your Microsoft Dynamics CRM environment. If you cannot find the forms, fields, or security roles referenced in this book, contact your system administrator for assistance.

> **Important** You must know the location of your Microsoft Dynamics CRM Web site to work the exercises in this book. Check with your system administrator to verify the Web address if you don't know it.

Mapping Data

Most data import tools allow users to import simple values into text fields. For more complex data importing—importing into drop-down lists and lookup fields, for example—you usually need to enlist IT resources to write code to map the data. These tasks usually have to go through a prioritization and scheduling process. By the time the data is finally imported, either the need has been met manually or the data is out of date.

The Microsoft Dynamics CRM Import Data Wizard solves most of these challenges. Although the wizard requires the import file to be mapped to the related Microsoft Dynamics CRM attributes, you can accomplish this without enlisting a software development resource. The process of mapping data may sound intimidating; fortunately, the Import Data Wizard does most of the work for you!

Microsoft Dynamics CRM uses *data maps* as the basis for translating how source fields convert into a related destination field. Consider the following example. You have a file of contacts you would like to import into Microsoft Dynamics CRM. Within your source file, there is a field named *First*, which contains the first name of a contact. In Microsoft Dynamics CRM, the related field is named *First Name*. In order to import the data in the source file, you need to map the First field in the source file to the First Name field in the destination (Microsoft Dynamics CRM).

In this exercise, you will create and upload a data map into Microsoft Dynamics CRM.

> **USE** the *ContactImport1.csv* file. This practice file is located in the *Documents\Microsoft Press\CRM4_SBS\ImportingData* folder.
>
> **BE SURE TO** use the Windows Internet Explorer Web browser to navigate to your Microsoft Dynamics CRM Web site before beginning this exercise.

1. In the **Settings** area, click **Data Management**, and then select **Data Maps**.

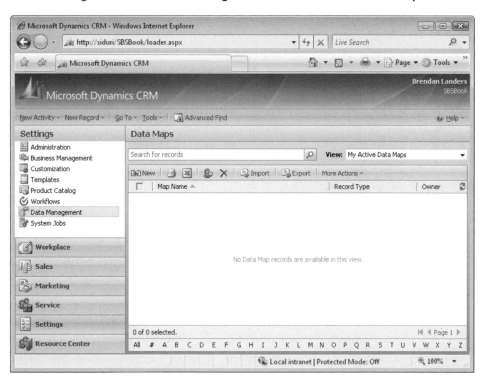

New Data Map

2. In the grid toolbar, click the **New** button.

The New Data Map form opens.

3. In the **Name** field, enter **Contact Import**.

4. In the **Record Type** list, select **Contact**.

Save

5. In the **Description** field, enter **Data map for contact import**, and then click the **Save** button in the form toolbar to create the data map without closing the record.

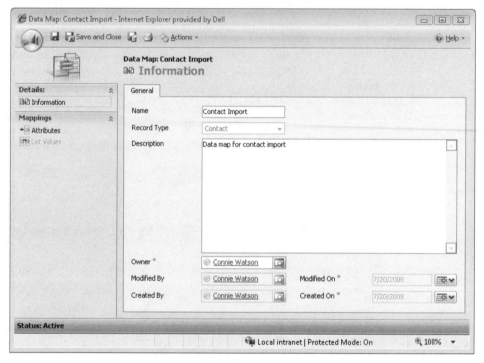

6. In the left navigation area, click **Attributes**.

The Attributes screen opens. This screen has two sections: Source and Target. The Source section will reflect the fields from the import file (after it is uploaded) and the Target section lists the contact fields from Microsoft Dynamics CRM. Within the Source section you can map the Source column headings to Target fields in Microsoft Dynamics CRM. These mappings are displayed in the Mapped Target Attributes column in the Source section. By default, the Source section is blank.

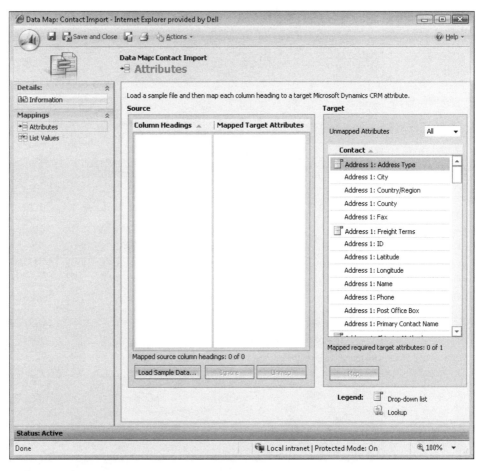

7. Click the **Load Sample Data** button in the **Source** section.

   The Select Sample Data File To Upload dialog box opens.

8. Click **Browse**, and select the *ContactImport1.csv* sample file.

> **Important** The sample data file must be in comma-separated value (*.csv) or text (*.txt) format.

The Source section is now populated with the column headings of the sample file.

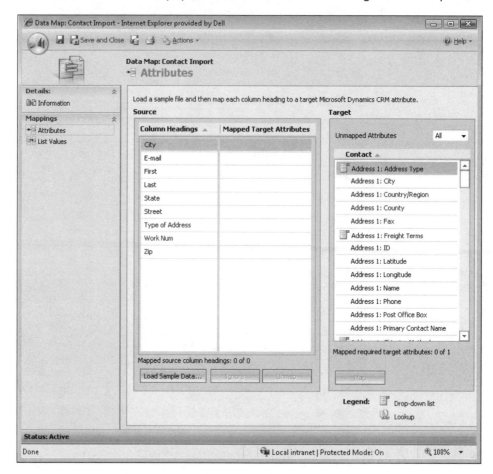

The next step is to map the columns.

9. In the **Source** section, select the **City** column heading.

10. In the **Target** section, scroll through the fields until you see **Address 1: City**, and then select the field by clicking it.

11. In the **Target** section, click the **Map** button.

The Mapped Target Attributes column is now populated with the value Address 1: City, and Address 1: City is removed from the Target section. The city field in the sample import file is now mapped to the Address 1: City column in Microsoft Dynamics CRM.

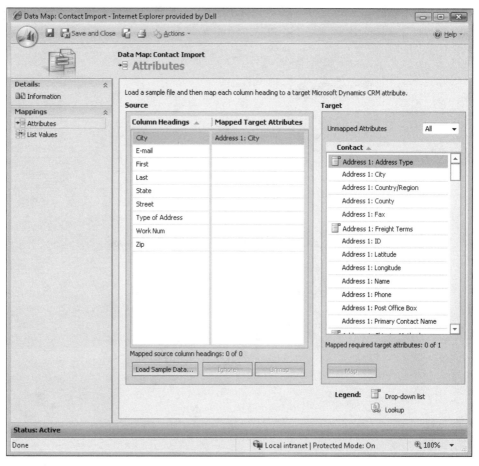

12. Repeat the process for the remaining fields, as follows:

Source column	Target mapping
E-mail	E-mail
First	First Name
Last	Last Name
State	Address 1: State/Province
Street	Address 1: Street 1
Type of Address	Address 1: Address Type
Work Num	Business Phone
Zip	Address 1: ZIP/Postal Code

> **Important** Notice the icon next to the Address 1: Address Type field. This icon indicates that the field is a list in Microsoft Dynamics CRM. You will need to manually map the list values to those in your Microsoft Dynamics CRM database.

After you have mapped the attributes, you will need to map any list values. In addition to list values that map directly to CRM values, in the *ContactImport1.csv* sample import source file is a list value called *Main* for the Type Of Address field. In Microsoft Dynamics CRM, the related value is called *Primary*. Therefore, you need to map the values so that the application translates *Main* into *Primary*.

13. In the left navigation bar, click **List Values**.

The List Values screen opens and automatically displays the list fields from your sample import file. Similar to the Attributes screen, the List Values screen contains two sections: a List Attributes section that shows the list fields from your sample import file and a Corresponding List Values section that allows you to map values from your sample file to the values in the mapped field in Microsoft Dynamics CRM.

14. In the Corresponding List Values section, select the source list value and corresponding Microsoft Dynamics CRM value, and then click the **Map** button for each list value, as follows:

Corresponding List Values	Microsoft Dynamics CRM Value
Other	Other
Ship To	Ship To
Primary	Primary
Bill To	Bill To
Main	Primary

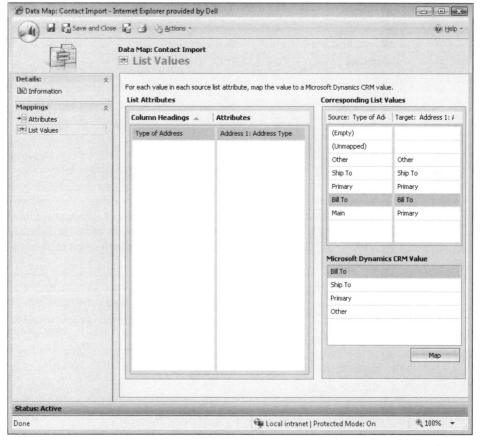

15. In the form toolbar, click the **Save and Close** button to complete the data map.

Save and Close

Using the Import Data Wizard

The Import Data Wizard is a simple and intuitive interface that navigates you through the import process. In just a few steps, you can import your records into Microsoft Dynamics CRM. Most entities are available for data import. By default, the following record types are available for import:

Account	Discount	Phone Call
Address	Discount List	Price List
Announcement	Document	Price List Item
Article	E-mail	Product
Article Template	Facility/Equipment	Quote
Business Unit	Fax	Quote Close
Campaign	Invoice	Quote Product
Campaign Activity	Invoice Product	Role
Campaign Response	Lead	Sales Literature
Case	Letter	Service
Case Resolution	Marketing List	Service Activity
Competitor	Note	Site
Contact	Opportunity	Subject
Contract	Opportunity Close	Task
Contract Line	Opportunity Product	Team
Contract Template	Opportunity Relationship	Territory
Currency	Order	Unit
Customer Relationship	Order Close	Unit Group
	Order Product	

> **Tip** Custom entities are also available for data import. It is impossible for the user to tell which entities are custom and which are native, so be sure to check the list of record types available in the Data Import Wizard. Contact your system administrator if you would like a list of custom entities.

Now that you have created a data map, you will import the data by using the Import Data Wizard. The Import Data Wizard contains four steps and requires you to input the following information:

- Data file to be imported
- File delimiters
- Target record type
- Data map
- Record owner
- Duplicate detection setting

In this exercise, you will use the Import Data Wizard to import data.

> **USE** the *ContactImport1.csv* file. This practice file is located in the *Documents\Microsoft Press\CRM4_SBS\ImportingData* folder.
>
> **BE SURE TO** use the Internet Explorer Web browser to navigate to your Microsoft Dynamics CRM Web site before beginning this exercise.

New Import

1. In the **Workplace** area, click **Imports**, and then click the **New** button in the grid toolbar.

The Import Data Wizard opens.

2. Click **Browse**, and then locate the *ContactImport1.csv* file. Click **OK** to select the file as the data source for your import. Leave the default **Data delimiter** and **Field delimiter** options.

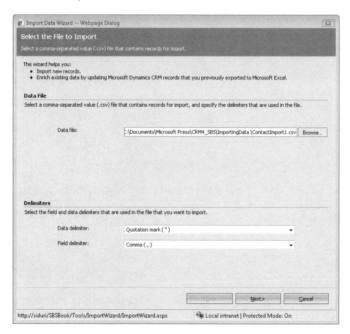

> **Important** A delimiter is a character or series of characters that indicates a boundary in certain files. In comma-separated files, each value is separated by a comma, which is specified in the Field Delimiter field in the Import Data Wizard. The following line shows a record that has a Data Delimiter value of *Quotation Mark (")* and a Field Delimiter value of *Comma (,)*.
>
> *"Jesper","Aaberg","someone@example.com",555-0173*
>
> Depending on the input file, you might need to change the delimiter options.

3. Click **Next** to select the record type and map for your import.

4. In the **Record Type** list, select **Contact**.

Look Up

5. Click the **Look Up** button next to **Data Map**, select the **Contact Import** data map, and then click **OK** so that the data map created in the previous section is selected in the Import Data Wizard.

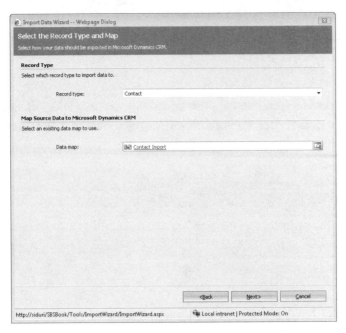

6. Click **Next** to proceed to the next step of the Import Data Wizard.

7. On the **Select Options** page, select the user to whom you would like to assign the records.

   This user will be the owner of the contact records that are created during the import process.

8. In the **Duplicate Detection** area, click **Import duplicate records**.

> **Troubleshooting** The Duplicate Detection option is present only if duplicate detection is turned on for data imports.

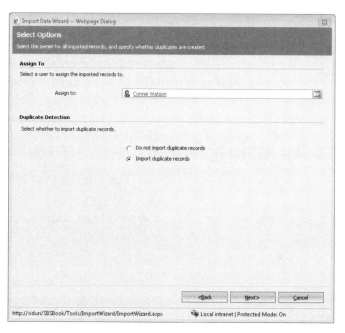

9. Click **Next** to proceed to the final step of the Import Data Wizard.

On the Confirm Import Details page, you can rename the data import, review a summary of your import settings, and indicate whether you would like to receive an e-mail message when the import is complete.

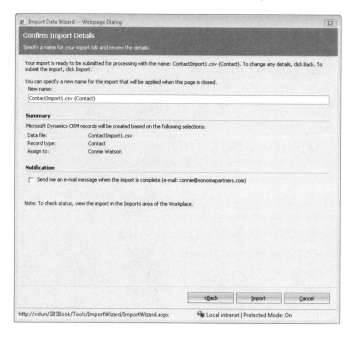

10. Leave the default options, and click **Import** to exit the Import Data Wizard.

The imports grid appears with a new record called *ContactImport1.csv {Contact}*, indicating that the import has been submitted to the system for processing. The status of the import updates automatically as the import is processed behind the scenes.

Importing Data by Using Automatic Data Mapping

As the previous exercises demonstrated, stepping through the Import Data Wizard is a straightforward process. The most time-consuming part of the process is creating a data map, which is a simple task that takes patience and an understanding of basic data concepts. To streamline the data import process, Microsoft Dynamics CRM allows you to create files that map automatically. This takes some set up using the Advanced Find tool, but you will find that it saves you valuable time in the long run.

See Also For more information about Advanced Find, see Chapter 15, "Using Advanced Find."

> **Tip** The key to automatic mapping is the column headers in your import file. If the column headers in your import file match the field display names in Microsoft Dynamics CRM, your file will automatically map. You can create a template for your import file by using Advanced Find, so that the column headers mirror the field values in Microsoft Dynamics CRM, and then use Copy and Paste to paste the rows of data you would like to import into the template file.

In this exercise, you will create an Advanced Find query that you will export to create an import file that uses automatic mapping.

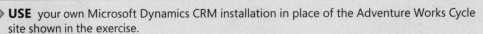

USE your own Microsoft Dynamics CRM installation in place of the Adventure Works Cycle site shown in the exercise.

BE SURE TO use the Internet Explorer Web browser to navigate to your Microsoft Dynamics CRM Web site before beginning this exercise.

1. In the application menu bar, click **Advanced Find**.

The Advanced Find form opens.

2. In the **Look For** field, select **Accounts**.

3. In the **Use Saved View** field, select **My Active Accounts**.

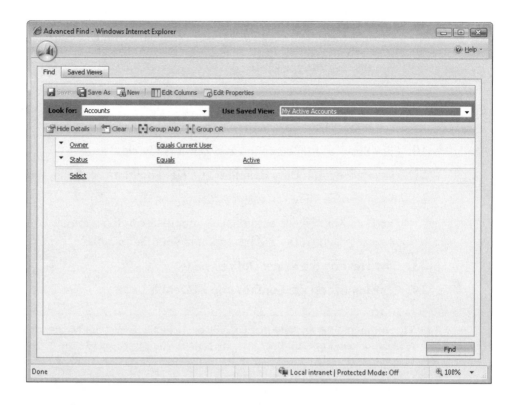

> **Important** If you cannot find the view referenced above, select one of the available views that will return at least a few accounts in the results, and continue with the steps.

4. Click **Find** in the lower-right corner of the Advanced Find query page.

The Results screen opens with the matching contact records.

Export to Excel

5. On the **Results** screen, click the **Export to Excel** button.

The Export Data To Excel dialog box opens.

6. Select **Static worksheet with records from this page**, and then click **Export**.

The File Download screen opens.

7. Click **Save**, and save the file to a familiar location on your computer as **MyAccounts.xls**. Then close the **Advanced Find** screen.

8. Open the **MyAccounts.xls** file in Microsoft Office Excel, save it as a CSV file named **MyAccounts.csv**, and then close Excel.

> **Important** Import files must be in a comma-separated value (CSV) format. To convert an Excel file to a CSV file, open the file in Excel and use the Save As feature. In the Save As Type list, select CSV (Comma Delimited).

9. Back in Microsoft Dynamics CRM, in the application menu bar, click **Tools**, and then click **Import Data** to launch the Import Data Wizard.

10. Click **Browse**, and locate the **MyAccounts.csv** file.

11. Leave the default **Data delimiter** and **Field delimiter** options, and click **Next**.

12. In the **Record Type** list, select **Account**.

The Data Map field is automatically populated with Automatic. This indicates that Microsoft Dynamics CRM has mapped your file for you.

13. Click **Next** on the **Select Options** page.

14. Click **Import** on the **Confirm Import Details** page.

> **Tip** Although it is unlikely that you will export a file from your Microsoft Dynamics CRM application and import it back into the system, you can easily use the output of the file as a template and paste import data into the file. Your file will automatically map as long as the column headings are not manipulated.

Reviewing the Import Status

The import will run in the background after it has been initiated. You can continue to use Microsoft Dynamics CRM during this time. The process can take a minute to several minutes, depending on the size of the import file.

You will want to review the results of the import to ensure that all desired records have been imported and, if necessary, troubleshoot import-related errors. Microsoft Dynamics CRM provides a tool that lets you easily obtain this information without leaving the familiar application interface.

After your import is completed, you can view its status in the Imports view, accessed in the Workplace area. Each import is displayed as a separate record in the imports grid, and by double-clicking a record, you can view the details of that import job. Each import record shows key information, such as the user who submitted the import, the date and time the import was submitted, and the import file name and file size. Additionally, you can view the records that were created during the import process and the errors for records that failed to import.

The ability to view failures for each import allows you to easily identify issues with your import file, so you can update it and re-import the records that did not get created during the import process. Each error row displays the information shown in the following table.

Column	Description
Sequence Number	An identifier for the error row
Description	A description of the error for that row
Column Heading	The name of the column in the import file that is causing the error
Column Value	The value that is causing the error
Original Row Number	The number of the row in the import file that is producing the error
Source Row	The full row of text that is failing

> **Tip** Any row that succeeds in the import process (and consequently does not show up in the Failures list) will be imported into Microsoft Dynamics CRM. Do not assume that no records were imported because a single row failed.

> **Troubleshooting** An import file can fail for several reasons. Each specific row in the Failures list can have a different error; therefore, you might need to diagnose more than one issue before attempting to re-import.

In this exercise, you will view the status and troubleshoot related errors for the import you submitted earlier in this chapter. Then you will research the failure in order to understand the root cause of the issue. Finally, you will correct the error and re-import the error row.

BE SURE TO use the Internet Explorer Web browser to navigate to your Microsoft Dynamics CRM Web site, if necessary, before beginning this exercise.

1. In the **Workplace** area, click **Imports**.

Note the row that contains the *ContactImport1.csv {Contact}* import you submitted in the "Using the Import Data Wizard" section.

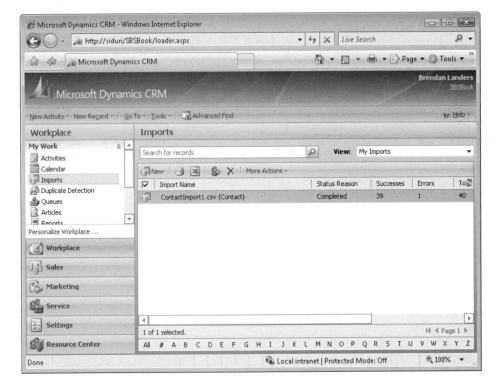

2. Look at the **Status Reason** value for the import.

The Status Reason will be set to Parsing, Transforming, Importing, or Completed. If the Status Reason is not equal to Completed, return at a later time.

3. Review the Successes, Errors, and Total Count values.

You should see 39 rows that have completed successfully, and 1 row that has errors.

4. Double-click the record to display additional information.

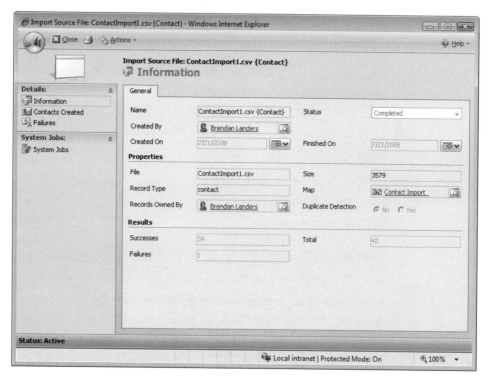

5. In the left navigation bar, click **Failures**.

The record that failed in the import process is displayed.

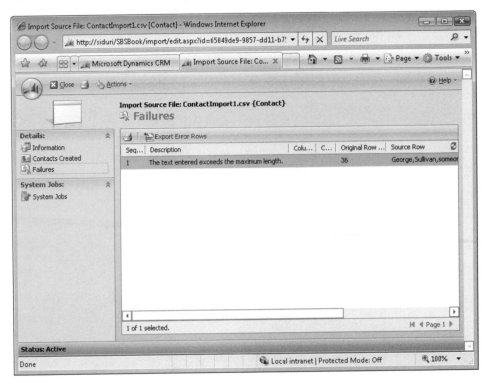

You can attempt to diagnose the error based on the message and data provided in the error row. You know that the issue is related to the 36th row in the import file, and the error description states that the text entered exceeds the maximum length. You can also see that the contact being imported was George Sullivan.

6. Locate and open the import file.

7. Find the text row with **George Sullivan**. Notice that the value in the Zip column is erroneous. Update the Zip to **60463**.

8. Delete the other (non-error) rows in the file.

> **Important** Do not delete the first row. The first row contains the column headers from the file.

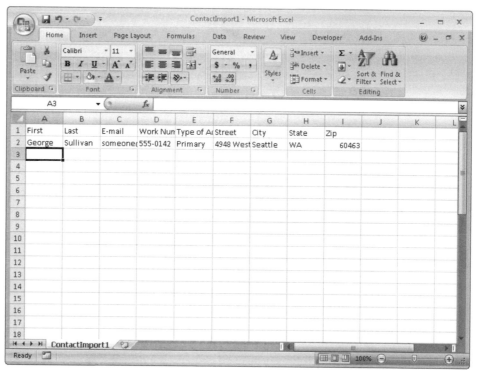

9. Save and close the file.

The next step is to attempt to import the file.

10. On the application menu toolbar, click **Tools,** and then click **Import Data.**

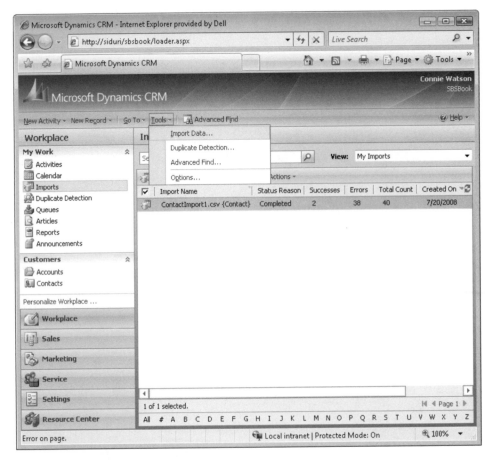

The Import Data Wizard opens.

11. Click **Browse**, and locate the *ContactImport1.csv* file.

12. Leave the default **Data delimiter** and **Field delimiter** options, and click **Next**.

13. In the **Record Type** list, select **Contact,** and then click **Next**.

14. Select the user to whom you would like to assign the records, and then click **Next**.

15. Leave the default options, and click **Import**.

Your error row should now be imported successfully.

Key Points

- The Import Data Wizard allows Microsoft Dynamics CRM users to import records in bulk by using a straightforward wizard that is available within the familiar application interface.

- Data maps allow users to map data from a source file to its Microsoft Dynamics CRM target field. Data maps are reusable for future data import needs.

- You need to provide a data map only if your column headings do not match the Microsoft Dynamics CRM column headings or if your list values do not match the values in the target mapping column.

- You can view the status of a data import in the Imports view accessed from the Workplace area, while the import is running and after the import process has completed. You can view successes and failures by opening the related import record.

Glossary

accounts Companies that might do business with your organization.

activating the quote The process of making a quote available to send to a customer. Before you send your quote to a customer, you must activate it.

activities General term used to describe interactions with your customers or potential customers. Activities can be created to remind a user to communicate with a customer or to record a communication that has already occurred. Eight types of activities exist natively, including task, fax, phone call, e-mail, letter, appointment, service activity, and campaign response.

allotment type Units of service, such as a case or a range of coverage dates, specified in a service contract that indicate how much access a customer has to customer service.

articles Text-based content stored in the knowledge base.

attributes Properties of an entity with a specific data type. Attributes are analogous to columns in a database table. When attributes are added to an entity form, they are displayed as fields that correspond to their data type.

campaign activities An activity associated with a specific campaign, such as a letter, fax, or phone call. Campaign activities include campaign-specific information, and must be distributed to create the individual activities for users to perform.

campaign responses A record of the communication you receive from a potential customer in response to a specific campaign.

cases A customer service issue or problem reported by a customer and the activities that customer service representatives use to resolve it.

contacts People who represent customers or potential customers, or individuals related to accounts; for example, individuals who purchase products or services for their own use, or an employee of an account. A contact may also be a person involved in a business transaction, such as a supplier or a colleague.

contract lines Line items in contracts that describe the service support to be provided. A contract line often includes pricing information and how support will be allotted.

contract template A framework for a contract used to ensure consistent layouts and content in similar contracts.

contracts An agreement to provide support during specified coverage dates or for a specified number of cases or length of time. When customers contact customer service, the level of support they receive is determined by their contract.

converting the lead Turning a qualified lead into an Account, Contact, and/or Opportunity record.

customer An account or contact with whom business units conduct business transactions.

customer relationships A way of relating customer records to other customer records. Customer relationships are reciprocal. The relationship defined for one record is also available in the other customer record.

direct e-mail To send a mass-mailing of the same message by using Microsoft Dynamics CRM e-mail templates to multiple e-mail recipients.

data maps A file that contains information about how data from a source system corresponds to data in Microsoft Dynamics CRM.

distribute To create campaign activities for each account, contact, or lead in a marketing list associated with a campaign, and then to assign the activities to the specified owners, or to perform the activities automatically (such as sending e-mail messages).

dynamic A value that updates in real time. A dynamic export can be refreshed with the latest data from the Microsoft Dynamics CRM database.

e-mail template A framework for an e-mail message, used to ensure consistent layouts and content in similar e-mail messages.

field mapping Streamlines data entry when creating new records that are associated with another record. When an entity has an entity relationship with another entity, you can create new related entity records from the associated view visible on the primary entity. When the user creates a new record from an associated view, mapped data from the primary entity record is copied to the form for the new related entity record.

Get Products Automatically adding products from an Opportunity to a Quote.

go online The act of connecting back to the Microsoft Dynamics CRM server from the off-line client for Microsoft Dynamics CRM.

going offline The act of disconnecting from the Microsoft Dynamics CRM server, providing the ability of working with a subset of data while not connected.

History Activities that have been completed or closed.

knowledge base A repository of an organization's information. This information is stored as articles, and is organized by subject.

lead source A resource through which your company obtains leads.

leads A potential customer who must be qualified or disqualified as a sales opportunity. If a lead is qualified, it can be converted to an opportunity, account, and/or contact.

list members Accounts, contacts, or leads included in a marketing list.

local data groups A set of filters that determines what data is available offline and stored on the local computer.

lookup A field that allows you to choose a value from data stored in a related entity.

notes Short text descriptions or file attachments related to a record.

marketing campaign Marketing programs that use multiple communication vehicles, intended to increase awareness of your company, products, or services.

marketing list Lists of accounts, contacts, or leads that match a specific set of criteria.

More Addresses Additional addresses for an account or a contact record.

opportunities A potential revenue-generating event or sale to an account that needs to be tracked through a sales process to completion.

order A confirmed request for delivery of goods or services based on specified terms. An order is a quote that has been accepted by a customer.

parent accounts An account record that is in a hierarchical relationship with a child record, where a reference to the record is stored in the child record. One parent account record can be related to many child records.

Product Catalog A compilation of all products that are available for sale.

queue Holding containers for activities that need to be completed. Some queues contain cases and activities in the Workplace, and some are articles in the knowledge base.

quick campaign A marketing communication method that creates a single activity for distribution to a group of marketing lists, accounts, contacts, or leads.

Quick Find A mechanism to quickly search for records in the database.

quote A formal offer for products or services, proposed at specific prices and related payment terms, which is sent to an opportunity, account, or contact.

Regarding field Used to link the activity to another record so that you can view the activity from the record. If you create a new activity from a record, this is automatically filled out.

reopen Opening a previously closed opportunity for further exploration.

share To allow another user or team to have a specified amount of access to a record, such as a case, account, or contract. For example, you can share an account with a team and specify that its members can read the account record, but cannot have write access to it.

static A value that remains the same and does not update in real time. A static export cannot be refreshed with the latest data from the Microsoft Dynamics CRM database.

sub-accounts A record in a hierarchical relationship with a parent account where a reference to the parent account is stored in the sub-account record. One parent account record can be related to many child account records, or sub-accounts. Sub-account records have lookup fields in the form to allow them to be related to a parent record.

subjects Categories used in a hierarchical list to correlate and organize information. Subjects are used in the subject tree to organize products, sales literature, and knowledge base articles.

Track in CRM To link between a record in Microsoft Dynamics CRM and Microsoft Office Outlook. Records that are marked for tracking are updated in both applications, including creating new activities.

view A filter applied to a list of records. Users can choose different views that contain all the records or activities of a particular type or that are a subset of that type.

Web client An Internet browser–based client for Microsoft Dynamics CRM.

write-in product A product that you add to a quote as you are creating it, without first needing to configure all of the details in the product catalog.

Workplace A pane in the navigation pane that contains the work a user has been assigned, is currently working on, and is available in queues to which the user has access. Users can accept, assign, and delete assignments from here. Users can also access their calendars and the knowledge base.

Index

A

accepting cases into queues, 300
accounts. *See also* records
  assigning, 53–54
  contacts, creating from, 44
  contacts, linking to, 41–42
  converting leads into, 120–121
  creating, 38–39
  defined, 423
  duplicate. *See* duplicate records
  linking to contacts, 45–46
  linking to Outlook contacts, 95
  notes in. *See* notes
  overview of, 35–36
  parent. *See* parent accounts
  primary contacts, specifying, 43
  relationships between, 39. *See also* parent
    accounts; sub-accounts
  sharing, 51
  sub-accounts. *See* sub-accounts
  viewing all related activities, 72–76
Actions button, 51, 68, 201, 241
activating quotes, 140, 156, 423
activating records, 51
active records, 49
Active status, 49
activities. *See also* records
  attaching files to, 67
  campaign. *See* campaign activities
  categories, unrelated to Outlook categories, 63
  converting to opportunities and cases, 70
  creating, 67–70
  creating, from contacts, 68–69
  creating, from parent accounts, 74
  creating, with workflow rules, 60
  data fields in, 62
  defined, 59, 423
  e-mail, converting to leads, 133–135
  filtering by date, 72
  follow-up, 67, 243–244
  linking to other records, 63–67
  managing. *See* Workplace
  prepopulated, 68
  Regarding field, 63–67
  status values, default, 71
  tracking, benefits of, 59–60
  types of, 61–62
  viewing overview of. *See* Workplace
  viewing related, 72–76
activity rollups, 72
ad hoc record sharing, 51
ad hoc reporting. *See* Advanced Find
Add Existing button, 198
address book in Microsoft Dynamics CRM for
    Outlook, 97–98
addresses
  alternate, 151
  bill to/ship to, adding to quotes, 145–149
  looking up, in forms, 148
Advanced Find
  AND vs. OR, 338
  automatic data mapping, 412–414
  bulk editing, 340, 342–343
  column width, changing, 332
  criteria, unlimited, 325
  formatting results of, 329–333
  opening, 326
  operators, 325
  OR logic, specifying, 339–340
  overview of, 324
  queries, creating, 326–328
  query columns, editing, 329–330
  query details, showing by default, 338
  query rows, adding, 327
  removing marketing list members with, 171–173
  saving queries, 334
  security settings and, 323
  sorting results, 332–333
  vs. SQL Server Reporting Services, 347–348
  updating marketing lists with, 173–175
Advanced Find button, 17, 326
Adventure Works Cycle company name, 4
advertisement responses. *See* campaign responses;
    lead source
advertising. *See* marketing campaigns
allotment types, 279, 423
alternate shipping addresses, 151
AND logic in queries, 338
Append privilege, 334
application areas, 17
  personalizing, 30
application menu toolbar, 17
application navigation pane, 17

About Sonoma Partners

This book's authors, Mike Snyder, Jim Steger, Kara O'Brien, and Brendan Landers, are executives at the Chicago-based consulting firm Sonoma Partners. Sonoma Partners is a Microsoft Gold Certified Partner that sells, customizes, and implements Microsoft Dynamics CRM for enterprise and midsize companies throughout the United States. Sonoma Partners has worked exclusively with Microsoft Dynamics CRM since the 1.0 prerelease beta software version. Founded in 2001, Sonoma Partners possesses extensive experience in several industries, including financial services, professional services, health care, and real estate.

Sonoma Partners is unique because of the following reasons:

- We are 100 percent focused on the Microsoft Dynamics CRM software product. We do not spread our resources over any other products or services.
- We have successfully implemented more than 150 Microsoft Dynamics CRM deployments.
- Microsoft awarded Sonoma Partners as the Global Microsoft Dynamics CRM Partner of the Year in 2003 and 2005. Microsoft recognized Sonoma Partners as one of three finalists for the 2008 Microsoft Dynamics CRM Partner of the Year award.
- More than half of our staff includes application and database developers, allowing our firm to perform very complex Microsoft Dynamics CRM customizations and integrations.
- We were named one of 101 Best and Brightest Companies to Work for in Chicago in 2007 and 2008.
- We are a member of Microsoft Dynamics Partner Advisory Council.

In addition to the multiple books we've written for Microsoft Press, we share our Microsoft Dynamics CRM product knowledge through our e-mail newsletter and online blog. If you're interested in receiving this information, you can find out more on our Web site at *www.sonomapartners.com*.

Even though our headquarters is in Chicago, Illinois, we work with customers throughout the United States. If you're interested in discussing your Microsoft Dynamics CRM system with us, please don't hesitate to contact us! In addition to working with customers who want to deploy Microsoft Dynamics CRM for themselves, we also act as a technology provider for Independent Software Vendors (ISVs) looking to develop their solution for the Microsoft Dynamics CRM platform.

Sometimes people ask us where we got our name. The name *Sonoma Partners* was inspired by Sonoma County, in the wine-producing region of Northern California. The wineries in Sonoma County are smaller than their more well-known competitors in Napa Valley, but they have a reputation for producing some of the highest quality wines in the world. We think that their smaller size allows the Sonoma winemakers to be more intimately involved with creating the wine. By using this hands-on approach, the Sonoma County wineries can deliver a superior product to their customers...and that's what we strive to do as well.

Mike Snyder

Mike Snyder is co-founder and principal of Sonoma Partners, a Chicago-based consulting firm that specializes in Microsoft Dynamics CRM implementations. Recognized as one of the industry's leading Microsoft Dynamics CRM experts, Mike is a member of the Microsoft Dynamics Partner Advisory Council, and he writes a popular blog about Microsoft Dynamics CRM.

Before starting Sonoma Partners, Mike led multiple product development teams at Motorola and Fortune Brands. Mike graduated with honors from Northwestern's Kellogg Graduate School of Management with a Master of Business Administration degree, majoring in marketing and entrepreneurship. He has a bachelor's degree in engineering from the University of Notre Dame. Mike lives in Naperville, Illinois, with his wife and three children. He enjoys ice hockey and playing with his kids in his free time.

Jim Steger

Jim Steger is also a co-founder and principal of Sonoma Partners. He is a Microsoft Certified Professional and has architected multiple award-winning Microsoft Dynamics CRM deployments, including complex enterprise integration projects. He has developed solutions and code for Microsoft Dynamics CRM since the 1.0 beta version.

Before starting Sonoma Partners, Jim designed and led various global software development projects at Motorola and ACCO Office Products. Jim earned his bachelor's degree in engineering from Northwestern University. He currently lives in Naperville, Illinois, with his wife and two children.

Kara O'Brien

Kara is a senior project director at Sonoma Partners and certified in Microsoft Dynamics CRM. Kara has led Microsoft Dynamics implementation projects for not-for-profit organizations as well as companies in the real estate, financial services, and other industries. Prior to Sonoma Partners, Kara worked as a marketing manager at Encyclopedia Britannica and as a software developer at Jones Lang LaSalle. She holds a bachelor's degree in communications from Northwestern University.

Brendan Landers

Brendan is a senior project director at Sonoma Partners and certified in Microsoft Dynamics CRM. Brendan has led numerous Microsoft Dynamics implementation projects for companies in the following industries: professional and financial services, education, healthcare, hospitality, and others. Prior to Sonoma Partners, Brendan worked at Information Resources, Inc. as a Director of Quality Assurance and Delivery where he led several data quality and business intelligence initiatives. He holds a bachelor's degree in management information systems from the University of Iowa.

What do you think of this book?

We want to hear from you!

Do you have a few minutes to participate in a brief online survey?

Microsoft is interested in hearing your feedback so we can continually improve our books and learning resources for you.

To participate in our survey, please visit:

www.microsoft.com/learning/booksurvey/

...and enter this book's ISBN-10 or ISBN-13 number (located above barcode on back cover*). As a thank-you to survey participants in the United States and Canada, each month we'll randomly select five respondents to win one of five $100 gift certificates from a leading online merchant. At the conclusion of the survey, you can enter the drawing by providing your e-mail address, which will be used for prize notification only.

Thanks in advance for your input. Your opinion counts!

*Where to find the ISBN on back cover

ISBN-13: 000-0-0000-0000-0
ISBN-10: 0-0000-0000-0

0 000000 000000

Example only. Each book has unique ISBN.

Microsoft®
Press

No purchase necessary. Void where prohibited. Open only to residents of the 50 United States (includes District of Columbia) and Canada (void in Quebec). For official rules and entry dates see:

www.microsoft.com/learning/booksurvey/